SCAPEGOAT

Scapegoat

How We Are Failing Disabled People

KATHARINE QUARMBY

Portobello
BOOKS

Published by Portobello Books 2011

Portobello Books
12 Addison Avenue
London W11 4QR

A CIP catalogue record for this book is available from the British Library

9 8 7 6 5 4 3 2 1

ISBN 978 1 84627 321 6

www.portobellobooks.com

Typeset by Avon DataSet Ltd, Bidford on Avon, Warwickshire

Printed and bound in the UK by CPI William Clowes Beccles NR34 7TL

This book is dedicated to all those – victims, survivors, families and friends – whose lives have been scarred by disability hate crime.

Contents

Introduction

When I first started writing on disability for the mainstream press in 2000, I believed that the long march towards equality was nearly over. I wrote articles and made films about inclusion in schools, the over-medication of disabled children and about women with mental health problems – the nitty-gritty of social affairs journalism. But I assumed that the struggle for the civil rights of disabled people had long been won. They were recognised, in law, as equal citizens. They had the right to independent living, and were speaking for themselves about the right to access to transport, shops and jobs. Paralympians such as Tanni Grey-Thompson were celebrated, a disabled politician, David Blunkett, had made it to the Cabinet, and there were even disabled presenters on the BBC. In 2007 I discovered just how naive I had been.

In the summer of that year I became news editor of one of Britain's leading disability magazines, *Disability Now*. In June 2007, on our monthly press day, news came through that sentence was to be handed down on three people from the Forest of Dean, responsible for holding captive and torturing a young man with epilepsy, Kevin Davies. The prosecutor told the court that Kevin had been 'kept like a dog in a locked garden shed at night'.[1] Astonishingly, two of the attackers, Amanda Baggus and David Lehane, had known Kevin well and he had treated them as his friends.

It emerged during their trial that the perpetrators had imprisoned and tortured him for weeks. Kevin died on 26 September 2006, weighing just seven stone. The three offenders were declared guilty of wrongful imprisonment and assault occasioning actual bodily harm – not murder or manslaughter. They were eventually sentenced to between nine and ten years in jail. I filed a terse story to meet our deadline and the next day I sat down to investigate disability hate crime – to prove that what had happened to Kevin Davies was in no way adequately covered by 'wrongful imprisonment' and assault.

Over the next few months, as I uncovered similar cases involving torture, rape and murder, I became convinced that there was a depth of hatred towards disabled people that had gone unmarked by the criminal justice system, politicians, the media and society at large. I spent more than a year assembling evidence to prove the existence of this 'invisible crime', before writing a report, *Getting Away with Murder*, published by Scope, *Disability Now* and the UK's Disabled People's Council. It argued that Britain had a serious and pernicious problem with disability hate crime – and with its attitude towards disabled people.[2]

As I looked more deeply into these cases, I found that the motivation of the offenders was shaped by our common history and by the fears and prejudices that have fuelled violence against disabled people for over 2,000 years. Commonly held beliefs from the past – that disabled people are a freakish spectacle, fair game for amusement and mockery, that they deserve to be treated as slaves, that they are blameworthy scapegoats for society's ills, even that they should not exist at all and should be destroyed – live on and even thrive amongst some people today. More recent controversial opinions, such as those of influential politicians hinting, strongly, that many people on disability benefits are cheats and frauds, have added to a toxic mix.

These discoveries confounded my own perception. Both the Conservative Government and New Labour had embedded legal rights for disabled people in statute in the 1980s and 1990s. They had tried to engineer social change through political reform. But attitudes in society had lagged far behind. Disabled people were, and remain, caught in the middle, between political rhetoric and the reality of their life in our community.

This book is the story of my investigation into disability hate crime, why it exists and what its roots are. It is not only an emotional story, for all of those families and friends of disabled people who have experienced such terrible crimes. It is also a physical journey around England, to the places where disabled people have been taunted, targeted, attacked and in some cases brutally murdered. Over the last year I have travelled all over England – north, to Hartlepool, where Christine Lakinski was urinated on as she lay dying, and further north to Sunderland, where Brent Martin was kicked to death for a £5 bet. I have travelled to the Midlands, to the town of Barwell, near Leicester, where Fiona Pilkington and her daughter Frankie and son Anthony were subjected to years of unrelenting abuse by neighbours and where the atmosphere remains poisoned by that crime to this day. I spent days in and out of court in Luton, just north of London, covering the case of Michael Gilbert, the 'big friendly giant' who was tortured, robbed and finally killed by a family who he considered to be as dear to him as his own, if not dearer. And I visited the West Country, travelling to the tiny hamlet outside Bodmin where Steven Hoskin was born, and St Austell, where a young girl stamped on Steven's fingers until he fell from a railway viaduct 150 feet to his death. All these journeys have helped me map disability hate crime onto geographical locations, where hatred has done violent harm.

It is a journey, too, back into our own common history, to Bedlam, Britain's most famous hospital for those once deemed 'lunatics', to the Hunterian Museum, where the last of the Victorian 'freaks' still entertain visitors, as well as east to Norfolk, to the quiet and beautiful village of Banham, where a headmaster, his brother and their henchmen abused disabled children for decades. I travelled to witch country, to the isolated Stour estuary on the Essex–Suffolk border, where Britain's biggest and most systematic witch-hunt started with a one-legged woman, Elizabeth Clarke – who had to be helped to the gallows and supported to put her head in the noose because of her impairment. I travelled deep into the

Essex countryside, to the Elizabethan village of Sible Hedingham, where in 1863 an old man who could neither speak nor hear, suspected of being a witch, was ducked in the local brook and stoned while a crowd looked on – a crime that culminated in England's last witch trial. I became convinced that our history has bequeathed to us a legacy rich in contempt, fear and hatred. Without recognising our history and what we have inherited from it, we have no hope of confronting disability hate crime and understanding the motivations of those who commit it.

This has been an emotional journey for me, as I have interviewed families and friends bereaved by hate crime and suffering in the aftermath, as well as survivors facing the hatred that some in society feel for them. But it is a political journey too: I have interviewed the senior police officers who investigated some of the worst crimes, disabled activists, academics and prosecutors, all struggling to understand why disability hate crime exists and what can be done to stop it. It has been a journey into darkness, but there has also been light. For this is also an optimistic story, of how disabled people and their families, friends, advocates and allies are coming together to combat disability hate crime and to identify its roots within society.

My job in 2007, as a campaigning journalist, was to gather the evidence that this crime existed and convince the public, the criminal justice system, the media and politicians that it was being missed, time and again. My task this time around has been to hear the testimonies that bear witness to the enduring pain of this crime and its bitter aftermath. But it doesn't end there. I have also looked for motivating factors and geographical patterns. I have searched for similarities between both victims and perpetrators. If we can identify danger signals and discover patterns of escalation early enough, perhaps we can prevent some crimes in the future. And I show some of the work that is being done, already, by disabled groups, the police, transport operators and other agencies, to combat this crime – albeit on a local and patchy level.

I end with a challenge to us as a society. Our own beliefs and prejudices about disability are reflected – magnified and distorted – in the actions of those responsible for disability hate crime. So when we ask who is responsible, the answer is: all of us.

Katharine Quarmby
London
January 2011

1

The Scapegoating of Kevin Davies

The village of Bream sits on top of a hill on the southern edge of one of Britain's most ancient woodlands, the Forest of Dean. As we drove up Bream Hill towards the centre of the village on an early summer evening, grazing sheep, out on the common, looked up at us incuriously. Bream is a quiet place, forgotten by history. That evening it was almost deserted.

This was the village where a young man with epilepsy, Kevin Davies, was tortured by one woman and two men who called themselves his friends, during the spring and summer of 2006.[1] I wanted to find out if a physical journey to the locations where disabled men and women were attacked and killed would reveal something about the nature of the crime. Over the summer and autumn of 2010 I travelled around the country on the same quest, tracing the source of this most pernicious of crimes. What would Bream, and the folk who live around and in it, reveal to me about Kevin Davies, and the men and women who tortured him until he died?

Bream is an ancient settlement, with the first dwellings recorded there in 1452. Its population was made up of miners, farmers and foresters. It has always been a poor area – in 1830, when its school was built, a local benefactor had to step in and pay for it, because the local residents were too poor to send their children to a fee-paying school.[2] Its population has increased, over time, to around 3,000. New council housing was built to accommodate the workers over the last thirty years. But the mines are closed now, and many Bream residents have struggled to find work. Although Gloucestershire itself is a relatively affluent region, the area around Lydney,

6

where Kevin was born and brought up, and Bream, where he was tortured and died, lie in one of the pockets of low rural income and multiple deprivation that scar and trouble an otherwise wealthy county. Lack of access to housing and services, child deprivation and unemployment are all problems in the southern reaches of the Forest of Dean.[3]

Perhaps all these factors go some way to explain the extraordinary sequence of events that led to the death of Kevin Davies, aged just 26. We had left London on a dreary summer's day, driving out west, through the golden Cotswolds and then further into the heart of the Forest. We drove through small villages, with neat houses decorated with hanging baskets. But as we neared Bream, the landscape started to change. It became grimmer and the houses smaller. Some cottages were falling in on themselves, despite being occupied, with leaking roofs and peeling paint.

The social housing in Bream had been crammed into a tiny footprint, despite the wide open spaces beyond. After turning left into the road that led to the housing estate where Kevin had lived, we had to slow to walking pace to get the car through the narrow lanes. One middle-aged man stared and his neighbour leaned on his gate as they watched us out of sight. We drove on, self-consciously, to Badger's Way.

Badger's Way is an unremarkable brown-brick estate, where the houses are huddled together, perhaps six foot apart at most. The house where Kevin was kept prisoner for three months, number fourteen, was clad in summer-flowering jasmine and it was hard to believe that a man was imprisoned here, in an ordinary shed from a DIY store. The estate was bathed in early evening light and children were playing ball in the road. The parents stared at us. I wanted to get out and go to the house itself, but I could see the suspicion in their faces. Eventually we backed out and drove around the corner, to the local chapel. From there I could see the back garden where the shed once stood in which Kevin was tortured and chained up. Clean washing hung on a line and a trampoline took up most of the garden. How could anyone, I wondered, in that close-knit, watchful and suspicious community, have missed the sound of a grown man crying for help, as he did, night after night?

In the rain, the next morning, we drove a few miles north to Lydney, where Kevin's mother and stepfather, Elizabeth and Greg James, live in a neat semi, with a well-tended garden. Kevin Davies was born there, in May 1977. He was a happy, placid child with a love of animals, especially dogs. Kevin's mother had described him to me, during our first long interview in 2007, as 'a gentle giant . . . he wouldn't hurt a fly'.[4]

Elizabeth and Greg's house is crammed with photos of Kevin and his sister as children. His sister Hayley is grown-up now. The photographs of Kevin end when he is a young man. There will never be a wedding photo of Kevin, nor photos of his children. Instead, shortly after my arrival, Elizabeth went upstairs and hauled down a huge suitcase, full of documents – all about Kevin.

But first we talked about Kevin's early life. Elizabeth recalled, smiling: 'He liked going up the woods, playing out,' and added, 'He'd be out in all hours, wearing his shorts, T-shirt and his wellies, he liked his wellies.' They led a simple, contented life, Elizabeth said. 'Kevin liked playing with his mates; he liked the dogs and Manchester United.' 'And *Countdown*,' Greg added, proudly. 'He was quick with his numbers.' But despite his mathematical talent Kevin did not enjoy school.

Things took a turn for the worse when, aged 15, Kevin was diagnosed with a very severe form of epilepsy. 'Nothing was ever done to help him except offer him medication. I asked for more help when he started falling out of bed and jerking about and bumping his head but it was just medication, medication, medication,' his mother had recalled in her earlier interview with me.[5] She asked for extra support to help the family manage his condition, but said she got none.

Kevin left school with few qualifications. He went to college, but dropped out because it was too far from where he lived. He started an apprenticeship as a welder, but his condition forced him to drop out and live on benefits instead. He roamed the Gloucestershire fields, looking for odd jobs. His mother says he had no contact with adult social care services, although he was given a housing association flat.

Kevin turned to his father, a sometime factory worker, for support. His father, although sympathetic, liked to drink, and didn't have a steady job himself. It was around this time, perhaps a year before he met his future torturers, that Kevin developed a liking for cannabis and alcohol. His life drifted and his mother felt she was unable to intervene. 'He left work because of his health, and he went to live with his dad, and that was the end of his jobs. Dad was a very clever man but he let the drink get to him; that's when Kevin started following in his footsteps. Kevin was his dad's son, I'm afraid.' But Elizabeth felt she had to step back and respect his right to independence and privacy. 'He was a young man, you can advise them all you like but whether they take any notice is a different thing. I suppose I lost touch with him a bit.'

In 2004 he came into contact with David Lehane and his partner, Amanda Baggus. Lehane, Mrs James says, befriended Kevin and offered him odd jobs. Like many disabled people, Kevin had become increasingly socially isolated and friendless – at this time, Lehane and Baggus were the only friends he really had.

When Kevin's father died of pneumonia Kevin turned to drink to drown his sorrows and grew closer to Lehane as a result, says Mrs James. On occasion he forgot to take his epilepsy pills, but insisted to his mother that he was 'all right'. In summer 2006 Kevin came to see his mum, who was working in a pub in Lydney, the Greyhound. 'I saw him in the July. All three of them come in, and he'd lost a lot of weight, and I did say to him, "Are you all right?" I put the weight loss down to the death of his father, he was very upset.'

It emerged in court that the sustained attack against Kevin had started when a three-wheeler belonging to Amanda Baggus had overturned in May 2006, and Baggus and Lehane decided to blame Kevin for the accident. Always the fall guy, the scapegoat, as his mother had told me, he was unable to defend himself. They decided that he should pay for the damage, and Baggus started to help herself to Kevin's benefits money. In the diary she kept, she recorded: 'Got Kevin's money, paid Sky.'[6] Just a few weeks after that event, police were called to the house when a dispute between Lehane and Kevin turned ugly. Kevin said something to the police, which led the duo to call him a 'grass' – with fatal results. It was then that the scapegoating took a turn for the worse.

Baggus and Lehane started to lock him in the garden shed and only let him out to be their 'slave', labouring to pay off the 'debt', and being fed scraps of food. When Scott Andrews arrived as a lodger in July, he found Kevin Davies locked in the shed. He told police later that he was surprised and shocked at Kevin's treatment. But instead of raising the alarm, he joined in the assaults. Both the police and prosecutors believe that he was responsible for branding a cross on Kevin's buttocks. (Andrews left on 7 September, a few weeks before Kevin was found by paramedics on the kitchen floor.)

Kevin's mother had tried, as usual, to stay in contact with him, phoning him regularly. He was forced to tell her that he was 'fine' and too busy to visit her. In fact, the torture of Kevin Davies was well under way. He was forced to swallow weedkiller, was beaten regularly and was branded with a hot knife on his arm. He was also burned with what pathologists think was an iron. His larynx and ribs were broken. By the time Kevin's frail body was examined in the mortuary, around 10 per cent was covered in burns and there were bruises all over.[7]

Police believe that it was Amanda Baggus, who at one stage was a care assistant and had a young child, who had instigated the plot to imprison Kevin. (Indeed the judge, in his summing-up, called her the 'initiator' of the 'maltreatment'.) They put a dog collar around his neck and dragged him around. She kept a detailed diary about Kevin's captivity. One chilling entry, in her childlike scrawl, reads: 'both Scott and Dave hit Prick until quite late, cause Prick made a load of shouting'.[8] Sadly, the nearest neighbour was an 84-year-old whose hearing was poor. No one intervened.

Towards the end of his torture, the trio, perhaps dimly realising that what they were doing was wrong, filmed a hostage video in which they forced Kevin to say that he was being treated well. On the video, Kevin, an emaciated shadow of the happy, golden-haired schoolboy he had once been, stumbles with his words. He is filmed crouching on the floor, as if for his own protection. He looks scared. He is prompted, aggressively, to talk: 'Speak! Speak! Speak!' one of the three shouts at him. He says, haltingly: 'I'm fine . . . I'm being fed perfectly, actually,' and adds that he is being kept inside for his own safety. A few days later, on 26 September 2006, after four months of torture and imprisonment, paramedics were called to the house by Amanda Baggus. Kevin was found dead on the kitchen floor.

When the police came to Lydney, to tell Elizabeth and Greg about Kevin's death, his mother thought that perhaps Kevin had mistakenly taken an overdose of drugs. She had no idea that his so-called friends were involved in his death. 'A few weeks prior to that, it was a Sunday lunchtime, the phone went and it was Kevin and he said, "I'm just phoning to let you know that I've gone to Cinderford with a bird," that was how Kevin spoke, and I said, "I hope you haven't given your flat up," and he said, "I've done that," and he didn't want to talk any more, he was just letting me know he'd gone to Cinderford to live with this bird. I did start to worry then, because Cinderford has always been a rife place for drugs, and so of course when police come and told me they had found Kevin dead I thought it was something to do with drugs. Of course my family came, I had to let them know, and my daughter, Hayley, and my sister went to Bream. I had a mobile phone number for David Lehane and I tried it a couple of times, thinking, Is he all right? I knew Kevin had been found in Bream, and I was concerned for David, and I phoned and it was switched off. Hayley even went to Bream to check on him. And all the time he was in police custody.'

The police arrested the three perpetrators on suspicion of murder. But the Crown Prosecution Service advised the police that they could not make a murder charge stick, as it was not clear whether

Kevin Davies had died following a seizure or as a result of his captivity. Instead, the three were charged with wrongful imprisonment and assault occasioning actual bodily harm. Sentenced to between nine and ten years in jail, Scott Andrews was due for release in April 2011 and Baggus and Lehane in November 2011.

I interviewed Elizabeth James for the first time just a few days after the end of the trial. She told me that the police had never asked her about Kevin's disability. Indeed, the senior investigating officer, DCI Geoff Brookes, was at a loss to explain the crimes at the time, saying that only those responsible 'knew what had motivated them'. I started to investigate other cases of disability hate crime, looking for patterns in the deaths of five disabled men – the others were Steven Hoskin, Barrie-John Horrell, Rikki Judkins and Raymond Atherton – and in this book I look at a number of those crimes again, in more depth.

There are many similarities between the cases – four of the men were attacked by friends, and they were tortured first, robbed and de-humanised.[9] They were forced to labour as slaves, what money they had was stolen and they were seen as less than human. These were not motiveless crimes, even if the perpetrators were unable to say exactly why they had done what they had done. They had picked the men out, blamed them for a crime and then punished them for it, and at the end expelled them from society by eradicating them. This was a crime with both ancient and modern overtones.

I have obtained more information about these cases and others, using Freedom of Information legislation and conducting in-depth interviews with families, friends and senior investigating officers. In the case of Kevin Davies, I acquired an audio transcript of the coroner's ruling on the case, as well as the prosecutor's opening statement and the judge's summing-up. These documents reveal new information about Kevin's death.

Mr Pringle, opening for the Crown, laid out the vicious nature of the attacks suffered by Kevin in the last few months of his life, saying that he had 'been kept like a dog in a locked garden shed', and concluding that the treatment was 'miserable and inhumane'. He made absolutely no mention of whether the three defendants were motivated by hostility towards Kevin's disability. But they knew that he had epilepsy and needed regular medication to prevent seizures (Baggus collected his prescription for him regularly and some of it was in his bloodstream, the pathologist said, as well as weedkiller).[10]

Mr Justice Gray, the judge, made reference to Kevin being 'gullible and naive' and dubbed him 'vulnerable'. Astonishingly, he even credited the three perpetrators for having 'befriended' Kevin when he was 'down on his luck'. He painted a graphic picture of the torture that Kevin had endured, as well as the fact that he had lost over three stone in weight since 2000.[11]

But other issues became clearer as I researched Kevin's death. One was that both Amanda Baggus and Scott Andrews had disabilities themselves. Baggus had mental health problems, and the diary she kept to record the torture of Kevin was in fact given her by a local mental health team to help her chronicle her mood swings.[12] Indeed, having read the mitigation for Baggus in court, it is clear that she could have been described as a 'vulnerable person' herself at that time – socially isolated, self-harming, unable to look after her child and almost unable to leave the house. Of course none of that in any way excuses what she did, but knowing it helps put the jigsaw together.

Andrews had been attacked in 2000 and suffered a brain haemorrhage, leaving him completely deaf in one ear and partially deaf in the other, as well as having a speech impairment and facial paralysis. None of the three had a steady job. This pattern has held true for almost every other defendant whose case I have examined. The three of them took work, mainly illegally, and both Lehane and Andrews had criminal records.

Geoff Brookes, a former detective chief inspector who has now retired from Gloucestershire Police, clearly recalled the Kevin Davies case, on which he was senior investigating officer: 'From the amount of time I'd be in the police service and investigating serious crimes you don't get shocked any more but it was extraordinary – to find some human being doing that level of abuse to someone they knew, to a friend.' Why had nobody intervened? 'We did house to house inquiries: you would have thought they would have heard something, seen something, how can you have someone kept in a garden shed? It's incredible, but we came back with a big blank.'

The motivating trigger, he believed, was Baggus overturning her car on a corner, though why Kevin was blamed for it was never clarified. Was he just the easy person to blame? I asked Mr Brookes if Kevin's disability and his vulnerable situation had inflamed the atmosphere. 'It's an aspect that I think is dreadfully sad, that Baggus and Lehane, more Baggus, had the motivation and the ability to control him. I don't think anybody put pen to paper to ask whether he had any psychological needs, or that he had special needs, but you would regard him as vulnerable and meek and mild, he was compliant.' He believes strongly that Amanda Baggus was the principal perpetrator. 'Her persona was calculating, she misrepresented herself, she was the motivating factor behind the abuse of Kevin, she got off on it, and she enjoyed having the power and control.' But why? I asked again. 'You can see the mindset of the attacker coming: they have the opportunity, they have a sense of power, and they get heady on it.' That thrill-seeking element, present in so many hate crimes, rings true. And, of course, in all the cases I have examined, nobody stops them.

Shortly after my analysis of those killings was published in 2007 in *Disability Now* – under the headline 'If these are not hate crimes, what are?' – things started to shift, at least a little. At a parliamentary meeting in November 2007, Sir Ken Macdonald, the Director of Public Prosecutions, conceded that there may have been 'an underlying hostility' towards Kevin Davies. He told me a few months later, in our first interview: 'I was particularly struck by the idea of locking someone in a shed and treating them like an animal, there is a very disturbing level of violence in the cases you have highlighted, I completely accept that, it is a campaign of sadistic violence.'[13] This was the first crack in the wall of the apparent complacency of the CPS regarding disability hate crime.

Then on 29 February 2008, after Elizabeth James had pushed for an inquest, the Gloucestershire coroner recorded a verdict of unlawful killing on the Kevin Davies case. This followed clear evidence from the pathologist that he did not believe that Kevin's epilepsy had caused his death. The coroner declared: 'I am satisfied so that I have no reasonable doubt that Mr Davies died from multiple blunt force trauma.' He said that the final blow – the blow that killed him – was delivered by Baggus to the head with a plastic jug.[14] This new evidence was forwarded immediately to the Attorney General, Baroness Scotland.

But her response was that she did not consider the evidence worthy of a retrial, because there was no 'new and compelling evidence'.[15] She also said that Baggus, Lehane and Andrews would be released automatically after serving just half of their sentences. Amanda Baggus, indeed, was spotted in 2010 working in a charity shop, on day release from prison – to the horror and disgust of Elizabeth and Greg James.

Just before I left Elizabeth and Greg, she showed me a picture of Kevin unwrapping a present when he was two years old. Dressed in a smart red romper suit, Kevin is smiling with joy as he lifts his new toy, Kermit the frog, out of its wrapping paper. 'He loved his Kermit, he did,' said Elizabeth. 'I thought about it, and in the end I buried Kermit with him. It seemed right.' I left them, with their memories, their photographs, a suitcase full of documents – and the feeling that they, and Kevin, had never received justice.

Elizabeth and Greg still struggle to understand why Kevin died. This book is my attempt to understand Kevin's death, and so many other crimes against disabled people. It defies understanding that Kevin should have been scapegoated, tortured and imprisoned, just because of damage to a car. Something, perhaps unconscious, deep and dark, lies behind it.

This journey is into the heart and the roots of violence against disabled people like Kevin. To understand the present we need to journey back into time – into the stereotypes that have surrounded disabled people since recorded history began. Ancient archetypes – the scapegoat, the sinner and the freak, to name but three – play their part in motivating disability hate crime. So the first part of my journey is to classical times, and Greek and Roman civilisation, where the roots of our culture lie deep.

The Greek and Roman Legacy

In November 2010 I stood before the fragments of the Pantheon frieze in the British Museum, looking at some of the sculptures deemed the most beautiful in the Western world. The Greek and Roman rooms were, as always, full of people. Some students sat on their haunches, absorbed, sketching. Tourists snapped photographs in front of their favoured statues, and children with clipboards wandered around, spotting clues and images for school projects.

My eyes settled on the horses and horsemen, full of energy. Nostrils flared, manes full of wind, their riders urge them on towards battle. Yet they are fragmentary, broken. We experience them, uncritically, as beautiful, yet for thousands of years they have not been whole. Even when they were first carved they were not whole for long – marble is a brittle stone to work and jointed limbs often break off. The Venus de Milo, for example, now in the Paris Louvre, judged by many to be the most beautiful Greek statue of all time, has two fragmented arms. She is the epitome of female beauty. Greek and Roman statuary is one of the cornerstones of our aesthetic imagination. They are broken, yet beautiful.

I am reminded of the controversy when the artist Alison Lapper, a disabled woman with short arms and legs, was sculpted, pregnant, by Marc Quinn and the statue displayed on the fourth plinth in Trafalgar Square in 2005.[1] Many said it was grotesque. But Alison was, and is, beautiful – and she, too, questions why so many find her grotesque and yet the Venus de Milo stunning. She writes, in her autobiography, 'One particular book I was looking at fell open at a photograph of the Venus de Milo. It showed a white marble statue, in the ancient

Greek style, of a woman with both her arms missing. There was a flash of recognition – hey, that's me!'[2] 'Her version of herself as the Venus de Milo has challenged many, as has Marc Quinn's. Why, he has argued, are the fragments left behind by time seen with an un-conditional acceptance, when those who lack living limbs are seen as grotesque or mocked as a freak show?

As Alison Lapper says herself, many non-disabled people aren't in-terested in seeing the 'aesthetic beauty that may live in depiction of impaired forms. If we walk along the beach and find a stone with a hole in it, we don't look at it with revulsion simply because most other stones don't have holes in them. In fact, we may be entranced by the variety of shape that the stone with the hole has brought to our attention. However, we don't respond in that way to the human form when it varies too much from the accepted norm.'[3]

Our attitudes to imperfection and disability descend directly from the concept of the body beautiful of Greek and Roman culture. Those cultures, and the stereotypes and prejudices they developed towards disabled people, were and remain very powerful – from the disabled person carrying a stigma, being cursed by the gods because of an innate sin, to the singling-out of disabled people as scapegoats to be sacrificed for the common good, and the increasing exploita-tion of disabled people as monsters and curiosities, to be collected and exhibited in freak shows – and, of course, for some, being erad-icated at birth as not worthy of life. All of these deep-seated cultural beliefs underpin disability hatred and help to explain a general dis-comfort with disability today.

One of the most powerful archetypes, which lives on today, is that of the scapegoat. When a crisis or disaster struck a Greek city, bring-ing down the ire of the gods upon mortals, the citizens would select an offering to appease the divine wrath. The scapegoat – or *pharma-kos*, in ancient Greek – would sometimes be expelled for ever from the city state, sometimes even sacrificed. All too often the offering that cleansed and purified the state was a 'useless' person[4] or an 'out-cast' (translated from the word *katharmata*), 'beggars, below the rank of men'. Someone 'mistreated by nature' was often targeted, it seems.[5] All these words suggest that disabled people were frequently selected as perfect candidates for scapegoating.

Daniel Ogden, a classical scholar, explains it thus: an unsatisfactory individual is born in a city state (either a bastard or a deformed person), who either 'embodies a *loimos* (pestilence, sterility), or brings *loimos* on it' and therefore must be expelled. This is done by exposing the individual (the *teras*, or deformed baby) at birth, or by scapegoating the individual as an adult. 'The evil deformed child that must be expelled to avert *loimos* finds an adult correlate in the figure of the scapegoat. The expulsion of the scapegoat was similarly intended to secure fertility and ward off sterility: like the *teras*, the scapegoat was a pollution.'[6]

Ogden quotes from a text of the time: 'when a famine or something else of things which are deprecated occurred among the Greeks, they would take the man who was most odious and a cripple, a victim of nature, a lame man, people of that sort, and they would sacrifice him to be rid of the evil that was troubling them.'[7] Another similar text states: 'When a disaster of any sort fell on a certain city they burned with barren logs the most deformed and unpleasant man on behalf of that city cursed by God.'[8]

Being born with a disability in ancient Greece was a misfortune indeed: you were viewed from the outset as unworthy of life. Children were selected and inspected at birth. The Greek physician Soranus, in the Gynaecology section of his *Manual for the Head of Household*, from AD 2, wrote that a child should 'be perfect in all its parts, limbs and senses, and have passages that are not obstructed, including the ears, nose, throat, urethra and anus. Its natural movements should be neither slow nor feeble, its limbs should bend and stretch, its size and shape should be appropriate, and it should respond to natural stimuli'.[9]

The most respected of Greece's ancient moral philosophers agreed that only the fit should survive. In Sparta, according to Plutarch, in his account of the founder of the state, written in the first or second century AD, it was a legal requirement of citizenship that all children should be examined. 'Whenever a child was born, it was taken to a council of elders for examination. If the baby was in any way defective, the elders dropped it into a chasm. Such a child, in the opinion of the Spartans, should not be permitted to live.'[10] Plutarch wrote that 'ill born or misshapen children are sent to the place called Apothetae, a ravine at the Mount Taygetus'.[11]

In Book Five of Plato's *Republic*, Socrates is quoted as saying, 'The offspring of the inferior Guardians, and any defective offspring of the others, will be quietly and secretly disposed of.'[12] Aristotle concurs, declaring in *The Politics*: 'With regard to the choice between abandoning a child or rearing it, let there be a law that no cripple child be reared.'[13]

Nobody knows for sure whether these edicts were utopian or were actually enacted (the scholar Rosemary Garland Thomson contends that few were actually killed).[14] Daniel Ogden agrees that there is a paucity of solid archaeological evidence either way (baby skeletons tend to disintegrate quickly), but points to one example, where the excavation of an Attic well revealed 175 baby skeletons at its base.[15]

However widespread or not this practice might have been, those who led the moral thinking of the Greeks were agreed on the need to cleanse the state of disability. Two of the most famous Greek depictions of paradise, Plato's *Republic* and the vision of Utopia described by Diodorus Siculus, were places where disability was banished. Plato not only said that disabled babies must be killed, but that disabled priests were strictly forbidden. In Diodorus's utopian work, anyone acquiring a disability was instructed to kill themselves.

Those attitudes towards 'good breeding' and banishing defection resonate today, and helped to inspire the twentieth-century obsession with eugenics. In a chilling passage, Plato argues: 'we must . . . mate the best of our men with the best of our women as often as possible',[16] a reminder of Hitler's obsession with Aryan children and his experiment, *Lebensborn*, to breed a master race.[17]

Plato also makes a plea for what we would call assisted suicide and 'do not resuscitate' notices, arguing that doctors should not attempt to cure those whose constitution is basically diseased: 'by treating them to a series of evacuations and doses and which can only lead to a prolongation of life, and the production of children as unhealthy as themselves'.[18] He also argues, in the *Laws*, that marrying someone with a disease or a 'deformity' of either mind or body can make life 'unbearable'.[19]

If someone acquired an impairment or somehow grew up with one, their fate was uncertain. Words used to describe impairment and disability can be neutral – in Aristotle's *Politics* disability is described in a variety of ways, including 'weakness' (*astheneia*), but also in more pejorative terms such as 'ugliness' (*aischros*) or even 'disgrace' (*aischos*).

Disability was, as it is too often today, seen as shameful. Even Hephaestus, a god, was banished from heaven because of his impairment. His mother, Hera, in the *Hymn to Apollo*, says: 'my son Hephaestus, whom I bear, was weakly among all the blessed gods and shrivelled of foot, a shame and a disgrace to me in heaven, whom I myself took in my hands and cast out so that he fell in the great sea'.[20] Indeed, Hephaestus, in *The Odyssey*, internalises this hatred, describing himself as 'misshapen' and bewailing his birth. And Aphrodite took a non-disabled lover to compensate for her husband being a 'cripple' – and therefore thought of, even today, as impotent and unmanned.

Disability is also connected with evil – a prejudice that gains even more traction in the Middle Ages and beyond, in the era of the European witch-hunts. Hephaestus is often represented with one leg shortened to denote his lameness; and throughout the Middle Ages it was popularly believed that his cloven hoof was the one feature that the Devil was unable to disguise. As Frederick Hall wrote: 'Hephaestus, Vulcan and Loki, each lame from some deformity of foot, in time joined natures with the Pans and satyrs of the upper world; the lame sooty blacksmith donned their goat-like extremities of cloven hoofs, tail and horns; and the black dwarfs became uncouth ministers of this sooty, black, foul fiend.'[21]

Lameness acquired in battle, or limbs lost, however, were accepted

– up to a point. Indeed, men with a variety of physical impairments participated in the military. Agesilaus, a Spartan king, was lame, as were many Roman soldiers. Artemon, in Plutarch's *Pericles*, was very lame. But disabled soldiers did not escape mockery – in the *Iliad*, Thersites is mocked for being lame, a hunchback and ugly, although he was not excluded from the army.

Disability is also a stigma. As Erving Goffman writes in *Stigma: Notes on the Management of Spoiled Identity*, the Greeks coined the term 'stigma' to refer to bodily signs designed to expose something unusual and bad about the moral status of the signifier. The signs were cut or burned into the body and advertised that the bearer was a slave, a criminal or a traitor – 'a blemished person, ritually polluted, to be avoided, especially in public places'.[22] (In later chapters I discuss how many disabled victims of crime are branded, even today.) Goffman argues that there are three different types of stigma. One is that of disability – what he calls the 'abomination' of the body, when it is deformed. Then there is the blemish of individual character. And thirdly there are the 'tribal stigma' of face, nation and religion.

Goffman's analysis of stigma could be taken as a description of hate crime today: 'The attitudes we normals have towards a person with a stigma, and the actions we take in regard of him, are well known . . . by definition, of course, we believe the person with a stigma is not quite human. On this assumption we experience varieties of discrimination, through which we effectively, if often unthinkingly, reduce his life chances.'[23]

As the Roman Empire gained territory, and Greek power de-clined, one legacy remained: hostile attitudes towards disability. The Romans, indeed, extended the abuse of both disabled children and adults in their open enjoyment of 'freakery' and spectacle. They also, discriminated against disability from birth. According to Dionysius of Halicarnassus, Romulus, the founder of Rome, demanded that 'de-formed or monstrous' children should be killed at birth, at the behest of the father. The Roman Law of the Twelve Tables stipulated that the deformed child should die, after being shown to five neighbours.

Methods varied. The usual way seems to have been drowning (in the River Tiber), although other methods were also used. Another author from the era of early imperial Rome, Philo of Alexandria, described the various ways in which infants may have been killed: 'Some of them do the deed with their own hands; with monstrous cruelty and barbarity they stifle and throttle the first breath which the infants draw, or throw them into a river or into the depths of the sea, after attaching some heavy substance to make them sink more quickly under its weight. Others take them to be exposed in some desert place, hoping, they themselves say, that they may be saved, but leaving them in actual truth to suffer the most distressing fate. For all the beasts that feed on human flesh visit the spot and feast unhindered on the infants, a fine banquet provided by their sole guardians, those who above all others should keep them safe, their fathers and mothers.'[24]

The Romans also developed and refined the archetype of the scapegoat – which they called a '*devotio*'. Walter Burkert describes two models for it: 'Either the victim must be termed subhuman, particularly guilty, or "offscourings" to be dumped, or else he is raised to superhuman level, to be honoured for ever. The extremes may even be seen to meet, deepest abasement turning into divinity.'[25] Both the aristocrat and the 'cripple', therefore, were called upon, at times, writes Burkert, to give their lives for the state. In *The Sorrows of the Ancient Romans*, Carlin A. Barton notes that the scapegoat was often disabled: 'They were the recipients of many of the blows aimed at deformity . . . Embodiments of chaos and representatives of the society, the *stupidi*, were types of the scapegoat.'[26]

But it was perhaps in their fascination with the 'freak show', the spectacle, that the Romans can most clearly be seen to have passed their ideas about disability down to the Victorians and beyond, into present-day crimes. Cicero talks about deformity and disfigurement making for good comic material – something that holds true today. Carlin A. Barton observes that the Roman populace shared with aristocrats an enormous appetite for 'novelty in spectacles', noting that Seneca the Elder, organising the *Controversiae*, encouraged combat between dwarfs, women and animals, a practice that delighted Romans. 'Roman bestiality formed part of the extended repertoire of pleasures which included the enjoyment of the available array of monsters, freaks, fools, exotic persons, animals, and food.'[27] The monsters – disabled people – were seen as wonderful spectacles. Dwarfs, hunchbacks and 'fools' were all in demand as entertainers.

Indeed, Plutarch and Longinus note that children were even deliberately deformed by being bound and confined in boxes so that they could be sold at the *teraton agora* or 'monster market'. Barton notes: 'There are those at Rome – the *curiosi* – who, according to Plutarch, pass by the handsome boys and girls for sale and proceed to the monster market, the *teraton agora*, and search out those with three eyes or ostrich heads or weasel arms.'[28]

As in Victorian times, human deformity became a marvel of the natural world, and disabled people collectors' items. Pliny the Elder records two such, in his catalogue of human wonders, *Natural History*: the giant Gabbara, bought in the age of Claudius, and the dwarf Cinopas, kept by the granddaughter of Augustus, Julia, as a pet.[29] 'Naturals' or 'fools' were also bought, and prized as pets, for their naive wit.[30] Roman emperors were particularly fond of dwarfs, often giving them confidential positions at court (a practice that originated in Egypt). Tiberius, Claudius, Nero and Domitian are all known to have employed disabled slaves as close confidants.

The Romans, too, saw disability as a stigma – as something that might make the disabled person powerless in themselves, but powerful in that they could pass on their sin to others. Pliny writes: 'We spit on epileptics in a fit, that is, we throw back contagion. In a similar way we ward off witchcraft and bad luck which follows meeting a person lame in the right leg.'[31] Carlin A. Barton describes the monster or disabled person as both rejected by the gods and expressing godly power at the same time – a paradox that explains the toxic mix of fear and contempt even now experienced by disabled people.[32]

Even the Emperor Claudius, who escaped death at birth only because he was from the highest echelon of Roman society, was subject
to abuse from both the Roman nobility and Roman guards because
of his disability (now thought to be cerebral palsy and resulting mobility impairments) prior to taking the imperial throne. His mother
Antonia treated him with contempt and referred to him as 'a monster
of a man, not finished by nature and only half done'.[33] But Claudius was in fact highly intelligent, and to some extent enlightened.
He presided over partial democratisation, gave freedmen new duties,
improved the rule of law and was less corrupt than many of his
counterparts.

However, the picture is not completely bad. Some writers, like
Pliny, could see that disability was part of nature. In his *Natural History* he writes: 'deformed children may be born of healthy parents
and healthy children, or children with the same deformity, may be
born of deformed parents'.[34]

As in Greece, disabled soldiers were tolerated, perhaps because they
had once been whole – although they too were seen as cursed by
the gods and therefore not worthy of approaching the deities, as this
passage from Pliny reveals of one eminent soldier, General Sergius:
'He had a right hand made of iron for him and, going into battle
with this bound to his arm, raised the siege of Cremona, saved
Placentia and captured twelve enemy camps in Gaul. All these
exploits were confirmed by the speech he made during his term as
praetor, when his colleagues tried to keep him away from the sacri-
fices, as one who was disabled.'[35]

As Greek culture fell into decline in the Alexandrian era, artists started to sculpt new types of figure not conforming to a rigid
aesthetic of beauty – hunchbacks, older people and black people.
Many statuettes of disabled people are known as 'grotesques' and are
thought to have been created to ward off the evil eye, but others are
more sympathetic and speak to us poignantly, even today. Egypt and
Mesopotamia took a more generous attitude towards some disabilities. One ancient Egyptian text, the *Instruction of Amenemope*, declares:

Do not laugh at a blind man
Nor tease a dwarf
Nor cause hardship for the lame.
Don't tease a man who is in the hand of the God
Nor be angry with him for his failings.

Another ancient Mesopotamian myth, of Enki and Ninmah, describes the creation of humanity, according to the scholar Neal Walls, in a way that celebrates and explains the origin of 'normal' and 'abnormal' human forms.[36] It also suggests a function for people with different impairments – a blind man can be a musician, a man with weak hands a servant, and a man with paralysed feet a silversmith. 'Rather than naming disability as a means to exclude some persons from city life, this myth recognises an "otherness" to each of Ninmah's children.'[37]

It was only when the Egyptians feared genetic contamination that they 'enforced normalcy', in the words of Lennard J. Davis.[38] Some texts suggest burying children with a condition that is similar to Huntingdon's. But it was not a common fate for disabled children. The only category of impairment that was associated with sin was skin conditions, in particular leprosy and dropsy according to Neal Walls, who concludes that disability was socially acceptable in Mesopotamia – unlike Ancient Greece and Rome.[39]

Unfortunately, however, the civilisations of Greece and Rome have influenced our culture more than those of Egypt and Mesopotamia. Our legacy from those times is one rich in contempt for disabled people. Sinner, slave, scapegoat, stigma and spectacle – a human without humanity, who should be banished from sight and segregated permanently – these images of and prejudices towards disabled people are rooted deep in our culture. Later images – the disabled person as a scourge, bringing down death and disaster on those around them, sexual beings without the restraints of 'normal people' and the suspect scrounger, undeserving of state handouts – also fuel the attitudes behind disability hate crimes. We understand more about disability hate crime perpetrators and their motivation than we think, and that understanding comes from history. But reversing attitudes that we have lived with for thousands of years is not an easy task.

3

Sin, Disability and Witch-Hunting

During the civil war that devastated England in the 1640s, a lawyer of sorts, one Matthew Hopkins, decided to take it on himself to search out witches, torture them until they confessed, and then have them put to death, earning a handsome profit in the process. He styled himself the Witchfinder General, as if the Government had appointed him, although in fact he had no mandate at all.[1] By the time he had finished his evil work he had interrogated some three hundred 'witches', almost all women, and around one-third of them had been hanged, victims of a terrible hate crime epidemic that swept across Europe.

As is the case with many hate crimes today, Hopkins started with his neighbours, in the small East Anglian town of Manningtree. Manningtree is an isolated spot nowadays, inland on the Stour estuary, not far from today's great ports of Harwich and Felixstowe. But in the seventeenth century it was a busy and thriving town.

In 1644 Goodwife Rivet took to her bed in Manningtree, with a wasting illness. Her husband John was at his wits' end with anxiety and consulted another woman, Goodwife Hovey, as to the cause. She in turn blamed an 'ageing' woman, Elizabeth Clarke, a one-legged woman who lived alone in the town, saying that she had laid a spell on the sick woman. Matthew Hopkins took an interest in the case and, along with his accomplice John Stearne, visited Elizabeth Clarke, suspecting her of witchcraft.

Malcolm Gaskill provides a vivid account of that time in *Witchfinders*, his heartbreaking history of the tragedy: 'as their eyes adjust-

28

ed to Clarke's faintly illuminated figure – an old beldame in rags, balanced on a stool, crutch in hand, Stearne and Hopkins made their menacing demands that she divulge the names of her accomplices'.[2] Some twenty-nine witches, Elizabeth Clarke amongst them, eventually stood trial in Chelmsford, at the Assizes, on 17 July 1645. Hopkins and Stearne had deprived them of sleep, had them stripped and searched by other women and marched up and down to prevent them from resting. Among them was another neighbour of both Hopkins and Clarke, Anne West. She had always expressed pity for Clarke's disability and poverty, telling her 'there was wayes and means for her to live much better than she did'. One witness of the time, Arthur Wilson, was sympathetic. He said of the witches that they were the 'poor and unfortunate, the decrepit and diseased'. Most, however, lacked his pity. Elizabeth Clarke was the first to take the stand, and was condemned to death. Eighteen of them were sent to the gallows, in Chelmsford, on 18 July. Elizabeth had to be helped up to a height where the noose could be put around her neck.

Manningtree, where Elizabeth lived, and nearby Mistley, where Hopkins is said to have ducked many of his victims in a pond under what is known locally as the 'Hopping Bridge', are quiet places now. The pond where so many women were ducked (and, some say, many drowned) is now part of an animal rescue centre. Flocks of geese and swans swim on the pond, or waddle over the road to the Stour estuary, where they gather in thousands on the mud-flats before rising and heading up and into the grey sky. The tourists that visit this place now are either birdwatchers or believers in the paranormal, who can join guided walks and lurk by the spots where ghosts are said to have been seen or heard. Hopkins, for his part, either died in his bed and is buried nearby or was ducked and drowned himself by angry locals. Nobody really knows. But the place feels saddened by its history, as do the small villages around, where so many women were put to death, violently, by men who sought to make a profit by targeting those who couldn't fight back.

It was not of course just disabled people, and women in particular, who were put to death on suspicion of being witches, but academics agree that the infirm, the different, the older and those with mental health conditions were more likely to be targeted. Brian Levack, who wrote the classic account, *The Witch-Hunt in Early Modern Europe*, says that although we know little about most witches, we do know that most were over 50. In Essex the median age was 60. In Levack's opinion, a reason for accused people being older 'lies in the fact that older people, especially if senile, often manifested signs of eccentric or antisocial behaviour which tended to make neighbours uncomfortable and to invite accusations of witchcraft'.[3] The powerful stereotype of a witch, as we know even today, was of an 'old, sexually voracious hag'.[4] But observers at the time also refer to the fact that many had impairments. A noted sceptic of the time and justice of the peace in Kent, Reginald Scot, says pityingly of them that they were 'commonly old, lame, blear-eyed, pale, foul, full of wrinkles . . . lean and deformed showing melancholy in their faces to the horror of all that see them'.[5] Another noted sixteenth-century Dutch dissident, Johann Weyer, describes them as 'poor ignorant creatures, old and powerless'[6] and argued against prosecution, saying that many of them were afflicted by melancholy (what we would now call depression). But many were genuinely feared, Levack argues, as disabled people sometimes are today: 'This popular view of the witch as a powerful woman reminds us that although the witch was often a scapegoat for the ills of society and a victim, many of her neighbours viewed her as both powerful and threatening. By having her tried and executed, her neighbours were not simply picking on a helpless old woman, but counteracting a form of female power.'[7]

This is no surprise. The concept of the disabled person as sinner, and as being in league with the Devil, or even being its 'spawn', gained tremendous traction during the Middle Ages and beyond. Small wonder that it ended in widespread slaughter, when two major Western religions, Judaism and Christianity, had reinforced such powerful, negative concepts about disabled people.

Ancient Jewish culture perceived impairments as ungodly and the consequence of wrongdoing. Indeed, Talmudic scholars listed 142 qualifying disabilities for not being priests. Leviticus, in the Old Testament, catalogues the imperfections that should divide God from disabled people – and keep them from sacred places: 'He must not profane the holy places, for I am the Lord who sanctifies them. None of your descendants throughout their generations who has a blemish may approach to offer the bread of his God. For no one who has a blemish shall draw near, a man blind or lame, or one who has a mutilated face or a limb too long, or a man who has an injured hand, or a hunchback or a dwarf, or a man with a defect in his sight or an itching disease or scabs or crushed testicles.'[8] The Book of Samuel, another sacred text for both Judaism and Christianity, declares equally sternly: 'the blind and the lame shall not come into the home'.[9]

Early Christianity, too, focused on 'curing' the lame and sick, who should battle their disability – and renounce the sin that caused it. In Luke, Chapter 5, Jesus exhorts the penitent sinner to 'take up thy bed and walk', and disability is seen as a punishment from God ('be cured if you sin no more') in John, Chapter 9. As Thomas Hentrich, a biblical scholar, points out, there was an obligation of charity towards disabled people, but they were also considered to be carriers of God's wrath for an unnamed sin in the past. On the other hand, Jesus approaches and heals disabled people, despite their perceived impurity.[10]

Disability was either viewed as a sin, or as a possession, or as an illness that must be fought and overcome – as long as the patient remained virtuous. (These attitudes are still pervasive today. People 'battle' cancer or 'lose the fight' against multiple sclerosis. 'Brave' amputee children are celebrated for their achievements, as are 'plucky' servicemen and women who lose limbs in modern battles.)

These attitudes pervaded Western culture during the medieval period. There were political developments too, with a clear legal distinction made for the first time between 'lunatics' and 'idiots', with the De Praerogativa Regis Act in 1324 giving the King custody of the land of 'natural fools' and wardship of the property of the insane. Lunatics and fools faced inquisitions from locally appointed King's Officers, known as Escheators, to determine which category fitted them.

The first asylum for 'lunatics', Bedlam, was founded in 1377, in the East End of London. We will return to Bedlam later, but at this point in its long history those who were confined there were chained up for hours on end and often starved, and deprived of fresh air, exercise and even water. As early as 1403 a Visitation had recorded a 'deplorable state of affairs' at Bethlem and a Royal Commission inquired into the conditions there two years later. When Thomas More visited over a century later, nothing much had changed. He wrote in *Four Last Things*, published in 1522: 'For thou shalt in Bedlam see one laughing at the knocking of his head against a post, and yet there is little pleasure therein.'[11]

By the end of the fourteenth century the British Crown had developed the concept of the deserving and undeserving poor. Disabled people were mostly placed in the first category. The lucky ones were admitted to small hospitals in which were gathered 'the poor, the sick and the bedridden'. Those rejected by their families and the Church, on the other hand, drifted from parish to parish, as 'deranged beggars'.[12]

In 1487 a manual called *Malleus Maleficarum*, known as the 'handbook of the witch-hunters' and written by two German Catholic friars, Jakob Sprenger and Heinrich Kramer, stated that children with impairments were born to mothers who were involved with witchcraft and sorcery. Disabled people provided living proof of Satan's existence and of his power over humans. Thus, visibly impaired children were seen as 'changelings', the Devil's substitutes for human children. The book explained how to identify witches by their impairments, by 'evidence' of them creating impairments in others, or by their giving birth to a disabled child. It stated that 'creatures can be made by witches, although they necessarily must be very imperfect creatures and probably in some way deformed'.[13]

Scholars believe that many thousands of people, mostly women (Levack estimates around 50,000), were put to death as witches across

Europe between the fifteenth and seventeenth centuries. Many of those targeted were disabled. Woman herself, in *Malleus Maleficarum*, is a deformity: 'It should be noted that there was a defect in the first woman, since she was formed from a bent rib, that is, a rib of the beast, which is bent as it were in a contrary direction to a man. And since through this defect she is an imperfect animal, she always deceives.'[14]

Malleus might have lain unread, without much influence, had it not been endorsed and popularised by the religious leader Martin Luther, who initiated the Protestant Reformation. Texts written by him reveal the spirit of the times: the belief that many disabled or ill people are possessed by the Devil. He was particularly scathing about disabled women. He talks of women 'being tormented by jealous and spiteful old hags' who cast the evil eye and can harm children or put a devilish changeling in their place.[15]

In *Table Talk*, a collection of his writings published in 1532, Luther declared: 'In all grave illnesses the Devil is present as the author and the cause . . . all dangerous diseases are blows of the Devil.'[16] He repeated those views at other times, claiming that many disabled people were possessed by the Devil. In another infamous text, Luther is reported as saying that he had seen the Devil in a disabled child, a 12-year-old boy, living at Dessau, who had no speech. He is thought to have advised the local ruler, the Prince of Anhalt: 'Take the changeling child to the river and drown it.' As this was a record of a dinner-party conversation, we do not know whether this is true, but many of his writings betray a very hostile attitude towards women and children with impairments.

Why were disabled people being targeted? Brian Levack explains that the witch-hunts came at a time of economic insecurity and, in England, a civil war. In a society full of anxiety and fear, people relieved these feelings by transferring them onto another person, i.e. a scapegoat. By depicting a poorer person who begged for money as a witch and therefore as a moral aggressor unworthy of support, a neighbour could rid himself of guilt for not coming to their aid.[17]

Although the Reformation began as a means of bringing enlighten-
ment, it actually intensified fear and guilt, increasing the witch-hunt.
Malcolm Gaskill argues that witches (like the *pharmakos* in ancient
Greece) were scapegoats. Their expulsion from society purified the
community.

Although Hopkins and Stearne terrorised East Anglia in the 1640s,
and were responsible for most deaths, there were witch-hunts in other counties too – including Devon and Cornwall, Lancashire, Cum-
bria – and Scotland. Some women escaped death by pleading natural
causes for their so-called possession, such as epilepsy, but other women with growths such as polyps or piles (or perhaps in some cases
tumours) were considered to have been suckled by 'familiars'.

The spirit of the time was 'febrile', notes Malcolm Gaskill, with
monstrous births and strange happenings, such as meteors, much in
discussion. Bizarre news stories proliferated in London during first
half of 1645, swirling around the writers and publishers working in
St Paul's Churchyard. One pamphlet discussed witches, ending with
a 'lurid account of the births of a limbless hermaphrodite and a one-
eyed, eight-footed kitten with the hands of a child'.[18] Another pamphlet from 1645 reports the birth of a monstrous child, with limbs
missing from both legs and arms.[19] Impairment, sin and witchcraft
were inextricably linked in society's collective consciousness.

Witches were scapegoats in a time of economic hardship. And the
classic depiction of a witch, of course, is of an old hag, stick in hand,
with a bent back or even a hump of sorts, often with a growth of
some kind disfiguring her face. They were a drain on resources and
often resented as such, particularly if they were unable to work because of their disability or age. (As Hitler would write in the 1930s,
'useless eaters' were 'unworthy' of life.)

Some feminist writers have pointed out that women were targeted
at vulnerable times during their life cycle: at childbirth, as they grew
older, if they were experiencing depression after childbirth or at
other times. Louise Jackson explains: 'Personal life crises such as suicide
attempts and depression were almost always seen as temptations from

the devil; desire to carry out acts which were considered morally bad was associated with evil.'[20] (Jackson goes on to argue that many women accused of infanticide and witchcraft at this time may have been experiencing post-natal depression.) The sixteenth-century writer Reginald Scot was particularly sympathetic to the plight of women troubled by mental illness. He wrote that many were suffering from 'not witchcraft, but melancholy' and pointed out: 'If our witches phantasies were not corrupted, nor their wits confounded with this humour, they would not so voluntarily and readily confess that which calleth their life into question.'[21]

Witchcraft is still prevalent today, as are attacks on suspected witches in India and Africa – and also in certain closed enclaves in our own society. Witchcraft in Essex was an intimate, local affair, as it still is. Walking through Chelmsford, where Elizabeth Clarke and her neighbours stood trial in 1645, it was difficult to conjure the spirit of that age. Everywhere I looked there were cheerful families, groups of young people out shopping in the busy high streets. The session house, where they stood trial (250 witches were to take the stand there, over just two years), was destroyed in the 1700s to make way for an impressive Georgian building, the Shire Hall.

Water is everywhere, for Chelmsford lies at the convergence of two rivers, the Chelmer and the Can, and locks, bridges and canals traverse the small and bustling city, with its fine old wharves that once saw seagoing vessels enter the nearby Heybridge Basin, until water-borne trade fell into decline with the rise of the railway. Here, in this terrain, water has witnessed so many crimes against both women and men – some of them quite recent, as I was to discover when I walked out to the Essex Police Museum on the edge of the city.

The Essex Police Force was one of the first county forces to be established, in 1840, after the 1839 County Police Act became law.[22] It prides itself on its long history and well-kept archives, and has a small museum celebrating that history. One of its most notorious cases was that of the last witch trial in England, held in 1863, following the death of Dummy, an old Frenchman who could neither speak nor hear, who was ducked at the nearby village of Sible Hedingham. The curator dug out the file relating to the case.

It was in Sible Hedingham that two villagers, the wife of a beer-shop-keeper, Emma Smith, and Samuel Stammers, a master carpenter, led a mob that ducked and stoned Dummy in the village brook. There had been witchcraft trials before Sible Hedingham, during the reign of terror of Hopkins and afterwards, but what happened to Dummy appeared, from the local newspaper reports at that time, which seemed accurate and fair, to be a clear case of disability hate crime.[23]

As one newspaper reported, Dummy was recognisable in the village for his impairment: 'Being unable to express himself, and being of a somewhat vivacious disposition, he was accustomed to make use of energetic and somewhat grotesque gestures, which were taken by the rustics generally as cabalistic and diabolical signs, and he was consequently regarded, for some time past, with considerable awe.'[24] He lived in abject poverty in a mud hut not far from the brook, where he scraped a living from superstitious villagers, who believed he could tell their fortunes.

On the night in question, Dummy went to the local pub, the Swan, for a drink. Emma Smith and Samuel Stammers were in the tap room, drinking. Emma Smith, on seeing Dummy, claimed that he had bewitched her and asked him to go back with her to her house, and she would 'use him well', so that he would take the curse from her. He refused, apparently frightened of her intentions.

The scene turned ugly, and another man forced Dummy to dance, while a crowd looked on and laughed. Dummy managed to break free, and went outside. Shortly afterwards, when the pub closed, the two perpetrators, along with a drunken crowd of around eighty people, dragged Dummy towards the brook and threw him in. Dummy tried to get out, but the mob stoned him and pushed him back into the mud. A witness, a 14-year-old girl, Henrietta Garrod, testified that 'the water covered him, and she could only see his arms'. Emma

Smith, she said, struck Dummy with a stick. Eventually he was pulled out. Henrietta recalled that he 'had tears in his eyes and was green and muck wet all over'[25] and he was taken to his hut, where he was left, wet, cold and alone. Witnesses said that he kissed the hands of those who took him home, in gratitude (although they did not stay to make him comfortable). A few days later, according to the same article, a Mr Fowke heard of him being 'ill-used' and went to visit him. He found Dummy shivering, cold and bruised, and took him to the workhouse hospital, in nearby Halstead. Dummy died there. His death certificate, of which there is a copy in the museum, records pneumonia as the cause of death.

The chairman of the Assizes, Mr Bernaldiston, sentenced the two perpetrators to six months' hard labour. They escaped a murder charge. But, unlike so many of today's judiciary, he did take note of Dummy's disability in his summing-up. He is quoted in the same newspaper account as saying: 'it was a fearful and disgraceful fact that at the present day an old and mutilated man should meet with such a fate and no one of all the crowd of men and women present should have interfered to save him'.

This story could have been told today – the presence of the mob, the deliberate targeting of a disabled person, the short sentence and the mockery – but at least the chairman chided the community for not intervening. Nothing remains of Dummy to display at the museum – he had no clothes, he lived in a hovel, no one ever took a photograph of him. But one letter in the file, from a villager who knew him, remembered him with affection. He used to come for lunch, the villager recalled, every Sunday, always wearing at least three hats.

But such affection had not been widespread during the medieval period or beyond. If anything, a hardening of attitudes towards disability was reflected in medieval literature and art. In *Richard III*, written by Shakespeare in the late sixteenth century, the king is portrayed as twisted in body and mind (it now appears he was neither) – as he says of himself, 'rudely stamp'd'. Like Hephaestus before him, he is rendered impotent by his physical limitations, impairments that also render him villainous. 'Then since the heavens have shaped my body so, let hell make crooked my mind to answer it.'[26]

Across Europe fools were collected and exhibited by world-weary aristocrats, particularly in Germany.[27] They were said to be able to ward off melancholy. The scholar Eric Midelfort suggests that the 'licensed misbehaviour' caused by fools was necessary to offset the strain of rigid etiquette at court. Midelfort notes that the court of Duke Wilhelm V of Bavaria 'bought, traded, and collected dwarfs, Turks, and Moors as well as simpletons, all evidence of the court's crude delight in the rareties and curiosities of human form and be-haviour. It was the budding age of the museum-cabinet of natural and artistic curiosities.'[28]

But it was not only the rich that delighted in such spectacles, the academic Colin Barnes points out: 'During the Middle Ages and thereafter, people with perceived "deformities" and intellectual im-pairments were often displayed for money at village fairs and on market days, festivals and holidays.'[29] This interest was reflected in art. Velázquez, in particular, painted disabled people, his two most famous depictions being *The Dwarf Sebastian de Morra* and *The Idiot of Coria*.

Folly literature was also popular in the sixteenth century. The best-selling book *The Ship of Fools*, by Sebastian Brant, an allegory of a boat afloat on the high seas with a cargo of fools, was first published in 1494. Nearly eighty editions had been published by 1787. Midel-fort observes that Brant, like other influential figures, linked folly to sin, and concludes: 'Renaissance Germany saw folly as "immoral", and madness thus became one of the basic moral categories of the sixteenth century.'[30] Those with learning difficulties were already outside the norm, but as the medieval period progressed, their posi-tion worsened. Midelfort concludes that fools became 'outsiders, to be beaten, manipulated, coddled and laughed at'.[31]

I visited Sible Hedingham on my way back from Chelmsford. I wanted to see for myself the Swan inn where Dummy was 'danced about with' and mocked and the brook where he was ducked. The Swan is now closed and the inn is dark. Its former owners believe it is haunted by Dummy's ghost and complain that he lurks in the cellar. Perhaps this is the reason why the inn failed. The brook to which Dummy was dragged, and in which he was ducked several times, runs clean and clear. It is a quieter, calmer stretch of water than it was at the time, because its course has been changed. And much of it is overgrown with brambles, thistles and nettles.

I drove home to London, passing near to another watery place, the Lakeside Shopping Centre, not far from Chelmsford where the witches were hanged four hundred years earlier. In March 2005 a man with learning difficulties, Mark Watts, drowned here. He was pushed into the lake by Jonathan Lawson, 20, and Sydney Quirke, 18, while a crowd stood there, watching, doing nothing. The youths filmed the attack on a mobile phone, and laughed as Mr Watts drowned. They were convicted of manslaughter and were both sentenced to just over a year in jail. As is usual, they served just half of that – the same sentence served by Emma Smith and Samuel Stammers, 150 years earlier, for near enough the same crime. The judge in this case, Sir John Blofeld, commended the mob that gathered and watched him drowning, for 'containing themselves'.[32]

So are witch-hunts really over now? No, sadly. Malcolm Gaskill points out that many innocent women, men and, more recently, disabled children are targeted, tortured and even murdered as witches, not only in India and Africa but also here in Britain, in communities still closed by culture and tradition to disability rights and equality.[33] Children with albinism, and those with epilepsy, have been feared down the ages and attacked as 'cursed'. And, as Gaskill observes: 'then, as now, witch-hunts involved not just savage persecutors tormenting innocent scapegoats, but ordinary neighbours with an affinity towards each other who also happened to believe in witchcraft powerfully enough to act out their most violent fantasies'.[34] How close that is to what happens today to many disabled people; it is called 'antisocial behaviour'.

The trial of Emma Smith and Samuel Stammers was Britain's last witchcraft-related trial. The time of targeting, hanging and burning the infirm, the vulnerable and the different as witches has largely passed – although I have observed that many crimes against disabled people, such as the killing of Mark Watts, Sean Miles, Raymond Atherton and others, involve water. Perhaps some folk memory connecting disability, ducking and water remains, buried deep in our collective unconscious.

Disabled people had entered the Middle Ages tolerated, even pitied to some degree. That changed. The medieval period and the Reformation were harsh times for disabled people, in which they were feared, mocked and even killed – just because of who they were. They were sinners, they carried a stigma and they were seen as freaks, just like too many today. And things weren't about to get better.

4

The Industrial Revolution,
Asylums and Freak Shows

Everyone in Britain, and many abroad, knows what Bedlam means. It is a dictionary term for pandemonium and chaos. But it is also one of England's oldest institutions, where disabled people have lived out their lives, often in great psychological and physical pain. I wanted to track down Bedlam, find what traces remained of the place that has become synonymous with so much that is tragic about the lives of disabled people, confined and put away, ostensibly for their own good, and what that history tells us, both about the roots of institutional violence and about disability hate crime today.

I started with what remained of Bedlam, in modern-day London. Nowadays the hospital is known as Bethlem, perhaps with a cautious eye on history. Bethlem, like Bedlam, is a variant of its original name, the Priory of St Mary of Bethlehem, which became a hospital for the insane at the end of the fourteenth century, overseen by the City of London.

Bedlam has moved a number of times in its history – from Bishopsgate, where what remains of it is now buried underneath Liverpool Street Station, then to Moorfields, where it was rebuilt by Robert Hooke, in grandeur. This was the time when it was thought great sport to visit Bedlam. The unfortunates who were confined to New Bethlem were put on display for a fee. One writer, Thomas Tryon, complained about this practice in 1695: 'It is a very undecent, inhuman thing to make . . . a show . . . by exposing them, and naked too perhaps of either sexes, to the idle curiosity of every vain boy, petulant wench or druken companion,' adding: 'admitting such swarms of people, with their noise and vain questions to disturb the poor Souls . . . they can never be at any quiet'.[1] It moved again in 1815 to Southwark, where it formed part of what is now the Imperial War Museum.

Bedlam moved again in 1930, to its current site, the Monks Orchard estate in Beckenham. In 1948, as part of the new National Health Service, it amalgamated with the Maudsley Hospital to form a single psychiatric teaching hospital. Ten years ago it became part of the South London and Maudsley NHS Trust.[2] A museum at the hospital, just one modest room, houses a small part of Bedlam's history.[3]

A small exhibition case holds a collection of restraints. Some, such as the strait waistcoat, could be tightened at the guard's will. Others, like the manacles that many patients wore routinely for hours on end in the seventeenth and eighteenth centuries, were put on and then snapped shut, but at least they could not then be tightened until the patient was in pain. A gag, to stop a raving patient biting their tongue out, is in the case too. Look closely and you can still see in the leather the teeth marks of those who wore it.

Bright pictures of cats, by the former Bedlam inmate and illustrator Louis Wain, adorn the walls. The cats are playing cricket, taking tea. They are free spirits – unlike their creator, who was confined here for years before moving to Napsbury Hospital, where he died, in 1939.[4]

Later I walked around the grounds. Modern-day Bedlam has many units, and many of the original villas that housed the patients are still in use. I wandered into the gallery, where a former patient, Peter Rowbotham, was exhibiting his art-work.[5] He had been in and out of Bedlam and other institutions for half his adult life, he told me, adding: 'Bedlam wasn't that bad. But in one of the other ones, the nurses would set us against each other to fight.' I thought that was all in the past, I said. 'No, they get bored, you see. And nobody believes us anyway.' That conversation with Peter stayed with me, because what he said is at the heart of disability hate crime. Nobody believed Peter and nobody believes so many of those who claim they have been attacked, whether or not they are in institutions or outside – particularly those living with mental health problems. And some staff still, as in the past, like to set patients upon one another, as I was to discover during my research.

The woods at the site stretch for miles and I walked down the quiet paths, eating luscious blackberries. Some of the units on site were open ones, and patients and nurses came in and out, indistinguishable from each other. But then I came across a unit surrounded by high wire, perhaps twenty foot high. Colin Gale, Bethlem's archivist, had told me about this – the medium secure unit, where some people with mental illness are confined, perhaps for just a short or medium period, until they are no longer a danger to themselves or others.

I asked Colin Gale to define what Bethlem means to him. He hesitated, and then said: 'A lot of ink has been spilled over what typifies Bedlam. It has always struggled against a bad public reputation. It's in the dictionary, after all, as a synonym for chaos and uproar. That's the general popular impression, that it was awful and that the doctors who worked there were sadistic. But the hospital was also a charity. One must remember that all hospitals were provision for the poor who could not afford to be treated and might die in the street. Conditions were poor inside but it was too much to hope for that the poor would have been treated as well as the rich.'

He has a point. Life outside Bedlam, for those living in poverty, was nasty, brutish and short. But to understand the history of disability hate crime, we do need to look at what Bedlam and other institutions were like, and why so many people were locked away for a period of over four hundred years. For Bedlam's legacy lives on, in its attitudes towards disabled people – both inside institutions and in the community – up to the present day.

The position of disabled people worsened as the Industrial Revolution gathered pace. As Pauline Morris wrote in 1969, in her influential critique of institutionalisation, *Put Away*: 'The operation of the labour market in the nineteenth century effectively depressed handicapped people of all kinds to the bottom of the market, and it is clear that among the legions of the destitute and vagrant who existed in Victorian England, there were many who fell into the category of the feeble-minded.'[6]

Disabled 'idiots' were, quite simply, surplus to requirements. Many became destitute. Although they were seen in the main as the 'deserving poor', they were also viewed as unnecessary and untidy (an attitude that sharpened even further in the United States in the mid nineteenth century, when a number of states instituted mendicant laws, dubbed the 'Ugly Laws', banning the unsightly – who were of course mostly impaired people – from streets, schools and restaurants, a practice that continued right up to the mid twentieth century).[7] Parish workhouses, private madhouses and local jails all had held disabled people in the eighteenth century, but that process accelerated as the Industrial Revolution took hold.

The medical profession was intrigued by disability, but wanted to study it away from view. So disabled people were excluded from the mainstream of community life – they were mad, bad or even dangerous to know. As the physician George Man Burrows wrote in *Commentaries on the Causes, Forms, Symptoms and Treatment, Moral and Medical, of Insanity*, published in 1828: 'Insanity is the scourge brought down on sinful men by the wrath of the almighty.'

The misery of those who were confined, often in straitjackets and manacles, is powerfully conveyed by a drawing by the artist George Cruikshank of a patient called William (or James) Norris, in a harness at Bethlem. Edward Wakefield, a Quaker, who commissioned the etching during his investigation of conditions in Bethlem, gave evidence to a Select Committee on Madhouses in 1815, saying: 'a stout ring was rivetted around his neck, from which a short chain passed to a ring made to slide upwards or downwards on an upright massive iron bar'.[8] Cruikshank also saw women chained up, naked except for blanket gowns.[9] Many there were chained, and some had frostbite. There were only four keepers for some 120 inmates, a good number of whom were paupers. Many were kept in the cellars, forced to sleep on straw, and were tortured and toyed with by their keepers.

Godfrey Higgins, who visited York asylum around the same time, was also shocked. He found 'maltreatment of patients, extending to rape and murder'. Many were chained, funds were embezzled, and the place was characterised by 'utter filth and neglect'.[10] He gave evidence to the Select Committee, saying that in one room, where thirteen women had to sleep, 'the walls were daubed with excrement . . . I became very sick and could not remain any longer in the room, I vomited.'[11] Another Quaker, Samuel Tuke, who visited asylums, reported, in words that remind me of what Peter Rowbotham told me in the Bethlem art gallery: 'madmen appear to have been employed to torment other madmen, in most of the places intended for their relief'.[12]

Jon Rogers, the apothecary of two asylums for paupers, Warburton's Red and White Houses at Bethnal Green, gave evidence to the Select Committee that the institutions were infested with rats and fleas and that many patients had contracted tuberculosis and gangrene because conditions were cold and damp. Women were likely to be raped, he added, and beatings and whipping were commonplace.[13]

By the time the Select Committee submitted its final report, in 1815, Andrew Scull writes, 'there was a wealth of documentation to support the reformers' contention that what they perceived as appalling degradation and inhuman treatment were the lot of madmen in every sort of institution in which they were confined'.[14] The Select Committee wanted to construct new, better asylums and bring in a far more rigorous system of inspection, but there was much opposition, both inside Parliament and beyond. However, the much watered-down 1828 Madhouses Act, a result of the Select Committee report, did legislate for better conditions in madhouses, including education and recreation – on paper at least.

But one aspect of institutionalisation, the unequal power relationship between staff and inmates, proved impossible to shift (and persists even today). Just two years after the Madhouses Act the superintendent of Bedlam, Dr Edward Wright – also, at that time, the president of the London Phrenological Society – was found at night with unclothed female patients. He denied any wrongdoing, as many abusers do today, knowing that their disabled victims cannot testify against them or won't be believed if they do. Wright called them 'unreliable' – just as so many disabled people are known as 'unreliable witnesses' today.[15]

A new set of Poor Laws was introduced in 1834, followed by a new building programme – for both 'lunatics' and 'idiots'. The decision to confine came from the political elite. Although the 1840s saw the advent of non-restraint in some asylums, the system as a whole remained largely unregulated. And the impetus to shut away grew stronger. In 1844 Parliament published the Lunacy Report, with Lord Ashley apparently startling the Home Secretary with his assertion that there were 12,000 pauper lunatics roaming the streets, many of them, in his view, 'absolutely dangerous' (not unlike some of the views about community care just a decade or so ago).

In 1886 the Idiots Act was passed. By this time a link had been established between 'feeble-mindedness' and 'degeneracy', a link that lingers today. An Italian criminologist, Cesare Lombroso, declared that social 'atavism' correlated with physical abnormality, and the influential physician Walter Fernald expounded similar beliefs in 1912, when he wrote that 'every feeble-minded person, especially the high grade imbecile, is a potential criminal'. Whilst some poets, like Wordsworth in his poem 'The Idiot Boy', urged a different view, the social and political elite believed, on the whole, that disabled people were poor, criminal and carried sexual diseases.

As Pauline Morris has observed, society now felt that the best way to deal with the 'threat' of many disabled people was to separate them as problematic individuals. But the separation did nothing to dispel prejudice. Indeed, Morris notes: 'the presence of a building set apart from the rest of human settlement gives some substance to the vague folk beliefs concerning the individuals who spend their lives in comparative isolation from their fellows'.[16]

Between the late 1840s and the late 1860s, five voluntary institutions for 'educable idiots', mostly for the middle classes, were founded in England. They focused on health, nutrition, exercise and 'moral training'. The task was to create 'economically independent and morally competent individuals', and lift the burdens of financial dependency and lifetime care from families. Some doctors, particularly in France, argued that those with learning difficulties could be 'trained'. This led to a medical trend in which people with learning difficulties were rigidly categorised as 'subnormal, idiot, imbecile and feeble-minded', with different strategies and expectations for each group. Pauper asylums for 'idiots' were set up from the 1870s onwards.

By 1881 there were 30,000 'classified idiots' in institutions, some of which had also become a dumping ground for paupers, unwanted wives, orphans and lunatics. By 1890 there were some sixty-six county and borough asylums throughout the UK. A few thinkers stood out against the tide. Wilkie Collins wrote about the confinement of women by jealous husbands in *The Woman in White* and John Stuart Mill, in *On Liberty*, declared: 'the man or still more the woman who indulges in the luxury of doing as they like is in peril of a commission de lunatico and of having their property taken from them and given to their relations'. But such dissidents were few and far between, and most were more interested in keeping the sane out of madhouses rather than improving conditions for those with mental illness.

The rich had their own 'madhouses' – even the Royal Family confined its disabled members, such as George III, to houses for 'single lunatics', or for the select few, which were comfortably appointed but nothing less than private prisons where those who shamed their wealthy families could be hidden from view. Even better-off disabled people could be abused and the houses became known as 'mansions of misery', run by profiteers. Daniel Defoe, writing as early as 1728, said they should be closed down, particularly when used to confine unwanted wives as a form of social control. 'If they are not mad when they go into these cursed houses, they are soon made so by the barbarous Usage they there suffer.'[17] Women were routinely chained, whipped, starved and raped.

Literature reflected these harsh attitudes towards disabled people, with writers like Charlotte Brontë painting an uncharitable picture of the 'madwoman in the attic', Bertha Mason, Mr Rochester's wife in *Jane Eyre*, in 1847. (Ironically, she dedicated the book to Thackeray, little knowing that he had confined his own wife, Isabella, in an asylum for insanity. She had had severe post-natal depression after the birth of their third child.) In Dickens's *Great Expectations*, Miss Havisham, who was jilted at the altar and is clearly depicted as having mental health problems, is also presented unsympathetically.

Being sent to the workhouse or the asylum was something that some disabled people fought hard to avoid. Indeed, some had a choice, if they could support themselves – most eloquently represented in the story of Joseph Merrick, who was immortalised as the Elephant Man. Like a number of other disabled Victorian people, particularly those who had gigantism or dwarfism, he chose to be exhibited in a freak show rather than be confined to a workhouse. Freak shows had been popular since Tudor times, but the Victorians became interested to the point of obsession, with one *Punch* cartoon in 1847 satirising what it called 'deformito-mania'.[18] The Skeleton Man, Claude Amboise, was a popular draw, as were giants, dwarves and black men.

One popular exhibit, Caroline Crachami, a child of very short stature, was brought from Italy to London for medical reasons by a Dr Gilligan, who exhibited her to defray medical expenses (apparently men could pay a little extra to handle her physically). Gilligan made a handsome profit from exhibiting her in 1823. The famous surgeon Sir Everard Home even showed Caroline to King George IV. He observed (denaturing and dehumanising her): 'It was brought to London and shown as a curiosity. It died just after it completed its ninth year. I saw it several times while alive, and it came into my possession after death . . . It could walk alone, but with no confidence. Its sight was very quick, much attracted by bright objects, delighted with everything that glittered, mightily pleased with fine clothes, had a shrill voice and spoke in a low tone; had some taste for music but could speak few words of English; was very sensible of kindness and quickly recognised any person who had treated it kindly.'[19] Caroline died in early childhood, far from her loved ones. Everard Home continues his account, without irony: 'In the accounts of her death in the newspapers of the day, it is stated that she had been "for some time afflicted with a cough," and that "on Thursday last she was exhibited as usual, and received upwards of 200 visitors; towards the evening a languor appeared to come over her, and on her way from the exhibition room she expired." '[20]

Joseph Merrick, the best known of the Victorian 'freaks', believed that his deformity (a condition now thought to be Proteus syndrome, which causes benign tumours to develop on the body, asymmetry and gigantism of the limbs and thickened areas of skin, described at the time as elephantine folds) was caused by his mother having been knocked over by a runaway elephant when she was pregnant. Merrick was born 'perfect' around 1860, he recalled in his autobiography, but around 21 months he started to develop tumours. He also limped after damaging his hip in a fall. His mother sent him to school, but he was bullied because of his impairments. After his mother died, and his father remarried, Merrick's life worsened. In his own account of his life, he said that he became the 'family outcast', targeted by his stepmother while his father looked on, either incapable or unwilling to intervene.

His uncle tried to help him and Joseph lived and worked with him for a time. But as his deformities worsened, he found it harder to work on the streets, and he was followed around and mocked wherever he went. He ended up penniless and applied for admission to a workhouse. But he hated being confined. A liberation of sorts came when he was 'freed' by five businessmen, who organised a syndicate to exhibit Joseph as a freak in 1884. But as Michael Howell and Peter Ford recount in *The True Story of the Elephant Man*, he had little or no choice: 'it is perhaps too easy to see nothing but degradation in

Joseph being forced to uncover his bizarre body to the public's gaz-
ings and ill-informed wonderings. Yet short of a miracle, there had
been for him no other conceivable life of escape from the grinding
limbo of workhouse life, which could only ever spiral downwards
to end in the unmarked shadow of a pauper's grave.'[21] As Merrick
admits in his autobiography, it was a rational decision: 'my deformity had grown to such an extent, so that I could not move about the
town without having a crowd of people gather around me . . . so
thought I, I'll get my living by being exhibited around the country.'[22]
It was the lesser of two evils.

Even those who considered themselves enlightened were initially
horrified by his appearance, considering him less than human. When
the surgeon Frederick Treves first met him he remembered that his
showman, Tom Norman, called on Merrick to stand up, 'speaking
harshly, as if to a dog'.[23] Treves himself recalled: 'The thing arose slowly and let the blanket that covered its head and back fall to the ground.
There stood revealed the most disgusting specimen of humanity that
I had ever seen . . . at no time had I met with such a degraded and
perverted version of a human being as this lone figure displayed.'[24]

Attitudes towards freaks in Britain were hardening, so Merrick's
managers took him abroad. Eventually, after a disastrous tour of Belgium, he became stranded at Liverpool Street Station, where a mob
surrounded him and jeered at him. He was rescued by Treves, who
created a flat for him at the Royal London Hospital, paid for after an
appeal in the London *Times*, where he lived peacefully for the rest of
his life, until his death in 1890 at the age of 27.

Treves realised later how wrong he had been to dehumanise Joseph
Merrick. In his recollections, he wrote: 'I supposed that Merrick was
imbecile and had been imbecile from birth. The fact that his face was
incapable of expression, that his speech was a mere spluttering and
his attitude that of one whose mind was void of all emotions and
concerns gave ground for this belief. The conviction was no doubt
encouraged by the hope that his intellect was the blank I imagined it
to be. That he could appreciate his condition was unthinkable. Here

was a man in the heyday of youth who was so vilely deformed that everyone he met confronted him with a look of horror and disgust. He was taken about the country to be exhibited as a monstrosity and an object of loathing. He was shunned like a leper, housed like a wild beast and got his only view of the world from a peephole in a show-man's cart . . . I came to know that Merrick was highly intelligent, that he possessed an acute sensibility and – worse of all – a romantic imagination . . . I realised the overwhelming tragedy of his life.'[25]

Merrick was more than aware of his humanity. Indeed, he ended his autobiography with a poem, which he adapted from 'False Greatness' by Isaac Watts:

> *T'is true my form is something odd*
> *But blaming me is blaming God*
> *Could I create myself anew*
> *I would not fail in pleasing you.*
>
> *Was I so tall, could reach the pole*
> *Or grasp the ocean with a span*
> *I would be measured by the soul*
> *The mind's the standard of the man.*

What happened to Joseph Merrick was part of a wider fascination in the nineteenth century with feral children, the most famous being Victor, the 'Wild Boy of Aveyron', who was discovered living wild in the Pyrenees in 1800. The philosopher and writer Rousseau developed his notion of the 'noble savage' from the national discussion of such cases in France, and further afield, about what constituted a human being. Disabled people like Joseph Merrick were seen, like feral children, as being between the beast and the human – an 'elemental being', according to the writers Peter Graham and Fritz Oehlschlager.[26]

Treves said that what Merrick wanted most of all was to 'make the acquaintance of men and women who would treat him as a normal and intelligent young man and not as a monster of deformity'. While Merrick was, eventually, shown some kindness towards the end of his life, his case was the exception. The tide was about to turn. Therapeutic optimism had failed. There were to be no cures for lunacy and idiocy. Instead, a tide of therapeutic pessimism swept Europe, as social Darwinism and the theory of 'survival of the fittest' took hold. Darwinism saw insanity as an incurable degenerative disease, a hereditary taint. Women in particular were inspected for signs of impairment. As Elaine Showalter writes in *The Female Malady*, lunatic tendencies were thought to be indicated by physical signs, such as badly shaped heads, flat foreheads and big ears.[27]

In 1867 the London Metropolitan Asylums Board was set up to establish relief for the infirm and build new asylums for lunatics and idiots, so that workhouses could, once again, admit only non-disabled people. By 1888 the London County Council had banned the freak-shops, partly because they felt it was exploitation – but partly also to tidy away the 'grotesques' from view. The next logical step was to prevent the incurables from 'infecting' decent society – as the eugenics movement took hold.

You can still see the mortal remains of some of those who starred, unwillingly or otherwise, in the Victorian freak shows. The impressive skeleton of Charles Byrne, the so-called Irish Giant, greets visitors as they enter London's Hunterian Museum, on the southern edge of Lincoln's Inn Fields. Visitors cluster around, exclaiming at his height and his damaged metatarsals. Caroline Crachami, or at least what purports to be her skeleton, is tucked away at the back of the museum, in a room used for children's educational activities. Her shoes and cream silk stockings are carefully preserved – so small that they could fit upon my fingers. A collection of fine paintings includes one of Mary Sabina, a child slave with a skin condition called piebaldism, and several pictures of people with short stature, as well as that of Daniel Lambert, a man with an endocrine condition that made him obese, who also exhibited himself as a freak after he was no longer able to hold down his job as an innkeeper.

The collections are testament to an age that medicalised and codified difference, and they live on, to be drawn by children, studied by medical students and observed by tourists – albeit, as far as I could tell, with compassion. I wish that Caroline could now be buried with dignity, along with the other people who have been seen, for too long, as medical curiosities rather than human beings. They have been on show for long enough. The age of the freak show isn't really over – it lives on, in a different shape.

5

No Better than Poison: the Eugenics Movement and the Holocaust

Gerhard Kretschmar was born in 1939, the son of Richard Kret-schmar, a farmhand, and his wife Lina. Gerhard was born blind, with short limbs. His father, who lived near Leipzig in eastern Germany, wrote to Hitler's office in early 1939 asking for permission to kill his son. Karl Brandt, Hitler's personal physician, visited Gerhard and his family. Later he testified: 'The father of a deformed child wrote to the Führer, with a request to be allowed to take the life of this child or creature. Hitler ordered me to take care of this case. The child had been born blind, seemed to be idiotic, and a leg and parts of the arm were missing.'[1]

Brandt, indeed, took care of it. After consultation with the family's doctors, Gerhard is believed to have been injected with luminal, causing unconsciousness or death, after three days. Just three weeks later Hitler issued a decree, stating that the killing programme of disabled children should start in earnest.[2]

What happened in the Holocaust, in which tens of thousands of disabled newborns, children and adults were murdered, was the logical conclusion of a movement that started here, in the UK. It was called the eugenics movement. The word eugenics has a Greek root, meaning 'noble in heredity', and was first used by the British scientist Francis Galton (a cousin of Darwin), around 1883. Galton and his wife both had mental health conditions, and his sister a disabling condition, curvature of the spine. Perhaps it was this background that inspired his research into eugenics (and, indeed, the couple never had children).

Galton's research inspired social radicals such as H.G. Wells and other Fabian luminaries including the Webbs and George Bernard Shaw – but was also embraced by English aristocrats, including Ottoline Morrell. Along with Wells, Galton became more and more interested in 'negative eugenics' – preventing or restricting recessive genes from reproduction by restricting the rights and opportunities of disabled people to 'breed'.

The movement started in Britain and spread rapidly to the United States, where it was eagerly embraced. British and American political activists, philosophers and scientists, from across the political spectrum, to a large extent inspired the attitudes towards disabled people that underpinned their widespread slaughter during the Holocaust. What is even more disturbing is that the most famous and fervent eugenicists of this time, and later – Galton, Darwin, President Roosevelt and Prime Minister Churchill – all had impairments.

Ironically, the late nineteenth century had seen an increase in humanitarianism, often based on the values of Christian charity. Several charities were established at this period, including the British and Foreign Blind Association, now known as the Royal National Institute for the Blind (RNIB), which was set up in 1868, followed by the National Society for the Employment of Epileptics in 1892 and the National Association for Promoting the Welfare of the Feeble-Minded in 1896.

But none of this charitable do-gooding averted the horror of eugenics and, later, the Holocaust. The first step along the way was the British Royal Commission on Mental Deficiency, which was constituted in 1904 and reported in 1908.[3] This commission was taken over by the eugenics movement as it gained in popularity.

It is ironic that, as other writers have pointed out, the three great emancipatory social movements of the late nineteenth century and early twentieth century – Darwinism, early feminism and Marxism – all consolidated negative attitudes towards disabled people.[4] Marx saw labour capacity as the cornerstone of citizenship rights (much as today Iain Duncan Smith talks about work making people 'free' and being an obligation of citizenship). But many disabled people could not work. Segregation therefore became even more intense – disabled people who could not gain respect through work should be shut away as they were, in effect, worthless.

Early feminist writers, such as Charlotte Gilman, argued that disabled children were conceived and born because women were unfairly confined and denied educational opportunities. Indeed, many women on both sides of the Atlantic became enthusiastic eugenicists, with the American suffragist Victoria Woodhull (who had a disabled son) arguing as early as 1891: 'the best minds of today have accepted the fact that if superior people are desired, they must be bred; and if imbeciles, criminals, paupers and the otherwise unfit are undesirable citizens they must not be bred'.[5]

Charles Darwin's pessimism was particularly influential at this time. In 1871, in *The Descent of Man*, he argued: 'we civilised men, on the other hand, do our utmost to check the process of elimination; we build asylums for the imbecile, the maimed and the sick . . . thus the weak members of civilised society propagate their kind. No one who has attended the breeding of domestic animals will doubt that this must be highly injurious to the race of man.'[6] His theories on natural selection and evolution were taken up by eugenicists, who believed that the human race and the Empire could only be safeguarded by cleaning up the gene pool. As Mary Dendy argued in the 1890s, in her influential tract *Feeble-Mindedness of Children of School Age*, children classified as mentally handicapped should be 'detained for the whole of their lives' as the only way to 'stem the great evil of feeble-mindedness in our country'.[7] The 'mentally defective' were convenient scapegoats for social problems such as vagrancy, crime, prostitution and poverty. Disability was a threat to society.

In 1907 Francis Galton became president of the Eugenics Education Society. His beliefs, and those of the Society, were clear. He declared a year later: 'One person in every 118 in our population is mentally defective, being either mad, idiotic or feeble-minded.'[8] The *Morning Post* (and other newspapers) popularised these views, proclaiming in 1909: 'It is difficult to express with sufficient force the gravity of danger to national life which the existence of these persons uncontrolled in any sufficient manner implies. For from these unfortunate men and women the ranks of paupers, drunkards and criminals are continually recruited.'[9]

Powerful political voices agreed – among them Winston Churchill, who supported sterilisation and made inquiries about it when he was Home Secretary in 1910–11, according to his biographer Martin Gilbert. As early as 1899 Churchill had written to his cousin Ivor Guest: 'The improvement of the British breed is my aim in life.'[10] In 1910 Churchill requested Home Office officials to inquire into sterilisation (which had been introduced three years earlier in the American state of Indiana). He asked about the best medical operation and what legal powers would be necessary before proceeding. The Chief Medical Adviser of Prisons, Horatio Donkin, replied that the Indiana experiment was a 'monument of ignorance and hopeless mental confusion'. But Churchill was undeterred. In a letter to Prime Minister Asquith in December 1910, he wrote about the 'multiplication of the unfit' that constituted a 'very terrible danger to the race' and concluded: 'I feel that the source from which the stream of madness is fed should be cut off and sealed up before another year is passed.'[11] They must, he argued, be kept segregated until the case for sterilisation had been made and won.[12]

Churchill and others were much influenced by a British physician, Dr A.F. Tredgold, an expert adviser to the Royal Commission, who delivered an influential lecture in 1910 called 'The Feeble-Minded – A Social Danger'. He said of 'idiots': 'These are . . . incapable of being employed . . . their care and support absorbs a large amount of the time, energy, and money of the normal population . . . many . . . are utterly helpless, repulsive in appearance, and revolting in manners . . . In my opinion it would be an economical and humane procedure were their existence to be painlessly terminated . . . It is doubtful if public opinion is yet ripe for this to be done compulsorily; but I am of the opinion that the time has come when euthanasia should be permitted at the request of a parent or guardian.'[13]

Churchill was instrumental in the drafting of the Mental Deficiency Bill of 1912, a product of the recommendations of the Royal Commission. It did provide for some limited education for some groups, such as those with Down syndrome, but it also gave the Government powers to detain and segregate some other groups. It categorised four grades of 'mental defectives' who could be confined for life. Its precursor, the Feeble-Minded Control Bill, which made it a criminal offence to marry a 'mental defective', had been withdrawn after liberal newspapers had protested and a few dissenting voices, such as the social reformer Josiah Wedgwood (although at other times disparaging of people with learning difficulties), had denounced it as a 'monstrous violation' of individual rights. Roman Catholic leaders said the Bill was 'contrary to Christian morals' (as some would also protest, at extreme risk, in Nazi Germany). But the Mental Deficiency Act passed into law in 1913, not least because of the great pressure exerted by eugenicists, whose first International Eugenics Conference was held just after its Second Reading. Churchill had not managed to secure sterilisation and thereby stop the 'stream of madness'. But the next best thing, confinement, was now rubber-stamped by Parliament.

Progress was duly made to confine disabled people. In 1914 the House of Commons was told: 'Institutions and homes provided by religious and philanthropic associations, and by individuals, have come forward in considerable numbers . . . In addition to these there are the nine hospitals and institutions formerly registered under the Idiots Act which have become certified institutions or houses under the Mental Deficiency Act.'[14]

However, as the First World War progressed, thousands of soldiers began to return with what became known as shell shock. At first they were confined to district asylums, but soon specialised war hospitals were being built – with the emphasis on health care, rather than asylums, because of the stigma that attached to the latter. The advent of psychoanalysis, and the possibility of recovery from some conditions through 'talking cures', did open some minds to the horrors of segregation. Soldier-poets like Siegfried Sassoon and Wilfred Owen documented in pitiless verse the cruelty of shell shock (and the viciousness of the response by the British Army). Sassoon's poem 'Survivors', written when he was recovering in one such hospital, Craiglockhart, in 1917, bears compassionate testimony to the mental distress suffered by so many soldiers:

> *No doubt they'll soon get well; the shock and strain*
> *Have caused their stammering, disconnected talk.*
> *Of course they're 'longing to go out again,' –*
> *These boys with old, scared faces, learning to walk,*
> *They'll soon forget their haunted nights; their cowed*
> *Subjection to the ghosts of friends who died, –*
> *Their dreams that drip with murder; and they'll be proud*
> *Of glorious war that shatter'd all their pride . . .*
> *Men who went out to battle, grim and glad;*
> *Children, with eyes that hate you, broken and mad.*

But reform was slow and patchy and certainly did not affect how those with learning difficulties, and so-called pauper lunatics, were treated. Indeed, the political legitimisation of segregation for such groups continued apace. In 1929 the Joint Departmental Committee on Mental Deficiency published the Wood Report, stating that they were a threat to society: 'Let us assume that we could separate all the families containing mental defectives . . . this would include a higher proportion of insane persons, epileptics, paupers, criminals, habitual slum dwellers . . . If we are to prevent the racial disaster of mental deficiency . . . we must deal with . . . the whole subnormal group.'[15] Defectives, as the committee termed them, were a social problem group, concentrated in the lowest 10 per cent of society, and alarmingly their number had doubled since 1908. In a debate on the report, Neville Chamberlain told the House of Commons that this rate of increase 'must give serious anxiety and apprehension amongst all who care for our future physical and mental condition of our people'.[16] The Wood Report urged segregation, to prevent social evil and facilitate medical study.

A few dissenting voices, among them some scientists, protested. The lower social classes, the zoologist Julian Huxley argued, had produced few geniuses not because of an innate deficiency, but because they were condemned by lack of opportunities to be 'mute and inglorious . . . vast reservoirs of innate intelligence untrained in children from the lower social strata'.[17] The psychiatrist and geneticist Lionel Penrose argued for years that a society should be judged by how it cared for those who were 'mentally incompetent . . . there is no menace of feeblemindedness'.[18] Writers, particularly James Joyce and G.K. Chesterton, also protested. Chesterton wrote in his book *Eugenics and Other Evils*, published in 1922, that it was appalling to turn common decency – such as being married to an invalid – into a social crime. He declared: 'Eugenics itself is a thing no more to be bargained about than poisoning.'[19]

But eugenics, and its legacy, was to poison the air, nationally and internationally, for many years – most violently in the United States and Nazi Germany. The United States, always a more enthusiastic nation for wholescale change than the UK, adopted eugenics with enthusiasm. By 1914 almost every US state had made it illegal for 'feeble-minded' and 'insane' people to marry.

The so-called Ugly Laws (first adopted in the 1880s), marriage laws, coerced institutionalisation and involuntary sterilisation all arrived on the agendas of state legislatures as the political expression of increasing cultural intolerance for human differences. The Ugly Laws forbade the unsightly to be seen on the streets. The Chicago Municipal Code, sec. 36034, contained an ordinance which read: 'No person who is diseased, maimed, mutilated or in any way deformed so as to be an unsightly or disgusting object or improper person to be allowed in or on the public ways or other public places in this city, or shall therein or thereon expose himself to public view, under a penalty of not less than one dollar nor more than fifty dollars for each offense.'[20]

That was bad enough – but it was the mutilation of disabled people's bodies in America, through sterilisation, that would encourage the Germans in their genocidal tendencies just a few years later. A moral panic in the US towards the end of the nineteenth century, similar to that in the UK, led to statistical researchers calculating that the number of feeble-minded individuals in the country had increased tenfold between 1850 and 1890. Indeed, the advent of statistics as a discipline gave the eugenics movement extra momentum – as now scientists could chart what they saw as a deterioration in the gene pool.

The prevailing view in the US, as in the UK, was that disabled people should be hidden away from sight. But in 1907 the state of Indiana took things one stage further, permitting the sterilisation of the 'feeble-minded' and 'unfit'. About thirty more states followed suit, some also sterilising criminals. Miss May Krueger of the Seattle Humane Society declared of the Indiana Plan that sterilisation could prevent further harm to 'helpless, unfortunate children of the degenerate and criminally depraved who are brought into the world handicapped at their birth, cursed before they see the light of day, stunted mentally, morally and physically'.[21] Thus was disability linked with moral corruption, a metaphor that remains powerful today.

One of the most influential scientists of the time was Henry H. Goddard, director of research at the Vineland Training School for Feeble-Minded Girls and Boys in New Jersey from 1906 until 1918. This was the first laboratory to study so-called mental retardation. He published two influential texts, asserting that feeble-mindedness was hereditary and should be bred out. The first, *The Kallikak Family: A Study in the Heredity of Feeble-Mindedness* (1912), documented a family, its recessive gene and its intelligence over several generations. He followed it up with *Feeble-Mindedness: Its Causes and Consequences* (1914), in which he speculated that feeble-minded people were a form of undeveloped humanity, 'a vigorous animal organism of low intellect but strong physique – the wild man of today'.[22] He concluded that it would be better for both society and the feeble-minded individual in question if the latter had never been born, and claimed that prostitution, unemployment, poverty and insanity were all linked to feeble-mindedness. He advocated the segregation of the feeble-minded in institutions like his own, where they would be taught various forms of menial labour. Goddard also introduced the IQ test into America, from France, which was then used to divide people with learning difficulties into categories such as the moron and the idiot. He suggested setting up colonies where the feeble-minded could be hidden from view.

The idea of hereditary mental illness that could be halted by sterilisation remained widespread for many years. In 1927 in the case of *Buck v. Bell* the distinguished justice Oliver Wendell Holmes, then in his twenty-fifth year at the US Supreme Court, closed the 8–1 majority opinion upholding the sterilisation of Carrie Buck – who along with her mother and daughter had been labelled 'feeble-minded' – with the six words: 'Three generations of imbeciles are enough.'[23] Carrie's daughter Vivian was said by her teachers to be intelligent. This did not save her from sterilisation. She died of measles, in childhood, in 1932. In 1928 the Canadian province of Alberta passed the Sexual Sterilisation Act of Alberta, allowing the Government to perform sterilisation on 'mentally deficient' people, with the involvement of the Alberta Eugenics Board. During the forty-three years of the Eugenics Board, 2,832 sterilisation procedures were performed.[24]

Another eugenicist, Charles Davenport, who established Cold Spring Harbor laboratory in the US, started to look for heritable traits such as albinism, Huntington's chorea, epilepsy and insanity. His views on race continue to be influential today.[25] He emphasised the importance of 'negative eugenics' – preventing the proliferation of the bad. If the family history of immigrants could be investigated, he argued, people with hereditary 'imbecile, epileptic, insane, criminalistic, alcoholic and sexually immoral tendencies' could be kept out of the United States.[26]

Soon the prejudices of the elites had spread to the people. At the Kansas State Fair in 1920 the first ever 'fitter family contest' was held. Notices were put up which declared: 'Unfit human traits such as feeblemindedness, epilepsy, criminality, insanity . . . run in families and are inherited exactly the same way as color in guinea pigs.'[27] Another exhibition, in Philadelphia, had a flashing board that revealed that every fifteen seconds $100 of 'your money' went to the care of persons with bad heredity, and that every forty-eight seconds a mentally deficient person was born in the US.[28] This totting-up of the costly burden of disabled people was something that the Nazis were soon to embrace with enthusiasm.

It is therefore not surprising that the American people were willing to accept the extensive sterilisation of disabled people. As early as 1889, at the Pennsylvania Training School for Feeble-minded Children at Elwyn, superintendent Dr Isaac Newton Kerlin sterilised a small number of children, albeit with parental consent.[29] But, as the practice became more widespread, the concept of permission disappeared. It is estimated that 8,000–9,000 people were sterilised in the US between 1907 and 1928. And the impetus came from the top. Franklin Roosevelt, who successfully hid his own physical impairment (he became a wheelchair user after contracting polio in his late thirties) when he was President, wrote to Charles Davenport in 1913: 'Someday we will realise that the prime duty, the inescapable duty, of the good citizen of the right type is to leave his or her blood behind him in the world; and that we have no business to permit the perpetuation of citizens of the wrong type.'[30]

One of the prejudices that fuelled sterilisation was the notion that disabled people had disturbing sexual proclivities, with 'feebleminded women' seen as particularly promiscuous. As the historian Daniel Kevles observes: 'Eugenicists gave a good deal of attention to the sexual behaviour of the "feebleminded", with some authorities discerning excessive sexuality among the males, others claiming that mentally deficient males were actually undersexed. Whatever the disagreement about males, there had long been no dispute about females, they were reputed to be sources of debauchery, licentiousness and illegitimacy. In the 1880s, the trustees of the New York Custodial Asylum for Feebleminded Women had argued, typically, that retarded women required special care because they were "easily yielding to lust".'[31]

One particularly influential doctor, Walter Fernald, said of women with learning difficulties: 'the high grade female imbecile group is the most dangerous class. They are not capable of becoming desirable or safe members of the community. They are not able to support themselves. They are certain to become sexual offenders and to spread venereal disease or to give birth to degenerate children.'[32] These views are widely shared today, and mask the ongoing sexual exploitation of women with learning difficulties and communication problems, who are seen as easy targets because nobody believes them when they say that they have been attacked.

The legitimisation of eugenic views throughout Europe and America ended in a logical, if horrifying, outcome: the systematic murder of thousands of disabled people in Germany after the Nazis came to power in 1933. The National Socialist Party wanted to create a pure Aryan nation and eradicate the taint of the Jewish people (as well as homosexuals and gypsies). But less well known was their view that 'degenerate', impaired Aryans should also be eliminated. In some ways what happened to Jewish people was a tragedy foretold in the slaughter of innocent disabled children and adults, used to perfect the killing technology that was then practised on the Jews. Racial hygiene, as Hitler called it, started with the social cleansing of disabled people.

The artist Liz Crow has spent the last two years investigating the process that led up to what was known as the T4 Euthanasia Programme, for her art installation *Resistance*. (T4 was an abbreviation of Tiergartenstrasse 4, the address in Berlin where the programme was coordinated.) She has identified a systematic 'softening up' of the population so that they would be prepared for the programme. One part of that campaign was to open asylums to the public (as in the Victorian freak shows), to promote the racial hygiene laws. Thousands visited in the mid 1930s, including many members of the SS. Each tour, Liz Crow notes, 'culminated in a lecture illustrating, via the inmates, symptoms and the necessity for eugenic measures'.[33]

Another strand of the campaign was through film and posters, stressing the cost of disability (similar to the less systematic but equally negative campaign in the US).[34] One example she has found, from a sequence in a Reich Ministry propaganda film, shows disabled people lying in cot beds, with the strapline: 'Life is just a burden'. Another, which combines the Nazi attitudes towards minority ethnic groups and disabled people, is of a film of a black man holding out a begging bowl, with the caption: 'Mentally ill negro, English, sixteen years in an institute costing 35,000 Reich marks.' Crow concludes: 'what happened to this disabled community served as a prototype for everything that came later . . . Had people intervened at that point, presumably, what came next would have been, in some way, different . . . disabled people were the guinea pigs for the next phase.'[35]

The first law that the Nazis had passed on coming to power was the Law for the Prevention of Genetically Diseased Offspring, on 14 July 1933. Those with deafness, schizophrenia and other 'malformations' such as learning difficulties were prevented from breeding by sterilisation. The law was based on the laws functioning in Chicago, drafted by Henry Laughlin. Indeed, there was much admiration as early as 1936 by Nazi doctors for American eugenicists – they even awarded one an honorary doctorate.[36]

Hitler and other leading Nazis were also much influenced by ancient Sparta, where Hitler admired 'the exposure of sick, weak deformed children, in short their destruction, [which] was more decent and in truth a thousand times more humane than the wretched insanity of our day which seeks to preserve the most pathological subjects'. Nazi propaganda against disabled people continued to increase, labelling them 'unworthy of life' and 'useless eaters' and highlighting their burden on society in print and films. Hitler's Strength through Joy campaign prioritised getting rid of the 'syphilitics, consumptives, hereditary degenerates, cripples and cretins'. He wrote in *Mein Kampf* that 'the lame and the defective are a scourge on humanity'.

The decision to eradicate disabled children started with Gerhard Kretschmar, and accelerated shortly afterwards, apparently when other families with disabled offspring also petitioned Hitler for permission to kill their children (although some German writers were advocating this solution as early as 1920).[37] It is estimated that at least 5,000 children, from newborn babies up to juveniles, were murdered. Some were starved, others gassed.

In July 1939 the planning of the T4 programme of 'mercy killings' began. An experimental gassing procedure was carried out in the winter of 1939, and the Reich Committee for the Processing of Serious Genetic Diseases was also formed that year, collecting data on infants and 'deformed newborns'. German doctors took part voluntarily in the programme, and the earlier, related programme of sterilisation. The German paediatrician Hartmut Hanauske-Abel, who has examined many of the official documents relating to both programmes, suggests that they did so because they were convinced of the rectitude of eugenics, the programme was profitable for them and it released corpses for medical experiments. (When he first published his findings in *The Lancet* in 1986, he was suspended from practising as a doctor in Germany. He later won an appeal against his suspension.)[38]

Hanauske-Abel stresses the significance of the programme: 'The practical experience obtained in the killing hospitals of T4 provides the core for the annihilation technology of the death camps, often implemented by the same technical and medical personnel.' He concludes: 'Changes which today are interpreted as causing the downfall of the German medical community were at that time warmly welcomed by the widest segments of that highly educated biomedical and scientific elite.'[39]

Chief Nurse Irmgard Huber, who was involved in the children's killing programme at the Hadamar facility in northern Germany, one of the six institutions where disabled people were murdered, said at her trial in 1947: 'The lives . . . are just as valuable as my life, but I couldn't change anything there. I didn't have any say. I couldn't report anything. I avoided the matter.'[40] Instead, she distributed sweets to the children before they went to the gas chamber.

No one abroad seemed very interested – except other euthanasia enthusiasts. When Germany started to practise euthanasia against disabled children and adults in 1939, one officer in the American Eugenics Society commented it showed 'great courage'. Indeed, it is estimated that by 1941 the numbers of those sterilised in the US had reached nearly 36,000.[41] Joseph Dejarnette, a doctor from the state of Virginia, commented that 'the Germans are beating us at our own game'.[42] In 1942 an article in the journal of the American Psychiatric Association called for the killing of all 'retarded' children over five.[43]

Hitler signed the order to start killing disabled adults on 1 September 1939, giving permission for those who were 'incurable' to be 'accorded a mercy death'.[44] Grey buses, with blacked-out windows, would arrive in villages and outside local asylums and hospitals to take disabled people away. They were known to children as 'the murder box' and mothers would frighten their children, saying that they would be taken away in them if they were naughty.

By the end of the war it is thought that around 200,000 disabled citizens had been murdered, among them the insane, the disabled, the tubercular and the retarded, as the Nazis called them. The killing, the writer Hugh Gregory Gallagher has commented, was methodical and scientific: 'What was interesting and important about the killing program is not the mad-dog killers, but rather the careful, orderly and quite medical manner by which the full German medical and scientific establishment proceeded to kill its patients over a period of years.'[45]

One witness recalled that when the killing first started, beds were made with fresh linen and warm blankets. When people arrived to be killed, they were given hot coffee and warm rolls. Of course we will never know whether this was genuine compassion or a desire to make the killings easier to achieve. Soon, however, the numbers of those due for killing rose and the system became strained. The Nazis began to reuse coffins (by designing them with a flap that opened in the bottom to allow the corpse to fall out) and started to dig mass graves, especially for children.

Some churchmen remonstrated. The Bishop of Limburg protested in 1941, writing to the Minister of Justice: 'the citizens of Hadamar watch the smoke rise out of the chimney and are tortured with the ever-present thought of the poor sufferers'. Another, the Bishop of Paderborn, declared: 'among those unhappy beings who are destined to be killed or who have already been killed, there are many who aside from partial disturbances are mentally completely clear and who know what is going to happen to them'.[46] However, one influential Catholic, Joseph Mayer, became an apologist for the Holocaust, writing: 'moral law applies only to the mentally normal, rational individuals. Mental patients do not belong in the moral order, neither as subjects nor in terms of implementation.'[47] Later he prepared a report saying that there were reputable moral arguments for and against sterilisation on both sides. Before long, the regime was killing First World War veterans and even shell-shocked soldiers fresh from the front line. However, this policy was short-lived, partly because it affected troop morale.

There were poignant scenes. In one village, Absberg, the villagers and abbess protested against disabled residents of the abbey being taken away in 1940. The abbess said a special mass for them, and one eyewitness reported: 'They were seen as stirred up, like animals,' and refused to go. One woman declared, 'I don't want to go.' The people of the town gathered and waved goodbye to their friends, causing widescale disgust as the news spread.[48] In another village not far away, Bruckberg, those who were about to die visited almost every house in the town to say goodbye.[49]

The Absberg and Bruckberg protests did have an effect. The secret of the grey buses was secret no longer. The villagers of Absberg protested to their bishop, Von Galen, who thundered from his pulpit that what was happening must stop. T4 was officially cancelled shortly afterwards, in August 1941. But unofficial killing continued – in what is known as the 'wild phase' of the programme.[50]

The banality and playfulness of the evil often perpetrated against disabled people is best exemplified in what Hugh Gregory Gallagher claims happened when the staff at Hadamar were assembled, in midsummer 1941, to celebrate the 10,000th murder in the institution. The staff toasted the anniversary with beer and wine, in the same room where the people had been put to death. The body of the murdered man was adorned with flowers and laid on a gurney, decorated with small Nazi flags. The hospital bookkeeper, Mr Merkle, in the words of one witness, 'turned his collar about, put his coat on backward, and intoned a burlesque eulogy of the deceased insane person'.[51]

The physicians who participated in the euthanasia campaign have mostly never been successfully prosecuted. They did not stand trial at Nuremberg, unlike other Nazi mass murderers, because their crimes had been, in the main, perpetrated against other German citizens rather than foreigners. As a result, Professor William Seidelmann writes, 'Absent from the dock were the leaders of the medical profession of the Third Reich, in particular the academic and scientific elite. It was this elite who legitimised the devaluation of human life and set the stage for medical crimes – crimes in which leading academics and scientists were either principals or accomplices.'[52] There may have been another reason for the paucity of trials. Liz Crow argues that the Nuremberg prosecutors were clear in their minds that what happened to the Roma, the Jews and other groups was abhorrent. 'But they were confused about whether killing disabled people was a public service. The prevailing attitudes about disabled people, that they were inferior, pitiable and burdensome, defined their judgement.'

Back in Britain, the return of the war wounded did increase public sympathy for the physically disabled and those with shell shock and other mental health conditions. Churchill, too, had mellowed. One of his last acts as a war-time prime minister was to commit the so-called 'mental millions' to support those returning from war with their nerves in shreds. One-third of servicemen invalided out of the army had been discharged on mental heath grounds. Disabled people had become angry at last: veterans from both world wars lobbied for the right to work, through organisations such as the National League for the Blind and Disabled, holding sit-ins to force the Government to ensure their right to employment.

The end of the war did achieve two things for disabled people: it confronted Britain and America with the ugly reflection of their own ideas in Nazi Germany, and it created more sympathy for some categories of disabled people, though not all, within British society. Disabled war veterans, in particular, normalised physical impairment for many. And the end of the war was also the beginning of the end for the institutions – but with numbers reaching a record 150,000 in 1950, it was to prove a very long journey.

As for Gerhard Kretschmar, his identity was concealed for over fifty years, known only as 'child K' in official terminology. His short and miserable life was hidden in the Stasi files in East Germany, and only came to light when a German historian, Ulf Schmidt, un-earthed it after the fall of the Berlin Wall and wrote about him in his biography of Hitler's physician, Karl Brandt.[53] Gerhard's murder was recorded not as euthanasia but as heart failure, like so many others. Many of the other victims of T4 remain nameless even now. Aston-ishingly, those responsible for murdering their 'patients' could escape responsibility – by claiming that the patients they had killed had a right to medical confidentiality.

The last victim of T4, Liz Crow notes, was a 4-year-old disabled boy, Richard Jenne.[54] 'The American forces moved into Bavaria, the last area they liberated, and they put a protective ring around the local institution for disabled people, not knowing about T4. He was killed, four weeks after peace was declared.'

Too many of the victims of T4 remain nameless. And naming the dead, and what was done to them, matters. I believe that Gerhard's story, Richard's story, and those of other disabled people murdered like them, should be known and taught in British schools. They were human beings, not beastly burdens who should be put out of their misery. We owe it to them to remember them, and to give them their rightful place in our common history. For if we do not learn from history, we cannot guarantee that it will not be repeated.

6

Scandalous Institutions

Ann Macfarlane was born just before the Second World War. At the age of 4, with her father away fighting, Ann became seriously ill and was admitted to a children's acute hospital. She was later transferred to various institutions and, at the age of 9, was placed in what was termed a 'long-stay hospital'. Her experience there was particularly traumatic.

Ann was sent to an institution in north Norfolk, ostensibly an orthopaedic and TB hospital for children. She and other children had their bodies encased in plaster as a crude form of treatment. Ann recalls its removal as 'downright cruel'. She remembers: 'They put sticking plaster on our heads and when it had to be removed they would just tear it off, and the hair came with it. We were just low life.' The children were humiliated and assaulted, Ann continued. 'If you couldn't move because of the plaster and they didn't get to you in time when you needed the toilet, your head would be rubbed in faeces.' Some children were even put outside, all night, in their beds, as a form of punishment.

Parents were discouraged from visiting – Ann only saw her parents once a month, for two hours. This wasn't unusual: many children had no visitors at all. The children were, of course, ill and weak. Those who couldn't, or wouldn't, eat were force-fed and when they vomited they were made to eat it, or the food was left until a later time when it was force-fed to them again. Ann recalls: 'When the specialists came the place would be immaculate, we were dressed and the beds were nicely made. When the specialist was gone, everything would return to normal.'

Toys were routinely denied (as they were, academic research confirms, in many other homes). Her father came back from the war and brought Ann, she remembers, 'a fantastic doll'. But Matron refused to let Ann have it after her father left and threw it on top of a high cupboard, where Ann could see it but not reach it. She got it back when she left, as a teenager.

One incident has haunted Ann since her childhood. A young girl, Mary, was disliked by the nurses. Years later, Ann wrote a poem, 'Watershed', about what happened to Mary at bathing time:

> *We were quiet, hiding our fear*
> *Knowing in our nine-year-old hearts*
> *That we were about to witness something*
> *Frightening and evil.*
> *One cried quietly,*
> *And we clutched inadequate towels around our thin bodies*
> *As Mary, pretty and small, passive and unmoving*
> *Became the focus of all our attention.*
>
> *They lifted her effortlessly*
> *Into the deep porcelain tub*
> *And then, without warning*
> *Pushed her passive pale body under the water*
> *And held her there.*
> *We felt the fear through our ill-clad bodies.*
>
> *Mary was dead . . .*
>
> *Slowly their attention turned outwards to us,*
> *Unacknowledged, unwanted onlookers.*
> *One by one we were wheeled back to our beds*
> *Alone with our fearful thoughts.*
> *No one spoke of Mary again.*
> *It was as if she had never been,*

And yet she was our friend,
Part of our lives.

Nearly fifty years later, this scene comes and visits me.
Then, we knew we must stay silent.
Now I speak it for all the Marys
In institutions, in hospitals, in segregated schools
And for my nine-year-old self, who had no choice
But to sit and watch.[1]

Looking back, Ann reflects: 'It was just a kind of a thing, they did all sorts of things. Bathing was a communal thing, and they took a dislike to certain children, they either liked you and you got favours or they didn't like you. I don't think the nurses knew it would end in tragedy, they just pushed her down and it was too much for Mary. Most of the children, like her, who had TB, were very frail.' No one has ever been prosecuted for Mary's death, there has been no official inquiry and the records that remain from that institution are patchy and incomplete.

Not all establishments were as bad as Ann Macfarlane's, but the institutional system of social control of disabled children and adults created an environment where both abuse and neglect could flourish. The National Health Service, established in 1948, had taken over control of over 100 asylums, as well as long-stay hospitals, with an average population of over 1,000 patients. The National Assistance Act 1948 stated: 'it shall be the duty of every local authority to provide residential accommodation for persons who, by reason of age, illness, disability or any other circumstances, are in need of care and attention which is not otherwise available to them'.[2] But soon reformers were pressing for action, and arguing that confinement was not only unnecessary for many, but deleterious to their health and often cruel as well.

The World Health Organisation included a section on 'mental disorders' for the first time in its sixth revision of the International

Classification of Diseases in 1948. The same year also saw a 'Monster Kongress', as Anna Freud termed it, in London, of over 2,500 representatives of 42 countries, to learn from the experience of mental health problems during the war. In 1946 Mind, the charity for mental health, and Mencap, a charity for people with learning difficulties, were formed (at that time under different names). They started to press for reform, arguing for education and treatment rather than seclusion and neglect.

A few years later John Bowlby published his highly influential work on children and attachment disorder, from direct observation of hospitalised and institutionalised children. He argued that institutions were harmful to children and created a devastating rift between children, their mothers and their families generally.[3]

Pressure for reform grew. The National Council for Civil Liberties published a pamphlet in 1950, called *50,000 Outside the Law*, citing 200 cases of alleged false imprisonment of 'defectives'.[4] Churchill, too, had learned from the horrors of the Holocaust. In 1953 he announced a reformist Royal Commission on the law relating to mental illness and deficiency. It suggested community care and closing the asylums.

The 1959 Mental Health Act, introduced by Harold Macmillan's Conservative Government, was described in its preamble as 'An Act to repeal the Lunacy and Mental Treatment Acts 1890 to 1930, and the Mental Deficiency Acts, 1913 to 1938, and to make fresh provision with respect to the treatment and care of mentally disordered persons and with respect to their property and affairs; and for purposes connected with the matters aforesaid'. It built on the increasing knowledge about the disadvantages of care in institutions and the damage that they could do.

In 1961 Enoch Powell, then Health Minister, made his famous 'Water Tower' speech to the annual conference of NAMH (later called Mind). He envisaged closing psychiatric hospitals and replacing them with community care, calling for 'nothing less than the elimination of by far the greater part of this country's mental hospitals as they stand

today'.[5] His support and that of other right-wingers was also temper-
ed by expediency, with many believing that it would be cheaper than
hospital care. In 1968 the Seebohm Report suggested a decisive shift
to care in the community, and for education for 'subnormal' children
to be transferred from health to education authorities.[6]

The pressure to reform the system mounted as the institutional
scandals – Ely, Farleigh, South Ockendon and Normansfield – broke
and became front-page news. The Ely Hospital Committee of Inquiry reported in March 1969 that the hospital's regime had been
characterised by cruel ill-treatment, inhumane and threatening behaviour towards patients, the pilfering of food and clothes by staff,
and indifference by senior staff to complaints. It highlighted overcrowded wards and a lack of privacy for patients, who were allowed
few personal possessions. Buildings were old and poorly designed,
few patients were discharged, and food and clothing were inadequate.
Staff members who tried to complain were intimidated into silence.[7]

The Farleigh Hospital Committee of Inquiry reported two years
later. It found that few patients received visits and even fewer visited
anyone outside the hospital. In one ward, nearly all of the residents
never left the room. There was a lack of space, equipment and staff,
and a 'harmful over-use of drugs'. Suspicious deaths were not reported to the coroner. Three nurses were eventually jailed for ill-treating
patients.

In May 1974 the Report of the Committee of Inquiry into South
Ockendon Hospital again found worryingly poor standards of nursing care. The inspector blamed poor management and problems with
the handling of complaints. The hospital, he said, was overcrowded
and understaffed. Among other things, he pointed to a lack of funding. Staff tended to rely on tranquillisers, rather than providing activities, to control the patients. Side rooms on wards were used as
punishment areas for patients who didn't 'behave' or cooperate with
staff. Often, there would be just a mattress and blanket on the floor of
these punishment rooms – little different from the blanket dress and
the straw on the floors at Bedlam, two hundred years earlier.[8]

These scandals forced the Government to set up the Hospital Advisory Service (HAS), which had the remit of inspecting and improving the long-stay hospitals. It was abolished in 1975, after minimum standards were said to have been reached. But the scandals kept coming.

One such was documented in the Committee of Inquiry into Normansfield Hospital in November 1978, which found that the standard of nursing care there was extremely low and that difficult patients were routinely secluded. Faeces and urine were not attended to for days, and the inspector concluded that the hospital was 'generally speaking, filthy', the wards bare and reminiscent of workhouses. Patients had no personal possessions and no privacy.[9]

The scandals, of course, should have been anticipated. They had after all happened before, and been documented as such, by a select committee 150 years earlier. But institutional violence (which is still usually called by its euphemism, abuse) has almost always escaped the attention of the criminal justice system – a blind spot that is only now becoming apparent. Children, in particular, are prone to be abused in institutions, disabled children even more so. But they are rarely believed and so some abusive situations can persist for decades, unnoticed, unchecked, unchallenged and, ultimately, unpunished.

In the quiet and beautiful village of Banham, deep in the Norfolk countryside, a forty-five-minute drive south from where Ann Macfarlane was abused as a small child, off tiny, winding roads, one school has become notorious for a thirty-year abuse scandal.

In 2008, eighty-six former pupils launched a compensation claim against Banham Marshalls College, a special school, for the physical and psychological abuse that they experienced at the hands of the abusive headmaster and owner, George Robson, and his accomplices. Banham Marshalls College, formerly the Old Rectory School, was an independent day and boarding school run by Robson between 1975 and 2004. It received children with special educational needs from twenty-four local education authorities across the country, including Norfolk, Suffolk and Cambridgeshire.

Hidden away behind yew and laurel trees, the old vicarage, where the abuse took place, looks beautiful and well tended. There are flowers in pots outside the freshly painted exterior, where Robson's family still live. Just a short walk down the lane is the pond, where children were routinely ducked for any supposed offence. One claimant, Raymond Turner, who came to the school with emotional and behavioural problems after a family break-up, recalled the abuse vividly in his testimony. Mr Turner had already been sexually abused in another home by an older boy before arriving at Banham. But things did not get any better for him when he was placed there in September 1978, by Cambridgeshire Social Services, at the age of 9.

Raymond Turner's testimony is chilling: 'I soon learnt to be careful around Mr Robson, Mr Thomas, Mr Wilson and Mr Holesworth. I never felt relaxed around them as I knew I would be severely punished if I misbehaved . . . It was really strict there and they would quite often humiliate pupils in front of others.' One punishment, for talking after lights out, was to force an entire dormitory to stand outside in the rain, wearing just underpants. Mr Turner was also physically abused, beaten with a large stick or plimsoll – often in front of others – as were other children. 'Seeing other pupils get assaulted made me feel stressed as it was horrible seeing your friends in pain. I could not comfort them because I knew the staff would turn on me and punish me next.' On one occasion Mr Turner and other boys were forced to act as beaters when the teachers went game shooting. The children were also used as unpaid labourers and forced to pull sugar beet on Mr Robson's nearby farm. On another occasion he saw two other boys covered in cuts and bruises, who said they had been set upon by four teachers. He was thrown in the pond on three or four times during his seven years at the school. He recalls: 'There was always debris in the lake and stinging nettles on the edge of it. The water smelt rotten.' Mr Turner connects his depression with his time at the school. Andrew Grove, the solicitor acting for many of the pupils, says that what happened to Mr Turner was not unusual.[10]

Charles Jarman, another former pupil, recollects: 'The school was run under a regime of fear, but that fear was backed up on an almost daily basis of seeing people punched and children being broken in one way or another.' He, too, lives now with permanent physical damage as the result of the treatment at the school. 'I had two ribs broken by Tony Thomas, and when I was 10 years old George Robson took away the crutches I had been given because I had broken my hip. I had to hobble around without any crutches because he had just had a new floor put down and didn't want me to ruin it.'[11] Other children maintain that they were sexually assaulted at bathing time.

Detectives said they investigated hundreds of allegations against children aged between 7 and 16. 'The school was clearly run in a climate of fear with "control" of the children being of paramount importance,' said Detective Inspector Matt Sharman, who led the inquiry. He added: 'This has been a long and involved investigation looking into events that took place up to thirty years ago. The many victims in the case, some of whom had never come to terms with what happened to them, were traced to addresses all over this country and even abroad. Many of these people have been greatly affected by their treatment at the hands of George Robson and his team.'[12]

But the person accused of indecent assault, Lesley Beckett, died before he could stand trial. George Robson, the school's former owner and principal, and Anthony Robson, his brother, were eventually convicted of cruelty offences against pupils between 1975 and 1988. A former warden, David Clarke, admitted cruelty and was given a nine-month suspended jail term. The case for compensation is still ongoing. Not one person involved in the systematic abuse of many disabled children over a thirty-year period has spent a night in jail for the offences.

The case at Banham Marshalls was not an isolated one. Disabled children in the care system, as well as adults, have been systematically abused by those who should protect them. But eventually change was to come, induced not least by a number of highly critical studies, including the sociologist Pauline Morris's masterly dissection of a broken system.

In *Put Away: A Sociological Study of Institutions for the Mentally Retarded*, published in 1969, Morris painted a picture of a bleak, inhumane and neglectful set-up, where disabled people were housed in barren, comfortless conditions.[13] In 1968, when she was compiling her report, the sixties were in full swing. Britain was booming. But nobody cared about those who had been shut away: 'In a materially prosperous society, the conditions of overcrowding and dilapidation which we have described in this chapter bear testimony to the harsh paradox of private affluence and public squalor.'[14]

She painted a graphic picture of the long-stay hospitals, where the smell of incontinence lingered in the rooms, and where many of them, former workhouses, were poorly heated, overcrowded and draughty. It was a system that didn't even understand those for whom it was supposed to care. There was a tendency to assume that someone with physical disabilities also had learning difficulties.

Pauline Morris and her team visited 761 wards and found that nearly 80 per cent of inmates were kept in wards of forty beds or more. Some hospitals had as many as 600 'patients'. There was barely room for patients to stand between beds. Less than one-third of the disabled children had access to toys and those that they had were inadequate. She noted that these 'barrack-like institutions with Spartan provisions are a negation of what is normal in human experience'.[15] The vast majority of patients didn't own their own toothbrush – they were expected to share. Women did not even have their own bra. The amount of money spent on food and drink was half that spent in general hospitals. Relatives were discouraged from visiting and routinely excluded, as they were seen as 'obnoxious, a perfect nuisance'.[16]

She explained why nobody cared, in words that still resonate today: 'The "accommodation" possibilities that still exist for other groups of handicapped persons seldom exist for the subnormal, possibly

because attitudes towards them go so deep into the human unconscious . . . the Mongol child is a living representation of the monster
to which the young expectant mother fears she may give birth. The
child who "turns out" to be subnormal in a hitherto "normal" family
is indeed the changeling left by the evil spirit . . . their appearance
is often disturbing. Thus the physical isolation of the hospital is reinforced by the reluctance of the community to accept persons who
may both look "odd" and may behave in a strange way.'[17]

The result was that 'conditions in some places are Dickensian and
grotesque; in a few places there are certainly unnecessary unkind-
nesses'. And she blew apart the notion that these were places of care:
'These are not really hospitals . . . few are prepared to bring the
problem out into the light of public scrutiny if it means spending
money on people who are looked at furtively and with a degree of
embarrassment.'[18]

Morris concluded: 'the isolation, cruelty and deprivation of the
hospital organisation, as it must be seen to be, is of our own making. Because almost everyone – hospital management committees,
staff and public – regards the poor conditions of these hospitals with
comparative equanimity, because almost everyone adopts an attitude of untutored pessimism about the possibilities of educating
and occupying the handicapped, unjustifiably low standards of care
are tolerated. The hospitals have been gripped with a kind of creep-
ing organisational sickness, within which the handicapped have little chance either to fulfil themselves or enjoy the rights available to
other citizens.'[19]

Another writer, Maureen Oswin, also shocked the social care profession with her book *The Empty Hours*, written in 1971 and drawing on her personal experience of teaching children in long-stay
hospitals. It was a powerful chronicle of abuse and neglect – of children so thirsty that they would drag themselves outside to suck water from puddles. She had seen children living in cockroach-infested
wards, where some were routinely dosed with strong tranquillisers.
Many had little or no contact with their parents. The nurses didn't

care – they thought there was nothing that could be done for these children.

Oswin's description of 'forgotten children' hit home. She wrote of children being 'bright, intelligent, physically disabled, bored, lonely, no toys, no occupation, nothing to reach out to or touch through the bars of their cots. Like battery hens, void lives in cot cages.'[20] In a description of another hospital, she observed: 'the walls of the ward were painted grey, and there was grey mottled lino on the floor. There were no carpets, no armchairs, settees, curtains or wallpaper,' – documenting bleakly the 'long empty hours with nothing to do'.[21] Oswin was blacklisted by her local education authority and her promotion was blocked, because of her revelations.[22]

Erving Goffman's work in the 1960s in the United States chimed with UK research that institutionalisation was harmful for both adults and children. He observed in the introduction to his book *Asylums* that what he called 'total institutions' were incompatible with family life (hence the ritual exclusion noted by observers) and that being incarcerated in a 'mental institution', as he called them at the time, was effectively a prison for people who 'have broken no laws'.

He noted, too, the unhealthy power relationship operating in institutions: 'Staff tend to feel superior and righteous; inmates tend, in some ways at least, to feel inferior, weak, blameworthy and guilty.'[23] He also criticised the 'curtailment of self' by the removal of possessions, the loss of personal safety and the indignity of treatment.[24] He concluded that 'many total institutions, most of the time, seem to function merely as storage dumps for inmates' and called for them to be closed.[25] These observations remain true today.

In 1971 the Conservative Government published a White Paper, *Better Services for the Mentally Handicapped*, in response to continued reports about appalling conditions in the hospitals. This paper laid the foundations for the care in the community initiative, with the Government stating that at least half of those living in hospitals should be living in the community by 1990. A similar White Paper, *Better Services for the Mentally Ill*, was published in 1975 by the new Labour

Government, which wanted action to close down the asylums and the long-stay hospitals and replace them with community facilities. So the decision was taken, as Michael Bayley describes in his book *Mental Handicap and Community Care*, to make a decisive switch to community care. It was the right decision, made for moral as well as politically expedient reasons. But the way in which it was carried out – on the cheap – would fail the very people it was supposed to benefit.[26]

Brave New World?

It should have been such a brave new world – institutions closing, disabled people growing in strength and voice. But although the new disability activists supported the closure of the long-stay hospitals, they were also fighting on other fronts. The disability rights movement had started to emerge as early as the 1960s, although there had been forerunners. The National League of the Blind and the Disabled, a trade union, was established as early as 1899. But as one activist, Richard Woods, observed, 'People began to realise there was more to life than employment.'[1]

A key factor in the radicalisation of the disability movement was the realisation 'that disabled people were not sharing in the wealth of the affluent society that was emerging in the 1960s', as Jane Campbell and Mike Oliver argued in their influential book *Disability Politics*, about this period.[2] Jane Campbell had been one of the earliest activists in the new movement and one of the first disabled people with high support needs to go to one of only two universities, Warwick and Sussex, in the 1970s that would accommodate disabled people. As a young woman she felt extremely alone, she told me in an interview, with doctors frequently warning her that her condition, spinal muscular atrophy, meant that she could die. It is a measure of how far some disabled people have come that she is now an influential figure in the House of Lords and has confounded medical opinion.

Looking back, she explains the movement's success through social movement theory, talking about tension, mass movement, resource mobilisation and political process: 'There was clearly strain in society in the 1960s in that disabled people were not getting a fair share, or even any share, in the affluence that was emerging. It was also a time of rapid social change and, as well as being affluent, the 1960s were swinging as well. Disabled people, however, began organising collect-ively in order to secure a reasonable standard of life, not because they wanted to participate in rapid social change.'[3] The first such group was the Disabled Income Group, which from the late 1960s onwards pressed for a disability income for all.[4]

But things became political when a frustrated wheelchair user, Paul Hunt, who lived in residential care in Hampshire, wrote to the *Guardian* on 20 September 1972 calling for other people with physical impairments to join together to fight institutional care. He declared: 'severely physically handicapped people find themselves in isolated, unsuitable institutions, where their views are ignored and they are subject to authoritarian and often cruel regimes'.[5]

Other activists such as Maggie and Ken Davis joined the fray, arguing: 'Whilst there might have been a time when it was perfectly reasonable for disabled people to have been segregated and incar-cerated, the growth of technology and the availability of wealth in British society had reached the point where there was no longer any justification for disabled people to be left on the sidelines.'[6] Vic Finkelstein, a physically impaired South African doctor and anti-apartheid exile, got involved too, saying: 'Basically it goes back to the fact that disabled people are socially dead so you don't need a home.'[7] He too campaigned for the end to institutionalisation, which he described as being as iniquitous as slavery.[8]

Paul Hunt and Vic Finkelstein, along with others, founded the left-wing Union of the Physically Impaired Against Segregation (UPIAS) in the early 1970s, with a clear mission to end what they called 'incar-ceration' for those with physical impairments. One of its first position statements read: 'The reality of our position as an oppressed group can be seen most clearly in segregated residential institutions, the ultimate scrapheaps of this society.'[9] From the start the movement was large-ly white, male and dominated by those with physical impairments. Vic Finkelstein acknowledged this nearly ten years ago: 'There are,

I believe, good historical reasons why people who used wheelchairs did predominate in UPIAS. They tended to be less isolated and so had greater awareness of significant social changes that were already taking place in the health and welfare services as well as political struggles and the general state of the economy. Many had been able-bodied and were familiar with social movements.' He added: 'The visible prevalence of people using wheelchairs in UPIAS made some groups . . . awfully suspicious of what we wanted to achieve.'[10] When UPIAS members decided to broaden the fight in the 1980s, founding the British Council of Disabled People, the same problems remained.[11] Not surprisingly one key member described it in retrospect as 'the wheelchair brigade'. Jane Campbell characterises it as 'white and male', as well as being full of 'highly intelligent, academic disabled people'. Another early member calls it 'elitist and argumentative'.

None of this should denigrate its achievements, given the barriers disabled people faced at that time (most were poor and jobless, however talented, and had no support to live independently). However, many within the movement now agree that it excluded certain groups – those with learning difficulties and mental health problems in its early years, the very groups that were the first targeted for attack in the community. Jane Campbell speaks for many when she describes the effort of will it took to overcome her own attitudes towards some groups: 'I was horrible to people with learning difficulties at my special school. We were taught to dislike people with learning difficulties because we were "better" than them. It was internalised oppression; I would cross the road rather than be seen with a learning disabled person – when I was a child, I wouldn't be seen dead with one of them, because I was ashamed. It was much later, when I met other disabled people, that I was able to deconstruct my anger and feelings of not liking disabled people, even though I was one.'

The nascent British movement was inspired, to a large extent, by American activism – which was based around seeking individual rights, such as access, facilities and appropriate support. The American movement had its roots in the return of physically impaired veterans from the Vietnam War, who sought to reduce physical barriers to their inclusion in society. But soon students were active too, most famously at Berkeley in California, where Ed Roberts founded a group known as the Rolling Quads, with wheelchair users pushing for the right to go to college. In 1972 Roberts founded the first ever Center for Independent Living, influencing the next wave of British activism.[12] Disabled people in Britain saw their counterparts in America organising sit-ins, pushing for the right to access, and occupying health, education and welfare offices in the late seventies.[13] America also saw a parallel movement develop, as people with learning difficulties started to found 'People First' organisations, pressing for equality.

Gary Bourlet, a young British man with learning difficulties, visited the US in the eighties and saw for the first time people with learning difficulties speaking up and campaigning for themselves. In 1984 he came back determined to start the first British People First organisation. Like others in the emerging disability movement, he was almost penniless, as he recalls: 'I wrote 400 letters to disabled people, handwritten, I didn't have a computer, and I paid for the stamps out of my benefits money. We started off in Camden, with just twenty people in the room.' People with learning difficulties were still coming out of long-stay institutions and many were spending long hours in day centres. They wanted real jobs, real wages, better housing. But People First was not connected in any way with the mainstream disability movement – as Bourlet says, 'We were on our own, at that time.'

Before long the mainstream movement was evolving – and challenging the language around disability. Its slogan 'Nothing About Us, Without Us' still resonates today. Disabled people were speaking for themselves and didn't want charities, or carers, speaking for them any more. They challenged what they termed the 'medical model' of disability, the idea that disability is an individual medical issue that can be solved. Disabled activists didn't want to be made 'better' or cured and, given the way doctors behaved to them, certainly didn't want them to be in control of so-called treatment.[14]

The 'charity' or 'tragedy' model was also pilloried, for putting charities in control of decisions that would be made better by disabled people themselves. The charity model, as one writer explains, is promoted by welfare organisations: 'The images and ideas that charities portray of disabled people include pitiful, needy, helpless victims, external children, asexual, incurable, courageous, special, exceptional, and in need of care. But most of all, they need your money.'[15]

Disabled people wanted equal rights, not a begging box. The first demonstration to hit public consciousness was on 7 July 1988 at the then Department of Health and Social Security, at the Elephant and Castle in south London, where disabled people gathered to protest against benefit cuts.[16] It was followed by disabled people chaining themselves to, and protesting against, inaccessible buses and against having to travel in the guards van on trains.[17] Slogans included, on one wheelchair, 'I'm too sexy for a charity photo', 'Rights, not charity' and 'End apartheid for disabled people!'.[18]

The new disabled people's movement was going through an angry phase, with much of its ire directed towards the 'big seven' charities (Radar, Scope, RNIB, RNID, Leonard Cheshire, Mencap and Mind) which had carved up both financial resources for disabled people and media attention between them. Mike Oliver called the charities Scope and Radar 'downright dangerous'.[19] Jane Campbell dubbed them 'super-tanker charities', unable to change policy quickly: 'they have influenced disabled people to reject their bodies and minds, to regard their impairments as a tragedy that must be eradicated at any price, and to return to some myth of undamaged normality'.[20]

Bert Massie, who was at this time at Radar, one of the most influential charities, reflects that the movement had to 'attack the charities to attract resources', in order to move the pot of money away from the charities to the movement itself. Looking back, he says that he felt hated for working at Radar and calls the movement 'segregationalist' at that time, as it searched for identity. But the attacks had positive results, he notes: 'The charities did defend their positions, but they also had to look at what they were doing very carefully. The movement gave disabled people a sense of empowerment that the charities had failed to do. As charities we got the laws changed, we got things moving, but the movement empowered people.'

Mike Oliver coined the phrase the 'social model' of disability in 1983. As Michael Devenney explains: 'The social model asserts the idea that disabled people have their own identity as people with impairments within society . . . in this model the problems of impairment or disability are turned on their head and become the collective problems of society, not of the individual disabled person.'[21] Society's attitudes towards people with impairments are disabling, the social model argues, as is the environment that denies them access to buildings and public space. Public policies by insurers, banks, schools and the police are also disabling, such as disabled car users being routinely charged higher insurance premiums.

All of this was well and good, but the social model had its critics. One of the most prominent was the disabled academic Professor Tom Shakespeare, who argued that the model has both strengths and weaknesses. It boosted self-esteem and anger amongst disabled people, and increased the pressure for political reform. But it was largely articulated by heterosexual, white, physically disabled men and ignored the experience of women and people with learning difficulties. It also skated over the negative aspects of some impairments – denying, for instance, that disability can cause suffering. 'Most activists concede that behind closed doors they talk about aches and pains and urinary tract infections, even while they deny any relevance of the body while they are out campaigning. Yet this inconsistency is surely wrong: if the rhetoric says one thing, while everyone behaves privately in a more complex way, then perhaps it is time to re-examine the rhetoric and speak more honestly.'[22] He argued that the social model has become a sacred cow and that pushing for a 'barrier free Utopia' did not solve all problems inherent in disability.

There was another problem too. Articulating the new theoretical model consumed precious time and effort, as did the struggle for equality on so many fronts (the right to equal employment, access to

history . . . the clothes in the bundle often don't even fit'.[29] Some
came out with tragic stories about their confinement – one woman
had been put away for breaking a plate at the age of 16, another had
been subjected to an unnecessary enema every other day for some
long-forgotten medical reason.

No one seemed to know who was responsible for checking up on
the former long-stay patients when they were resettled. There was
confusion between the health authorities and social services depart-
ments. Many of the former patients seemed to have been abandoned,
and they didn't receive the visits from social workers that might have
given them some protection and the opportunity to report abuse.

The investigative journalist John Pring, in an interview for this
book, said: 'This was exacerbated by the fact that because the long-
stays were usually in the countryside, and few inner-city boroughs
had private homes in their own boundaries, an inner-city authority's
residents could be dispersed far and wide. There was no way that
social workers, even when they knew about people placed in care
homes miles away, would have the time to check up on them regularly. And they didn't. And because there was no slack in the system,
there were many inappropriate placements.'

It was John Pring, then a young reporter in Slough, who in 1994
would uncover the scandal of the Longcare residential homes, which
he wrote about in his book *Silent Victims*. By the mid 1980s the
number of smaller, private residential homes like those at Longcare
was rising by about a fifth every year. These institutions were spring-
ing up to cater for those who were not seen as being capable of
living independently. Ironically, some would turn out to be as
abusive as, if not more abusive than, the long-stay hospitals. Indeed,
as John Pring observed: 'The resettlement programme presented
many of the former patients with some new freedoms, but the way
it was managed also exposed many of them to grave new dangers
and poor quality care, in homes that were a long, long way from the
family-type settings that had been envisaged.'

Gordon Rowe, a former social worker who had worked at Broadmoor, knew when he set up Longcare in 1983 that there was a severe shortage of residential homes for learning-disabled people. Thousands of patients were being resettled into the community from the long-stay hospitals. Many of these people had been living in such institutions since they were very young children, often for more than fifty years. He set up two homes, with a substantial number of places (thirty-eight and twenty-eight respectively). John Pring explains what happened: 'The closure of the long-stays was exaggerating the tensions in the residential care system, and people like Rowe, with his social work contacts, were well placed to take advantage. With little or no oversight, Rowe saw, and took advantage of, the opportunity. For ten years, former social worker Gordon Rowe beat, raped, ill-treated and humiliated the residents of the two residential homes for adults with learning disabilities he owned and managed in south Buckinghamshire. Many, including those who moved to the Longcare homes, were just abandoned by the authorities. Those who went to Longcare were left at the mercy of a man who had already been investigated by police for serious sexual offences against other people with learning difficulties.'[30]

John Pring started investigating Longcare in 1994, on the *Slough Observer*, and his work led to the reopening of the police investigation into abuses at the homes. The local MP, Fiona Mactaggart, also took up the case after she was elected in 1997. The trial of the three managers (Gordon Rowe killed himself in 1996) took place in 1997. Paul Boateng, then a health minister, admitted after sentencing: 'This case has brought out real failings. We need a tough, transparent and clear regulatory system across the board.' The inquiry into Longcare, by Tom Burgner, reported in 1998 and recommended an independent element in the inspection and registration of care homes.[31]

Reflecting on that time, Pring believes that Longcare 'demonstrated every single flaw in the system – not enough social workers, shortage of good placements, poor registration and inspection procedures, poorly trained and paid staff, no links between homes and the communities around them, people with learning difficulties

treated as third-class citizens, not enough money put into learning difficulties services and lack of communication between the
agencies'. And such homes were as institutional as what had gone
before. They were a bit smaller, but that on its own wasn't enough
to stop appalling abuse occurring. The power relationship between
staff and disabled people had not changed.

Those who were deemed able to live independently in the community were also cast adrift. As Jean Collins concluded, they were
'pauperised and dependent . . . denied the opportunity to function
as independent and worthy human beings'.[32] Many were wholly un-
prepared for life outside. Some people were dispersed far from the
areas in which they had lived for years, and many in the community
did not want them as neighbours. Prophetically, Collins observed
that 'resettlement teams tend to find that the houses that are offered
by the council are in the most undesirable streets on unpopular estates. One resettlement officer said "do you leave the people in hospital or put them on the streets where no one else wants to live?" '[33]
And their self-esteem, experience of education and expectations
had been reduced too. They expected little of the community, Collins noted: 'their life of deprivation in mental handicap hospitals has
narrowed their horizons, limited their experience and lowered their
expectations'.[34]

There was also emerging evidence of hostility, as Michael Bayley
had found when he had investigated the start of the long-stay closure
programme in 1973. One mother of a disabled young person told
him: 'When we're out, boys, they can be very cruel.' Another said: 'I
was once told that if she was a nuisance to the neighbour they could
send her away.'[35]

The alarm was sounding, but few were listening. One academic, Margaret Flynn, studied nearly a hundred people who had moved out of
hospitals and hostels in 1988. Apart from social isolation, she found
that some were also repeatedly victimised and targeted. In words res-
onant of Fiona Pilkington, one single woman said: 'I've been robbed

three times in two years here. That's why I always keep my curtains closed . . . I'd like to move because of the kids. They throw eggs and all sorts at my windows. They call me names and throw things at me when I'm out. The window cleaner can't get the mess off the windows. The police can't do anything. No one can stop them.'[36]

Flynn warned that some were starting to isolate themselves, such was the level of victimisation: 'people who experience victimisation are unable to trust others and, regarding themselves as prey, they do not or cannot take the necessary steps to form relationships. Some people are too frightened to leave their homes and, inevitably, this reduces their opportunities to meet others.'[37]

Cast drift, disabled people who had been deinstitutionalised were an accident waiting to happen. Despite the brave hopes, the birth of the disability rights movement and the grand ideas of politicians, this was a tragedy foretold. Enough people knew that prejudice existed, that the folk memories of people had if anything become stronger because so many disabled people had been put away, regarded and treated as a race apart.

Nobody had asked the British people what they wanted, nor explained to them why this policy was put in place. There were elements of both altruism and political expediency – politicians thought it would save money, but they also felt that the scandals showed that institutionalisation was harmful. It was very harmful, and a grave injustice had to come to an end. But so too was dumping people back into a hostile society with little thought as to what would happen next – which was the rise of disability hate crime, a very modern version of an ancient crime.

In 2000 the Disability Rights Commission was founded, to push for equal rights for disabled people. It had a major job on its hands, listening to and acting on individual cases – access, transport, discrimination – and getting the 2005 Disability Discrimination Act onto the statute book. Sir Bert Massie, the DRC's chairman, recalled its heyday in an interview for this book. It handled 100,000 calls to its helpline each year, started one new legal challenge each week and won an impressive number of test cases, forcing equal citizenship for disabled people into the public arena for the first time.

In the same year, 2000, in the wake of the Longcare Inquiry, the Care Standards Act reformed the inspection and regulation of institutions. A year later, the Government published a new strategy for those with learning disabilities, *Valuing People*.[38] *Valuing People* seemed to set in stone a new compact for people with learning difficulties. At last, they were recognised as citizens, with the right to choice and independence.

Disability rights were in the ascendant. It looked as if the last great civil rights movement was nearing the end of its journey. But the reality was different. For too many disabled people, despite the rhetoric, weren't valued by all. The brave new world did not celebrate 'such people' as were in it once again. Quite the opposite.

8

The Terroring of Raymond Atherton:
Freedom's Betrayal

In May 2006 the body of Raymond Atherton, a middle-aged man with learning difficulties and mental health problems, was found floating in the River Mersey. Before he had died he had been routinely beaten and stolen from by teenagers that he had, at times, considered to be his friends. The two ringleaders were Craig Dodd, 17, and Ryan Palin, 15. They regularly broke into his flat, covered it in graffiti, used it as a location where they could have sex, daubed him with make-up, poured bleach over him, urinated in his drinks and burned his hair. They dubbed this process 'terroring' and they enjoyed it.[1] Social services felt powerless to intervene because Raymond, intimidated as he was, refused to ask for help.[2]

Lisa Ashton, the manager of Bargain Booze in Warrington, interviewed by the *Guardian*, reported that Raymond Atherton (also known as David) was often the first customer of the day. 'One day in April 2006 when he called in, it was obvious he had been beaten up,' she said. He told her that some young people had been in his flat and had 'done it for a laugh'.[3] On 8 May, the night that Raymond disappeared, a neighbour, Philip Ashton, saw teenagers beating him until he bled. They then led him off towards the River Mersey, while Ashton ran to get help. It later emerged that they had urinated on Raymond before pushing him into the river.

Detective Inspector Christine Hemingway was the senior investigating officer. She told me, in an extended interview: 'I became involved on 10 May. At that stage we were treating him as a "missing from home". We pulled out all the stops, we had a helicopter out and a search team, but it soon became clear that Raymond was a creature of habit, going to the same shops every day. So when we found out that his routine had been broken, we thought we wouldn't find him alive.' In fact the boys responsible led the team to his body. They had gone back to the scene of the crime, with two other youths, to the Mersey, to flaunt what they had done and show them his body. 'And the youths were shocked, one of them wanted to report it. A police car was passing, and saw them acting suspiciously, and the youths had just been shown the body, and they led the police to the river.'

His attackers were jailed for manslaughter in April 2007. Prosecutor Patrick Harrington declared: 'If one were to search for a single adjective to describe their behaviour, it would be feral.' Mr Justice Hodge told the teenagers: 'You both treated Mr Atherton as a punchbag. What you did was not opportunistic. It was premeditated, it was a savage attack: cruel, brutal and vicious, and on a very vulnerable man.'[4]

Although the police identified the fact that the teenagers had targeted Raymond 'for a long period of time, abusing him and his property and demeaning him', all markers I had identified as characteristic of disability hate crime, the crime was never viewed as such by social services or the criminal justice system. DI Hemingway reflected this thinking in her interview: 'I think he was targeted because of his vulnerability. The police weren't informed until social care had realised the enormity of the problem. Ray wasn't very forthcoming with names and details. You see, he was so socially isolated, so vulnerable, that he regarded them as his friends. He always let them in.' She added: 'If people had been named, it would have been followed up by us. It wasn't recognised as a hate crime, it didn't fall under the definition, but he was seen as vulnerable. He didn't want any action and what he did report was under duress.'

More light was shed on Raymond's case when I obtained, through freedom of information, an internal report that Warrington Borough Council carried out into the sad life and death of Raymond Atherton, a so-called 'joint review of a serious incident'.[5] It makes for grim reading, but it does shed light on the mentality of those dealing with disabled people, often deemed 'difficult' because they are both victims and, sometimes, perpetrators of crimes. The following account is drawn from that document.

In June 2005 Raymond Atherton came into contact for the first time with Warrington Social and Mental Health Services. He was described at this time as 'extremely vulnerable', and the intake team, which first assessed him, noted that he had beaten up on the streets. He was also diagnosed with schizophrenia. Several concerns about his vulnerability and about him being beaten up – through July, August and September – were noted, culminating in a social worker visiting his flat to find he had been burgled and Raymond saying that young people were using his flat, drinking and taking drugs. The burglary was never reported to the police. Just four days later young people entered his flat again, punched him and attempted to shave his head. This was reported to the police. In October 2005 the 'vulnerable adults' officer (a specialist officer charged with reviewing cases where adults are seen as being at risk of harm) requested more information on Raymond, believing that he had learning difficulties. Two weeks later a social worker and nurse discussed his diagnosis and referred him again for a psychological assessment.

A day later, a case meeting of professionals suggested a detox programme for Raymond and recommended rehousing, due to problems with youths. His learning difficulty was to be assessed and he was issued with a mobile phone. Housing officers were encouraged not to place other 'vulnerable people' in the area.

But no one was designated, the report notes, to refer Raymond to a psychologist, first mentioned over three months earlier. In November 2005 the social workers had a meeting with the housing antisocial behaviour unit, to discuss the 'Longford barmy army', a group of 'youths aged between 14 and 16 years who target people who are (a) vulnerable and (b) out of area'.[6] (Indeed, I was told during my research that a few days after attacking and killing Raymond, Craig Dodd allegedly attacked another disabled man.)

A social worker persuaded one of the young people in Raymond's flat to give the police a list of nine boys who were entering the flat, but the police never followed up this lead. Later it emerged that one of the names on that list was of one of the perpetrators. At last, eighteen weeks after it was first mentioned, a referral was made to a psychologist to see if Raymond had a learning difficulty. Throughout November Mr Atherton continued to have what the review calls 'numerous difficulties with local young people' – deemed so dangerous to professionals that they only visited in pairs. Raymond, for his part, had to face them alone.

Eventually, six months after suffering harassment at his property, Raymond was moved to St Katherine's Way. But, just one month after being moved, he had been assaulted again by youths and had a cut nose and bruised eye, and youngsters were once more using his flat. An outreach worker recorded one day later that it was 'obvious from his bin that he had been drinking for a long period, [he] stated he had been beaten up by a gang of kids, he had a big cut on his nose . . . later he changed his story, saying he had fallen when drunk'. When the police visited him he told them that 'six youths had been entering his flat, drinking his alcohol, eating his food and generally bullying him'.

A fortnight later the housing association recorded complaints from neighbours about loud music, and the antisocial behaviour unit became involved. Raymond's tenancy was under threat. In February 2006 Raymond told the social worker that the same youths were visiting him again. Later that month he turned up at the YMCA, too scared to go home.

One of the most tragic points about the case, said DI Hemingway, was that only Raymond could have told the youths where he was moving to, no one else would have divulged it. But merely moving him had not alleviated his social isolation. The group of young people who visited him was a mixed bunch, the inspector said. 'There were some girls in the group, who were quite kind and helped him to clean his house. It was only the odd character who picked on him.'

She added: 'It seems that he was willing to put up with the assaults to have the friendship.'

In March, an outreach worker visited to find Raymond asleep. His face had been painted black and striped with black eyeliner. The police decided not to attend. In April a plan was made to assess whether he was capable of living independently. Shortly afterwards, an antisocial behaviour officer stated that a number of youths had been issued with 'acceptable behaviour contracts' and were being closely monitored by police. But instead of this protecting Raymond, she feared that this explained why they were using his flat, as they could not be monitored there. The violence continued to increase. A new social worker visited, to find him with a black eye and swollen jaw. He stated that three men had poured cleaner on his hair and took turns punching him. The men had also taken his keys. The antisocial behaviour officer considered CCTV in the flat but worried that Raymond might tell visitors about it.

On 8 May Raymond was beaten up again in his flat. The social worker asked again for surveillance to be put in before the weekend. It was to have been put in on 11 May. Two days earlier Raymond went missing. The social worker who went to visit him that day found the flat had been trashed and there were blood spatters on the walls, door, sofa and pillow. The neighbour who raised the alarm, Philip Ashton, said he saw a group of men, aged between 17 and 27, assault Raymond with batons. Mr Ashton tried to intervene, but was assaulted himself. He managed to get Raymond away and took him to his flat. But while he was calling the police, Raymond was taken away by the men, never to be seen again.

DI Hemingway's inquiry led her to make two particularly interesting discoveries, in the light of what we know about disability hate crime. The youths, she established, had planned the attack at the flat belonging to another 'vulnerable' person they regularly exploited. That witness said that they had talked about 'going to see a man who had "done something", they were going to do him'. And, as Philip Ashton tried to intervene while Raymond was being led away, the youths explained: 'He's a paedo, he's been fiddling with my cousin.' This was untrue, and Mr Ashton intervened anyway, but without success. The charge of paeodophile, as we shall see, is one that is often levelled at disabled people before they are killed.

The second discovery was that Raymond Atherton was not the only disabled person the youths had targeted and used. Indeed, after they had killed Raymond, they went to the flat of another disabled person (with mental health problems) who they had assaulted in the past. They said, there, 'I banged him' and used the man's flat as a place where they could wash off bloodstains. Blood was found everywhere in his flat, on curtains and in the bath.

I asked DI Hemingway what the killers were like. They have never admitted assaulting him, nor killing him. She observed: 'They were rogues, feral youths, they didn't go to school, they didn't go home at night, they slept in, woke up at tea-time and moved around the town.' Their motivation? 'It was long-running, it seemed to be a sort of domination thing. And I think there's a whole generation of dysfunctional youths, they don't want to go to school, they don't want to be at home, and they have to find something to do, some purpose, and they need shelter. So it's quite easy to target vulnerable people, to drink in their houses, take drugs and take their money. We deal with it seriously if we find out about it, but we don't find out about the targeting bit until something reaches crisis point. Until a murder happens.'

All in all, Raymond Atherton had suffered five physical assaults over just nine months, and a further four crimes of damage to his property. From the internal report it seems that different 'concerns' – as many as fifteen, perhaps more – were noted by different agencies on different occasions. All sorts of different agencies were involved – social workers, police, housing, antisocial behaviour, drug and alcohol, the YMCA. But nobody saved him.

The review concluded: 'It appears that the incidents which started as damage to DA's [Raymond's] property soon became regular physical assaults which involved an element of degradation. However the police may have been dealing with these as one off incidents and not linking them . . . as DA was considered to have capacity his right to self-determination affected the ability of the police to intervene in the incidents.'[7]

Whether or not Raymond had a learning difficulty – which would have triggered extra support if he did not have capacity* – was never established. Instead, the psychologist felt it was more important for him to talk about the death of his sibling and of a child. If the Learning Disability Service had been involved, they said, they would have offered a service 'to support the team dealing with DA's communication and comprehension issues'. I asked DI Hemingway about Raymond Atherton's capacity. She replied: 'He had capability, even if he didn't fit in with social norms. There is a recognised capability test that runs alongside the diagnosis of disability. I think, he was set up, living independently, and that a diagnosis wouldn't have affected that.'

The report decided that there was 'evidence of good practice in the management of this complex case' but the lack of attention to Raymond's alcoholism and learning difficulty needed to be reviewed. It concluded, however, that the death was not avoidable. 'DA was not motivated to stop drinking and all the services involved were unsuccessful in influencing this, or in deterring DA's association with the youths that were eventually to be the perpetrators of his death.'[8]

Raymond Atherton's killers were originally jailed for life but successfully appealed against the length of their sentences.[9] This disappointed DI Hemingway, given the nature of the attacks. One is only serving three and a half years in jail and the other just three years, for their systematic abuse of Raymond Atherton which culminated in his death. They will be released in 2011.

The killings mounted, but few noticed. Although Mind and Mencap had published reports suggesting that people with learning difficulties and those with mental health conditions were being harassed and

---

* Capacity, also known as capability, is an assessment that a person has a right to make decisions unless it is proved that their impairment affects their ability to make that decision.

'bullied', they did not connect that everyday, relentless harassment to other more serious crimes of torture and murder.[10] Raymond wasn't the first to be attacked, targeted and murdered for the crime of living independently in a hostile society. Each of the crimes below was reported, but none of them was seen as part of a bigger picture, with similar motivations, similar patterns of attack and similar types of perpetrator.

In March 2005 Albert Adams, a man with learning difficulties living in Greenwich, was attacked by a woman who called herself his carer, Jennifer Henry. She stabbed him repeatedly and then concealed his body in his flat. Later she called 999 and declared that a 'little spastic' had tried to rape her (a false allegation) and said that she had murdered him.[11] The same month, Keith Philpott, a man with learning difficulties from High Grange, Teesside, was murdered by acquaintances who accused him (wrongly) of being a paedophile. They disembowelled him and stabbed him to death.[12]

Vicious, prolonged attacks, many of them ending in murder, piled up in 2006. On 1 May 2006 Sean Miles, a young man with autism and learning difficulties, was falsely accused of being a paedophile and was kidnapped, stripped naked, stabbed and then allowed to drown in the river at Oxford. He was poked with a stick as he floundered, to prevent him from getting out.[13] (Raymond Atherton died just seven days later.) In June Rikki Judkins, a man with learning difficulties who became stranded in Preston after a mix-up with his bus ticket, was punched, kicked, stamped and beaten with a large stone by Simon Unsworth and Aaron Singh.[14]

One month later, in Wales, another man with learning difficulties, Barrie-John Horrell, was assaulted by 'friends' Lee and Brett Davies, who, in the words of the judge, 'leached' off him and 'treated him like a dogsbody'. They accused him of being a paedophile and a grass and told him that they were out for revenge. In the end the two cousins abducted him, put a pillowcase over his head and drove him to a remote Welsh hillside, where they strangled him, beat him and set him on fire.[15]

Also in July, a woman with learning difficulties, Shao Wei He, was tortured, beaten and left out in sub-zero temperatures to die by her husband and his mistress, outside her husband's takeaway in Sheffield.[16] The same month, Steven Hoskin, a young man with learning difficulties, was found lying at the bottom of a railway viaduct in St Austell, Cornwall. He had been targeted, tortured and murdered by 'friends', who had accused him of being a paedophile and had dragged him around on a dog-leash.[17]

In September Kevin Davies was found dead in Bream, Gloucestershire, after being held captive, tortured, burned and starved by so-called friends, who called him a grass and dragged him around, like Steven Hoskin, by a dog collar.[18] In October Steven Gale, a young man with learning difficulties, was murdered by Andrew Green and two women. Green, who termed himself Mr Gale's carer, systematically abused him, starved him, tortured him and then murdered him. By the time he was murdered he weighed less than six stone.[19]

Eight deaths in just six months. Many more had passed almost unnoticed, each seen in isolation as motiveless murders. But further horrific killings, and other crimes against disabled people, were to come before such crimes were recognised as targeted disability hate crimes. I revisit many of these killings later in this book.

9

Steven Hoskin and the
Case of the Invisible Crime

The sun barely breaks through the thick canopy of old oak trees in Maudlin, where Steven Hoskin was born and raised, in a tiny hamlet clinging to the side of the National Trust's Lanhydrock estate, deep in the Cornish countryside. This is a beautiful and peaceful place if you are visiting it – and can leave again, after a wander in the woods and a look around a beautiful stately home. But if you have as few opportunities as Steven had in his short life, before his untimely end nearby, it is a different place altogether.

Steven was born to a mother who also had learning difficulties, and the tight-knit Hoskin family have supported them both for many years. Steven was mocked and taunted from an early age, particularly in school. At the age of 12 he became a weekly boarder at Pancalenick special school, returning home at weekends.[1]

He had few friends, except one or two adults who took pity on him – a local farmer and members of staff at a local coal merchant, where he helped out. At 16 he was admitted to an assessment unit for people with learning disabilities and mental health problems near Bodmin and also participated in youth training activities. Here he was targeted by other trainees. As he neared adulthood and the perilous time of transition from childhood, he was described by Margaret Flynn, who reviewed his case in 2007, as 'a lonely young man, who wanted friendship'.[2] A natural desire for an ordinary life, with friends, was to prove fatal.

In 2003, when Steven was 33, he moved away from Lanhydrock, with its fields and deep woodland, after a series of arguments and violent outbursts with his mother, culminating in his conviction for assault. Steven was bored and frustrated, and aware that he was different from other people. He started to drink, and a Housing Homefinder Application stated around this time: 'He is very vulnerable and can be taken advantage of due to the way he looks, i.e. his learning disability.'[3] After a while he moved to St Austell, where he fell in with those who would later kill him. But when he first met them, he told one of his few other friends that he was happy to have found them. He felt ordinary at last, all that Steven ever wanted to be.

The rain was falling on the day we visited St Austell, a neat, grey Cornish town. The town itself has a vast number of charity shops, and litter flew around the quiet streets. The few streets of social housing, not from the town centre, where Steven lived, were scruffy and rather desperate. The paint was peeling from the communal doorway to the block of flats where Steven was tortured, and a dirty pink hydrangea struggled to survive in the small front garden.

From the house where he lived you can see the railway viaduct where Steven was taken and from where he fell. As we walked up the hill towards it, the housing changed suddenly to neat, comfortable, owner occupied dwellings. The gardens were a riot of colour, with vibrant hanging baskets. One garden had a fine collection of gnomes. The change felt unexpected and incongruous – and a long way to be marched, uphill and drugged up, to your death, without anyone noticing.

The steep path off the road up to the viaduct itself was grassy and overgrown with brambles. I pushed my way through as far as I could, but gave up before I got to the railway line. They must have really wanted to kill him, at the expense of their own clothing and skin, to have pushed through the undergrowth on that grim day in July 2006.

As Margaret Flynn, who wrote the serious case review into Steven's life and tragic end, observed, the facts are stark. 'In addition to his bearing catastrophic injuries associated with falling 30 metres, a post-mortem examination confirmed that Steven had taken paracetamol tablets, had been drinking alcohol and had sustained recent injuries from cigarette burns. Further, he had neck bruises from having been hauled around his home by his own pet's dog-lead and the backs of his hands bore the marks of footprints. At the trial it was reported that on the night of his murder, Steven had been found "guilty" of being "a paedophile." While this claim was without foundation it was determined that Steven should die. Graffiti to this effect was written on a wall in Steven's bed-sit. Steven's final hours were harrowing, not least as he was required to revise his view of himself from being Darren's "friend" [Darren Stewart being the man who later murdered him] to being a "paedophile" – reviled and morbidly different from other men.'[4]

When Steven got back to his bedsit that July evening, Darren Stewart, Sarah Bullock and Martin Pollard, his so-called friends, were there, along with four teenage boys, two of whom joined in with the abuse and later witnessed the escalating violence towards Steven. It was five against one. He didn't stand a chance. As Flynn recorded: 'He was beaten about the head with a telephone charger, had his arm pushed up his back and was kicked, while held face-down on the floor. Two of the teenage boys also kicked Steven as they went to the toilet and as they left the flat.'[5]

Sarah Bullock put a dog's collar round his neck and Steven was later tied up by Darren Stewart. He was imprisoned in his own home, and his mobile phone taken away when he tried to call for help. Two of the boys (who had also been locked into the flat) were allowed to leave. They said they were 'disgusted' by what happened to Steven, but they did not intervene, nor did they report what was happening to police. Steven told Darren and Sarah that he was scared. Sarah pulled on the dog lead when he moved and forced him to call them 'sir' and 'madam'. Although neighbours heard screams that evening, nobody called the police.

The last two teenagers left the flat and Steven was forced to swallow what Margaret Flynn called a 'lethal dose of paracetemol tablets'. She concluded her grim account of that night's events: 'He could not repel his persecutors. Steven's final minutes of consciousness were bleak in the extreme. Having been made to leave his home and walk to, and onto, the railway viaduct, accompanied by Darren, Sarah and Martin, Steven was forced over the safety rail. All his life, Steven had been terrified of heights. Sarah ensured that he would let go by kicking his face and standing on his hands. He fell 150 foot to his death.'[6]

His family, living in the small village where Steven was raised, are still affected by their loss and unable to talk about his death at length, even now. It took Steven's mother, who also has a learning difficulty, a long time to understand why Steven would never come back, to walk the dogs, see the few friends he had and check in on her.

Steven's death was one of the five crimes I first investigated as possible hate crimes in the summer of 2007. I felt then, and still feel to some extent today, that disability hate crime is an invisible crime. (When I first 'googled' the phrase, in the summer of that year, I found that nobody had ever even written an article about it. I was, according to the disability charity Voice UK, the first British journalist to do so.)[7]

Steve Otter, the Chief Constable for Devon and Cornwall, who speaks on equality and diversity for the Association of Chief Police Officers, told me in an extended interview that the police force, both locally and nationally, learned much from the Hoskin case and the subsequent serious case review. The police learned, he said, that organisations working with disabled people were reluctant to involve the police and didn't recognise when they should do just that, in time to prevent people being attacked.

In Steven Hoskin's case, the attacks 'had gone too far, it was too late'. Like other disabled people, Steven was not seen as an 'ideal witness'. 'He didn't want to speak to the police, he was an adult with a significant impairment and there was a big difference between what he looked like and the risk that he carried because of his disability. And no one could believe that someone would do something as horrible as what those persons did, take him onto the viaduct, and stamp on his fingers, the whole torment of the thing.'

Steve Otter added, thoughtfully: 'He was in contact with a lot of authorities, but they just didn't understand that what was happening to him was a risk to his life. There has been a lot of focus on freedom, on the drive to independence, but you don't have to take away someone's freedom to recognise that something is happening that shouldn't happen.'

Right-minded people at this time did not believe that disabled people were being targeted. It was an invisible crime, for many reasons. The crime didn't show up in criminal justice statistics, police and prosecutors didn't believe it happened and no one was reporting it. Disability hate crime had been enshrined in law in 2003, a law that came into force in 2005. But it was hardly, if indeed ever, used.

Hate crime as a general concept had only really entered the lexicon in the UK in the 1980s, and academic and political attention was focused on racial and religious crime. The impetus for hate crime legislation came from the US, as the noted British academic Paul Iganski observes, where it was a product of the American civil rights movement.[8] That movement, given its roots, concentrated understandably on race equality. In Britain too the catalyst for change came from the racist murder of the black teenager Stephen Lawrence in 1993 and the subsequent Macpherson Report into the actions of the Metropolitan Police in 1999, which found that the force was 'institutionally racist'.[9] It is therefore no surprise that on both sides of the Atlantic the concept of racial hatred is far better understood than other forms of hate crime and that other groups offered 'protection' under the law – religious groups, homosexuals, disabled people and transgendered people – are still playing catch-up.

Hate crime has always existed, it has just not been recognised by the legal system. In America scholars point to the 'ethnocide' of Native Americans, the lynching of freed black slaves, and the hounding and execution of witches. In Europe we immediately turn to the Holocaust, and our own history of witch-hunting, and understand why it might occur. But recognition of the specific harm of hate crime has been contested, and is still contested, on both sides of the Atlantic, as an attempt to criminalise thought and as a dubious concept.

Hate crime, as Paul Iganski points out, still 'has no legal status in the UK. No law uses the term' and it remains, he says, a 'rather slippery' and elusive notion.[10] The Labour Government did introduce specific penalties for racially aggravated offences in the 1998 Crime and Disorder Act, largely in reaction to the murder of Stephen Lawrence. Religiously aggravated offences were added in the 2001 Crime and Security Act, following 9/11 and the Islamophobic backlash that followed. In 2003 hate crime sentencing provisions for sexual orientation and disability were added in Section 146 of the 2003 Criminal Justice Act, providing for sentence uplift or enhancement – but these were not separate offences.[11] As Iganski notes, although such offences are termed 'hate crimes' these words do not appear in the legislation – instead the word 'hostility' is used. It was largely irrelevant what word was used then anyway, at least as far as disability was concerned. The criminal justice system wasn't aware of disability hate crime then and the situation is patchy even now.

Those who advocate giving hate crime a special category point to its unique impact on communities and society at large. An attack on one of the group, advocates argue, is seen as an attack on all and, as such, affects their behaviour, where they go and how safe they feel in their everyday life. And, as the criminologists Jack Levin and Jack McDevitt observe in *Hate Crimes: The Rising Tide of Bigotry* (1993), hate crimes are associated with excessive brutality, multiple offenders, victimisation of strangers and extreme violence.[12] Another writer, Melissa Mertz, points out that some victims are subjected to overwhelming sexual mutilation and violence.[13]

But commonality with other forms of hate crime only went so far. As I started to dig deeper into the analysis of other forms of hate crime and look for patterns in disability hate crime, it became clear that this was, often, a different sort of hate crime. Different kinds of people attacked them, the attacks happened in different places and for different reasons too. They didn't look like other hate crimes.

And they were often obscured from view, with so many claiming they didn't exist.

Moreover, as the criminologists Neil Chakraborti and Jon Garland have explained, disabled victims are not always seen as sympathetic, and their evidence is often not believed: 'The victimisation of disabled people is rightly classified by the criminal justice system as a hate crime as it shares several characteristics with other forms of hate crime. Its continuing marginalisation from mainstream hate debates may be down to the fact that those who suffer disablist harassment are not commonly seen as "ideal victims" deserving of sympathy and only when this is rectified will disablist hate crime occupy the central place within the hate debate that it deserves.'[14]

But they were certainly being attacked, even if their experience was marginalised and trivialised by the criminal justice system. Talk to any disabled person about their experience of everyday life and they would tell you that it was a weekly, if not daily occurrence. It was higher for some groups – friends with learning difficulties were used to being spat at in the street, pushed around on the buses when schools were out, or called names. Other people I knew, with cerebral palsy, were only too used to being called 'spazzo'.

Reports by charity after charity confirmed that these weren't isolated incidents. *Another Assault*, a 2007 report by the mental health charity Mind, which surveyed thousands of people with mental health conditions, found that 90 per cent of those living in social housing had been targeted and 22 per cent assaulted.[15] One-quarter had been sexually assaulted and two-thirds called names such as 'schizo', 'nutter' and 'freak'. A similar study of people with learning difficulties by the learning disability charity Mencap found that nine out of ten of the respondents had said that they had been bullied.[16] One-quarter had been physically assaulted and 73 per cent taunted and bullied in public.

Significantly, however, neither charity sold their reports as being evidence of 'disability hate crime'. Others did, but the media was not particularly interested – and in any case the patterns linking the more serious crimes were not identified at this stage. A Disability Rights Commission report, in 2004, found that over half of all those interviewed had been attacked outside and a quarter at home.[17] Deaf people, too, were routinely targeted.[18] The National Schizophrenia Fellowship found a similar pattern of harassment from family, friends and neighbours.[19] And my own research, trawling through both very violent murders and assaults as well day-to-day harassment, showed that hardly any crimes were ever identified as disability hate crimes.

None of the disabled people I knew thought it was worth reporting the everyday taunts to the police. They knew that even if they made it to the police station (many police stations are still not accessible to wheelchair users, and many struggle to find interpreters swiftly, for instance for deaf people), they probably wouldn't be believed, especially if they had mental health issues or learning difficulties. If they had a sensory impairment, such as being blind or deaf, the police would often feel that the case was too hard to pursue.

As the national press became interested in my work, the most pressing question I was asked was 'Where is the evidence?' I had cited evidence from disability charities, but the crime was all but invisible in official data. Without that, it would be difficult to present a convincing case to sway public opinion. To get the public to take this crime seriously, I had to build a case that others in the media would feel was robust, well argued and watertight. My aim was to present fresh evidence that the crime existed and wasn't being prosecuted as such.

I felt that some original research was necessary too. So I spent the autumn of 2007 preparing an in-depth investigation of fifty crimes involving disabled people across the police forces of England and Wales. I couldn't do this work alone – I was lucky enough to be working with a number of disabled reporters who were keen to expose the truth about the real picture of disability hate crime. I divided the forty-three police-force areas in England and Wales between the reporters, myself and our deputy editor John Pring, who had run the investigation into Longcare. Then I started to identify crimes, both across the spectrum of disabilities (mental health, physical, learning difficulties and sensory) and across geographical locations.

There was no point in searching for them under the sobriquet 'disability hate crime' because nobody had ever done this before. I had to use other words to find the attacks, reflecting the language and attitudes of the general public and journalists towards disabled people. I used every search term I could think of – 'handicapped', 're-tard', 'mentally impaired', 'vulnerable' 'mental age of' and so on – to track down the missing crimes and start investigating them properly. By the time I had finished identifying crimes across half of the police forces in England and Wales, I had discovered many cases, from nasty everyday events – a young lad going out for the papers in Gwent and being spat at and robbed, a number of wheelchair users being pushed out of their disability scooters – to arson, kidnap, torture, rape, do-mestic violence and murder. The next job was to ask police forces if any of these crimes had been investigated as possible hate crimes.

Several times, our journalists would put the phone down and tell me, 'The police press office didn't know what a disability hate crime was,' or 'They said they weren't sure the law was in force yet,' or 'No, we don't have that problem here.' It was dispiriting to see how many cases that were clearly motivated by hostility towards disabled people had simply been missed by the police. We were investigating the in-visible crime.

But it wasn't just local police offices and prosecutors who had trouble with the concept of disability hate crime. The central Crown Prosecution Service press office became increasingly impatient with me, as I asked them for comments on case after case. One press officer eventually snapped, 'We can't go on providing this level of service to you.'

Where police and prosecutors saw a common assault, or a rob-bery gone wrong, or a vicious rape, and maintained it was enough to charge the original offence, I kept on asking them why they weren't using their powers to ask judges to increase sentences if the motiva-tion was disability hatred – after all, the sentence enhancement for such a motivation was enshrined in law. The dossier, when it was published, showed that just one out of the fifty cases we investigated had been viewed as a hate crime.

When I started my work in 2007 hate crimes motivated by race and religion were recorded separately because they are separate offences. This wasn't the case with those motivated by disability hatred. Because any crime can be a hate crime, if police did not mark the disability element with what is called a secondary tag or flag, it never showed up in the statistics. As the then Crime Minister, Vernon Coaker, confirmed in a written answer in 2008, 'statistics are collected on the number of racially and religiously aggravated offences, but no information is available on those offences which are specifically "disability hate crimes"'.[20] Until 2007 the Crown Prosecution Service did not separate out disability hate crime offences either. Even when it started to do so in 2007, because of the lack of reporting to police, just 141 incidents were prosecuted, compared to over 6,000 racial incidents.[21] It wasn't that the crimes weren't there – I knew that from talking to disabled people – but they weren't being identified properly as hate crimes.

The invisibility of the crime was not confined to the media. For far too long the disability movement itself had not seen the warning signs of trouble ahead. After deinstitutionalisation, the movement, which was still largely led by white intellectuals with physical impairments, was concentrating on other historical wins – one of the most important being the right to independent living, shored up by individual budgets.

Baroness Jane Campbell remembers this well. 'You see, things were good for a period. I was a baby boomer, who came out at the right time, you see. I didn't see much hate crime. All I could see was barriers to my inclusion. So I didn't notice it. I would say that people started taking the gloves off and being nasty about the time when we started becoming visible. And that's when I started to experience hate words or people telling me that we were asking for too much.

When there were more of us, more than one or two, people started saying, "You are asking for too much."' She continued: 'We did miss the warning signs. We were the sensible white middle-class disabled people, and we looked tidy. But the minute there were too many of us, and we were beginning to look like the unwashed, you did see a backlash. There was one article, for example, by a well-known writer, in which he referred to us as "weird and contorted".' But Campbell, like others, understandably connected violence against disabled people to institutional abuse. It was all to easy to miss the warning signs that violence was happening outside, in the community, partly of course because it wasn't happening to people like her.

Others did spot targeted violence earlier, such as the disability and human rights activist Rachel Hurst. She had been compiling a human rights violation database from 2000 onwards, cataloguing all kinds of violence, including so-called 'mercy killings', neglect and abuse, as well as possible hate crimes against disabled people.[22] But no one, she said, wanted to hear: 'We did raise cases but we weren't listened to because what we say is too difficult.' For the disability movement, it was difficult to talk about, Hurst believes, because many found it shameful, embarrassing and damaging: 'I think that we as individuals don't want to confront it because otherwise our lives would be intolerable . . . it's awful.'

Mike Smith, now a lead commissioner at the Equality and Human Rights Commission but then working in the financial sector, agrees but takes the critique wider still: 'I think there was a collective self-denial, because I think that many disabled people struggle to understand that disability hate crime actually occurs, just like the wider population does. The population at large can conceive how you can hate a gay person or a black person but the majority of people can't get their head around some people hating us, partly because of the charity model, which says that we should be pitied. But also, there was no data.' When Mike Smith himself was targeted because of his impairment (he is a wheelchair user) he too did not perceive it as a hate crime: 'I experienced antisocial behaviour and threatening behaviour in my property, in around '92 or '93. But even I didn't attribute it to hate crime, I was thinking it was to do with what was wrong with the perpetrator. They started painting swastikas on my front door, they would jam wooden stakes in my front door, I was consistently getting National Front, or swastikas, and even "cripple", spelt wrong, as graffiti on my property. They were clearly targeting me because I was disabled but all my focus was on why the perpetrator was doing it, he was so weak.'

Anne Novis, who credits Rachel Hurst as her inspiration, was another of the few who had been aware of disability hate crime for some time. She had run a reading recovery group for youngsters in a school, aided by an inspirational black teenager, Stephen Lawrence. When Stephen was murdered in a racist attack in 1993, Anne was deeply shocked. But she also learned much about targeted violence from his murder. When another friend of hers, a disabled man, Albert Adams, disappeared in March 2005 after voicing concerns about his money going missing, she quickly suspected that his so-called carer, Jennifer Henry, was responsible. When Albert was found dead in his flat with seventeen stab wounds, Henry was arrested and later convicted of murder. The local disability organisation, GAD, of which Anne was chair, was key in lobbying for the case to be treated as a hate crime.

They did not succeed, but when Anne became co-chair of the Metropolitan Police's Disability Independent Advisory Group later that same year she managed to get the case reopened and classified as domestic violence. And, along with Ruth Bashall, an inspirational disabled feminist, the two of them set about trying to reform the Metropolitan Police from the inside, with the help of key officers such as Dave MacNaghten and Paul Richardson of the Violent Crime Directorate, and Deputy Assistant Commissioner (DAC) Alf Hitchcock, who supported their work. But progress inside the Met to increase reporting and recording of disability hate crime was slow, requiring expensive resourcing.

Pressure, at least in the Met, was coming from the top, but attitudinal change in large organisations takes time. Alf Hitchcock, when I interviewed him in December 2007, was frank about the challenge: 'There has been a significant focus on race and homophobia and that work is fairly well established, but disability needs to be raised to that level of awareness. But it is catch-up.' He continued: 'It's the same for most police forces around the country – there is still room for improvement. When we have identified a crime as disability-related, I think we do appropriately and adequately investigate it, but the difficulty is always with the least experienced staff dealing with the incident and recognising it as a potential hate crime.'[23]

Sir Bert Massie was by then chairman of the Disability Rights Commission. The DRC had tried to include all disabled people from early on in its work, setting up a Learning Disability Group to advise the Commission. They started to mention the everyday problems they were having, on public transport, near their houses and in the streets. It was, Sir Bert explains, 'background noise' by the turn of the century. Around 2003 the DRC issued its first policy documents on hate crime, and produced a video of a man with a learning difficulty called *Just a Normal Day*, in which he was routinely insulted wherever he went. It was important that an organisation such as the DRC was putting hate crime on the agenda, and Sir Bert mentioned it in a number of speeches. But media awareness remained low, and the disability charities – and the rights movement – did little on the issue.

It was a difficult balancing act for the disability movement. Shout too loudly about this as an issue and face the risk of some powerful voices advocating the return of segregation, for safety's sake. It is understandable that the movement as a whole, with a few exceptions, concentrated on the big wins – better budgets, more human rights, independent living – faster, further, deeper, rather than talking about the negative side of deinstitutionalisation.

But disability hate crime could not remain invisible for ever. Justice was not being done, and too many people were being victimised. I hoped that the dossier I had put together would bring disability hate crime out into the light. When it was published in December 2007, under the title *No Hiding Place*, journalists and broadcasters started to interview me about the crime.[24] At last the awareness that disability hate crime existed was filtering through to the press – and to general consciousness.

It also had another effect, on the creaking supertanker that is the criminal justice system. The Director of Public Prosecutions, Sir Ken Macdonald, read the dossier shortly before I interviewed him that year for *Disability Now* magazine. He surprised me by saying, in that interview, that he thought disabled people should be angry because, in his words, 'they weren't getting justice'.[25] Sir Ken later told me, in an interview in 2010, that he had realised the situation was awful and that he had come to it 'much too late. You sent me a file with all the cases in it. I'd looked at some cases but I'd never before seen a package of cases.'

The case of Kevin Davies, in particular, triggered a childhood memory for Sir Ken. 'I had this very strong feeling about it, when I was primary school, there was a kid in my class that had Down syndrome, and we had rabbit hutches in the playground and one day some kids put her in the rabbit hutch and started to throw stones and I remember looking, then walking away and feeling awful, I felt awful. So when I started to read about these cases, particularly those where they were kept prisoner, the really bad ones, I just felt slowly that we had let people down, and we did.'

But other pressing issues were engaging much of the energy at the Crown Prosecution Service at that time, Sir Ken explained. 'Those were the years of terrorist attacks and we were pushing back very hard against the Government with its legislative proposals on detentions without trial, so we were fighting a lot of major battles. As far as discrimination is concerned there was no doubt whatsoever that we didn't pay enough attention to disability hate crime.' They were more engaged, he added, with race and homophobic hate crime. 'We were focusing on those, and disability hate crime is the one thing I'm really ashamed of . . . I don't think we recognised it as a major issue, and this is true broadly in society, we thought about race, then sex discrimination, the third thing would be homophobic, and disability discrimination would be way down there . . . we used to say there was no hierarchy but we were thinking of race and homophobia, disability hate crime was not on the radar.'

Sir Ken, and some key individuals around him such as equality experts Joanne Perry and Nadine Tilbury, set about reforming the criminal justice system's response to disability hate crime. 'I used to get all the senior people together and say this is shameful, we are letting these people down, this is a real mark of inequality before the law and that is the worst thing a prosecutor can do. But I think it was a two or three year project.' Time, however, was short. Sir Ken had just six months to change the CPS from the inside. It wasn't long enough. He stepped down as DPP in 2008.

10

Brent Martin and the
Tipping Point that Never Was

'Aye, he was a dead loving babby,' said Brenda Martin, the mother of Brent Martin, as we looked over photographs of Brent and his family and talked about his short life. But even from an early age, Brenda was worried about her son. 'He was soft, soft. Even when he and his sister had one of their little scraps, he always gave in. And then, as he got older and went out with the lads, he was the one who got the blame for everything.'

I had travelled north from Hartlepool, where I had interviewed those touched by the death of Christine Lakinski, to visit the family of Brent Martin. Their two deaths had happened within a month and thirty miles of each other in the summer of 2007. I had written about both deaths at the time, and at the time of the trials. Now I was going back, to look at the aftermath.

Brent was born in Sunderland in 1980, one of twins, the last-born children of Brenda and Alec Martin. It was a surprise pregnancy for Brenda, who already had four older children with her husband, but a welcome one. Brent and Danielle were lucky enough to be born into a large, loving and united family. But life wasn't easy. Brenda's older children took on the job of caring for the little ones because Alec had cancer. Brenda nursed him at home for the last five years of his life and went out to work as well, to keep a roof over their heads. Alec died shortly after the twins went to primary school.

Brent experienced discrimination because of his learning difficulty from an early age. He was bullied and teased at primary school for having a slight squint and for being what was then called 'slow'.

Although Brent was always tall for his age, his mother said, 'You never saw him in a fight. Boys would lash out at him, he got the blame for a lot of things, and got called a lot of names. But he never fought back.'

So bad was the harassment that Brenda took to following him to school and back, even when Brent reached secondary-school age. At first he went to the comprehensive all her other children had attended, but then the head told her that he didn't belong there. She lost the battle to have him educated in mainstream schools and, instead, he attended special schools. They were good, Brenda recalled, but still the harassment on the way to and from school continued and Brenda would follow him through the woods, hiding behind trees, to check he was not attacked.

Then, at 14, Brent changed. A few years earlier, Brenda remembered, he had come home sobbing at night, and had refused to tell her or his older brother what had happened. Instead he had asked to see the doctor, although later he changed his mind. Brenda is now convinced that he had been assaulted in an intimate manner and that his breakdown as a teenager related back to this earlier assault. One morning, Brenda remembered, he stood at the top of the stairs and said: 'Chocolate. I want chocolate. Chocolate.' Brenda was frightened. By the next day Brent was in hospital. He had experienced a breakdown. He spent the next ten years in and out of segregation, with Brenda and her family travelling to and from three different institutions. At times Brent was sectioned and, on occasion, violently restrained. Brenda complained to the police about his treatment but no one was ever charged. However, Brent eventually recovered, and by the summer of 2007 was ready to start a new life. He had also met a young woman in the last institution in which he had lived. Brenda said, smiling, 'They got on well, they went shopping together, just a normal boyfriend and girlfriend.'

In August 2007 Brent was on the brink of a new life – out of institutional care, he and his family hoped, for good. He was about to start a new job as a landscape gardener and live independently. He and his close-knit family were excited about his future. Brenda told me: 'His girlfriend was lovely, and I'd got him his new towels, one set of dark, and some white towels, a tea-set and a set of pans. He'd got his house, just near his sister. But it wasn't to be.'

Brent had around £3,000 in savings by the time he came out of institutional care and this news spread quickly around the tightly knit estates where he lived. 'He was all right when he came out. He enjoyed his freedom. But he got in with a bad crowd again, and he wanted his money out the bank.' At first, Brenda said, she was adamant. 'You won't have it, you're not getting it, you'll give it away,' she told him. But, eventually, after he kept on about it for a fortnight, she gave in, saying, 'I wish you had stopped in hospital till you were really better because I don't think you are now.' She feared the worst.

Brenda was right. Brent gave every penny away. It was soon known on the local estates that he had money he would lend out and lads came calling. After his death Brenda found a small book in his room. 'He kept a black book with the names of those who took his money – they knew he'd never get it back.' One or two of the killers were on the list, she said. 'They were on the list, they were on it. I didn't even know them; Brent had only just met them. He even asked my sister for money, he'd had money off his sister; they refused him because he'd wasted so much. But he was bullied into giving it away. It was a lot of money.' Eventually that money killed him. Brenda told me, sadly: 'He was trying to buy friendship. He'd been in hospital for eight years altogether and he just wanted to see some of the lads.' This wish for a normal life was to have fatal results.

Trainee boxers William Hughes, Marcus Miller and Stephen Bonallie had heard that Brent had money. They went out looking for him and started to get to know him, just days before they murdered him. He thought they wanted to be his friends.[1] Instead, on 23 August 2007, he was viciously attacked and murdered for a £5 bet. When Brent bumped into them that day, he bought them a bottle of vodka, with the last of his money. He had just £5 left in his pocket. The killers decided to see who could knock him out, with the winner taking Brent's money as a prize.

Over the course of several hours Brent was partially stripped, repeatedly beaten and chased through the streets of Sunderland. He was attacked by his killers in four different locations, in a number of adjoining housing estates. At first, according to witnesses, Brent thought that the youths were 'funning'. But as he was attacked time and again, he pleaded with them to stop. At some point that day Brent had lost his phone. He started to work his way towards home, across the estates, despite the beatings. But the last attack, just over the hill and behind the houses where Brenda lives today, was too ferocious.

Brent was finally knocked out in Bexhill Road, on the Town End Farm estate. His killers laid him out between two cars and posed, Brenda said, for photos by his body. One of the cars belonged to Brent's uncle Norman, who went out, thinking that someone was trying to steal a car. He found Brent's body, but he was so battered, especially around the head, Brenda told me, that Norman didn't recognise him. Instead he rushed in, got a sheet to lay over the young man and phoned for emergency help.

Brenda knew that night that something was wrong. 'When they came for me, at half past three in the morning, with me daughter Tracey, I'd had me coat on, I was out of me mind.' She had had two premonitions, she said, that something was going to happen to Brent. In bed, a few days earlier, her body had been twisted and pulled by invisible forces. Then, that night, she had phoned the taxi firm on the Town End Farm estate. 'He was late and I phoned Town End Taxis and I said, "Can you tell me if Brent's been?" They said no, and I told them, "If he comes and he has blood on him and no money will you bring him back in a taxi and I'll pay for him?" And when I was phoning them, he was already lying dead in the streets. That was another premonition and then there was a knock on the door, it was me daughter with a policeman. "What's the matter? Brent, where is he?" I said, and they said, "It's Brent, he's in the hospital, he hasn't got long to live." '

Brenda and the family were with him in hospital from Thursday night until Saturday, when he died. 'Two and a half days, it was. I sang to Brent, when he was in the coma, I lay beside him. I sang him all my favourites, the ones I used to sing to him, all the old-fashioned ones, like "Put your head upon my pillow, put your warm and tender body next to mine," all the old songs, that he had heard me singing to him over the years. After all, they say a person in a coma can hear. And the family left us on our own, and they went back into the waiting room. Then I came down and the family came back in so we were all together. And the priest was there. She said, "I'm going to anoint Brent with gold," and she did. Then they switched the machine off.'

The family was devastated. Brent's twin sister Danielle, in an interview with me around the time of the trial, said: 'Brent was looking forward to starting a new life. Words cannot describe the pain we feel. It will never go away.'[2]

Detective Superintendent Barbara Franklin from Northumbria Police led the investigation. Shortly after Brent's body was discovered, she had told local newspaper reporters: 'There is no motive for the assault but children (on the Town End estate, where Mr Martin was found dying) often bully people with learning difficulties.'[3] Despite this statement, the murder was never investigated or flagged as a disability hate crime, although a spokesman for Northumbria Police told me at the time: 'The Senior Investigating Officer and her team are aware of all the issues surrounding Mr Martin's disabilities and his family have provided comprehensive details about him. We also have his medical history. His disability has been a factor throughout the investigation.'[4] The police force refused to give me a follow-up interview for this book, saying that the investigating officer was too busy to spare the time to talk to me or even give me a statement.

The lax attitude of the local police force in investigating the disability aspects of the crime led to predictable results. In the judge's summing-up, no mention was made of disability hate crime, despite the fact that witnesses told the court that Bonallie, one of the defendants, had said: 'I am not going down for a muppet' (a common term of abuse for a person with learning difficulties). Instead, the judge called for an investigation into whether defendants were getting younger. William Hughes, the ringleader, 22, was sentenced to twenty-two years, Marcus Miller, 16, to fifteen years and Stephen Bonallie, 17, to eighteen years.[5]

In June 2008 Brent's killers successfully appealed against the length of their sentences as the judges agreed that the murder did not fulfil the legal definition of sadism. Despite the fact that the Lord Chief Justice, Lord Phillips, likened the attack to a 'pack of hounds on a fox', the three appeal court judges accepted arguments that the sentencing judge had wrongly categorised the murder as sadistic. Mr Justice Goldring added that he could 'well understand' how the judge came to his view, but concluded: 'Appalling though this behaviour was, it fell short of the behaviour contemplated as sadistic.' The sentences were reduced by two to three years each, to the anger of Brent's family and disability organisations.[6]

If their sentences had instead been increased because of disability hate crime, they would have lost their appeal. And, since the attack, more evidence has come to light. Brenda has talked to two witnesses who were not called at the trial. One says that she saw the killers 'lifting him up and dropping him' time after time. This witness heard Brent saying, 'Leave us alone, what are you doing this for?' She was never called as she was deemed an unreliable witness. Another witness, in a chilling echo of the Christine Lakinski case, said she saw the youths urinate on Brent as he lay dying. There were girls watching as Brent was attacked, again and again. None of them stepped in.

Some of those in the community where Brent lived never accepted him, never believed he had the right to live independently. Many did not see him as a kind and friendly human being, worthy of respect and dignity, but as a 'muppet' who could be exploited, robbed, mocked and finally killed for fun.

And it's not only Brent, and his family, who are affected. Steve Thompson, of a local disability group, Sunderland People First, told me at the time that the crime had had an immediate impact on local disabled people: 'It magnifies in people's minds and they won't go on the buses.'[7] A hate crime like that committed against Brent Martin resonates with other people in the same situation. Understandably, they self-segregate – they stop going out, and limit their own freedom. The murder had the effect that the perpetrators hoped it would have, sending a message to local disabled people that they were not free to walk the streets, that they were not equal citizens.

Brenda has a memory box, full of photographs and cards reminding her of Brent. On the front of the box is the Mother's Day card he wrote for her just a few months before he died. On it Brent has written: 'Happy Mother's Day mam, see you soon.' Inside the box is Brent's first pay packet, for £50.

Brenda feels Brent's presence still, as well as that of her dead husband Alec. She talks to them downstairs, she told me, and tells them: 'I know you're waiting for me, but it'll be a few years yet!' At night, when she goes upstairs to bed, she told me: 'I can sense Brent in my room. I always put my hand to the side of the bed, where he is, and I says, "Don't sleep here, go to the other room," but he says he wants to stay. So I say to him, "Put your head up the bottom of the bed, and your feet beside." Aye, I always touch that side of the bed, and I get comfort.'

Brenda is still suffering from the loss of Brent, but she is angry too. She is angry because she knows that Brent was attacked because of his disability – after all, he had been targeted because of his impairment right from boyhood – but also because the boys who killed him had their sentences reduced, which might well not have happened if it had been sentenced as a hate crime.

But Brent's was not an isolated case. In my next piece of research, I started to look at the kind of sentences handed down for racially aggravated murders, to see if they were longer than those handed down for murders with a disabled victim. I was staggered when I had completed my research. I looked at the murders of eight disabled men – Rikki Judkins, Colin Greenwood, Barrie-John Horrell, Sean Miles, Steven Hoskin, Keith Philpott, Albert Adams and Brent Martin. Of the seventeen people who attacked and killed them, just four were given sentences of over twenty years. By contrast, in five of the most notorious racist murders of the last few years (Kriss Donald, Anthony Walker, Isiah Young-Sam, Lee Phipps and Mohammed Pervaiz), ten out of the thirteen people responsible were given sentences of over twenty years and five of them, twenty-five years or more.[8] This is partly because Schedule 21 of the Criminal Justice Act 2003 (which gives advice to judges on the tariff, i.e. how long a prisoner should serve for murder) provides for 'sentence uplift' for murders where hostility is related to race, religion or homophobia, but not to disability.

There was clearly more work to be done, putting together the many articles I was writing on disability hate crime into a much larger report. The dossier had received good coverage, as had my interview with Sir Ken Macdonald and my work on sentencing. *Disability Now* magazine, where I then worked, along with the UK's Disabled People's Council and the charity Scope, agreed to co-publish the report. I started by tracking down the missing data. I felt that disabled people would be in official data, but that they might have been described differently. This was important. I wanted to close the circle between so-called qualitative research and anecdotal evidence and official data. What isn't measured in crime terms, one senior police officer told me, never gets tackled. So that needed to change.

I decided to see what data I could discover from the British Crime Survey that might relate to disabled people, even if it wasn't described in that way. I looked at all the tables relating to the experience of people who described themselves as 'long-term sick', the nearest equivalent to disability. Their experience of crime, and the fear of crime, was far more intense than people who described themselves as 'not long-term sick', and very similar to the experience of minority ethnic groups. They feared crime more, had less confidence in the police and experienced it more.[9]

I also wanted to challenge the notion that crimes against disabled people were isolated and motiveless. When judges and prosecutors talk about disability hate crimes they all too often describe them as 'motiveless' – as if you don't need a motive to attack a disabled person. Not so with racially motivated crimes, or homophobic ones for that matter. In the case of Anthony Walker, the judge, sentencing his attackers, declared: 'There is no difference between people of different races, trying to live out their lives in peace. In spite of your youth, deterrent sentences are vital.'[10] In the case of Jody Dobrowski, murdered by two men in October 2005, the judge said his killers had one intent when they attacked him: 'homophobic thuggery'.[11] It is vitally important for society to hear and see justice being done – for hate crimes to be named what they are. The law says that disabled people have equal right to justice. All hate crimes appear to be viewed as equally heinous by the criminal justice system, but disability hate crimes are not recognised or treated as such in practice.

This was something that Ken Macdonald felt, and still feels. When I interviewed him in 2010 he said it was crucial to mark the hostility towards disability, because it sends out a signal to society: 'You have got to mark the behaviour, because if you don't it sends out the worst possible message, that that part of the case doesn't matter. We used to say that about race crime: you are saying racism doesn't matter. The prosecution is not the Queen, it is the community against this person, saying, "We want to say to you this is out of order and we are going to make things difficult for you." If you don't do that, you don't make it, because you want a quiet life and a quick case. It sends out a bad message to people, particularly to people who have a disability and are suffering discrimination.'

In hate crime theory this is known as the 'declaratory effect' – that society is declaring that this hostility is unacceptable, and that society is turning its back on it.[12] One of the reasons that so many of the families I have interviewed are still in so much pain is that the specific nature of the crime that their family suffered has not been recognised as such by the criminal justice system.

By the time my report was published, the crime was invisible no longer and the glaring disparity between the way disability hate crime and other hate crimes were treated was also exposed. People with learning difficulties, and those with mental health problems, were routinely targeted, often with overwhelming violence. Wheelchair users too, and those with sensory impairments, were being targeted. They also experienced hostility. One feature however, continued to nag: the crimes that got publicity seemed to involve men, often with learning difficulties. Women and children were also being attacked, but in private, so the crimes against them were not apparent in the same way. They were the hidden victims.

Getting Away with Murder was published by the charity Scope, *Disability Now* magazine and the UK Disabled People's Council in the summer of 2008.[13] The report played some part in accelerating change, both in the criminal justice system and in public opinion. But much remained to be done.

11

The Humiliation of Christine Lakinski: Women and Children First

Detective Inspector Keith Groves, whom I interviewed in the summer of 2010, was clearly still affected by investigating the death of Christine Lakinski in 2007. He remarked thoughtfully: 'She deserved better than this. She was obviously physically and visually vulnerable and anybody who saw her would know that. She had learning disabilities and physical disabilities. I think to say that she had a difficult life was an understatement.'

'This' was what happened to Christine, who had mild learning difficulties and curvature of the spine, outside her house in Hartlepool in July 2007. Her brother, Mark Lakinski, a paramedic, described the attack in an affecting and emotional interview with me in 2008.[1]

'Christine died on her own doorstep after crawling on her hands and knees in pain across a cobbled street, not being able to call out for help, but only to groan and wish for it. There were people there, just across the street, who were getting ready to celebrate a birthday; they knew her, at least by sight. These were her neighbours. They knew she was in trouble, they had been told that she was, and they could see it, quite plainly, for themselves. However, Christine, my sister, was disabled and what happened next, I believe, was purely down to that fact. After all disabled people are just good for a laugh and it doesn't really matter what happens to them now, does it? Or at least that is how some of Christine's neighbours saw it.'

Christine Lakinski had become ill with pancreatitis on the way home from her closest friend, Angela Shotton, and collapsed in the street. Her brother continued: 'At this point three men, not teenagers,

131

came out of a house just across the street. They had been drinking and smoking skunk cannabis. One of them, a 27-year-old man, Anthony Anderson, had a towel around his waist. It was his birthday. He was getting set for a good night out on the town with his friends. All three men walked up to Christine, who was lying helplessly on her back on the pavement, with her eyes shut, bleeding from her head injury when she fell over. "I'll show you how to deal with her," said Birthday Boy and he then took centre stage for the next sixteen minutes, applauded and egged on by the other two. It started with a kick to Christine's feet which got no response from her, so a bucket of water was produced from Birthday Boy's house and thrown over Christine, who did in fact groan and move slightly at this.'

Then one of the men decided to record the scene on his mobile phone – first covering her with shaving foam. Mark continued: 'The final act was for Birthday Boy to pull back his towel and urinate all over Christine, all recorded on the mobile phone. "This is YouTube material," somebody yelled in the background and everybody laughed. Christine's laminated flooring, which she had been carrying home, was piled on top of her and she was left where she lay.' By the time somebody called an ambulance, Christine was dead. Just one of those who attacked her and humiliated her, Anthony Anderson, was arrested. His friend, who filmed her dying, was not convicted of an offence.

Keith Groves remembered the case well. 'We first got involved when we got a phone call from the ambulance service, about 10 p.m., they have been called out, when they arrive she's deceased, and she has a pack of laminate flooring on top of her, she is covered in shaving foam and it's in the street. They call the police, uniformed officers attend, but as in a case like this they call an on-call detective sergeant, and it was Alan Tod, one of the most experienced officers I've ever worked with. I can only think of one occasion when he's ever rung me as the DI, and it was for this case.' He added: 'I have twenty-one years in the job and I've been called out to a number of deaths and things like that, but this one was initially the strangest one and it was only later on, when the facts unfold, how disgusted you feel, how one human being can do this to another human being doesn't bear thinking about.

'We had no idea what had gone on until we interviewed a number of witnesses and it unfolds that Christine has come round from Angela's house, carrying this pack of laminate flooring, which is heavy, she is really struggling, she bumps into the wall, she drops the laminate flooring, she tries to kick it along the street, and she actually gets to her own front door when she then collapses. This is witnessed by a female who is visiting her boyfriend at Anderson's address; she makes them aware that there is a woman fallen over outside.' Anderson told the police later in his interview that he thought Christine was drunk and that he had kicked her feet to rouse her. DI Groves continued: 'She doesn't respond, except for a bit of a noise, then he thinks it's funny to get a dish of water and throw it over her. In his words "in an attempt to rouse her". She doesn't rouse obviously, though he didn't know at that time she's dead.'

DI Groves paused. 'And then he proceeds to urinate on her and cover her from head to toe in shaving foam and then pile laminate flooring on her and at this point it is videoed by another lad, on his mobile phone. We understand he cleared space, he did admit to videoing it, but we never found it.' It was only when the three men were ready to go out for a night on the tiles, and saw that she was still lying there, that one of them phoned for an ambulance.

Within a few hours Keith Groves had tracked them down. It wasn't difficult, he told me. 'There was a trail of shaving foam from Christine's body across to the house and down the drainpipe where Anderson had wiped his hand, next to the door, and then we found that it was the phone belonging to the other occupant of that address that had phoned the ambulance.'

A number of suspects were swiftly arrested on suspicion of manslaughter. But the pathologist's report showed that Christine had died of pancreatitis. This left police officers and the prosecutor, DI Groves freely admitted, scratching their heads, working out what the charge should be. 'We had to look for a charge and we spoke to the Crown

Prosecution Service about it. The only charge we could think of was outraging public decency. After all, it did outrage public decency. Anyone who has any morals at all was disgusted by what Anderson had done, and the other people who stood and watched, and laughed, probably. And videoed it. For me they were almost as responsible as Anthony Anderson.'

But just being there, part of a crowd, was not in itself an offence. DI Grove clearly regretted this. 'Had we been able to prove that the others had egged him on, we could have charged them.' Getting an aggravated factor for disability hate crime proved much harder. Keith Groves has compelling personal reasons why he was very aware of disability as a factor – he is more attuned to it, perhaps, than other police officers. But his comprehensive trawl through the evidence trail did not point conclusively to this as being a factor.

Groves looked at other crimes where Christine had reported being a victim – two attempted burglaries and the theft of some money, just a day or two before the attack. 'You would have to have proved why she was targeted, and that was the issue. Again, how do you prove it, if he had said something while he was doing it, such as "hunchback, cripple, spastic", and they are words that because of my circumstances I hate with a passion, if he had used those words and somebody had given us a statement, we would have made our case, or if we had recovered that video, or he had said why he had done it, but he didn't.' Instead, Anderson argued that he thought she was drunk – and excused himself for the same reasons, admitting he was 'intoxicated' with a mixture of cannabis and alcohol. Anderson was sentenced to just three years in prison.[2]

And yet according to Christine's closest friend, Angela Shotton, whom I visited in her house just around the corner from where Christine died, she was targeted frequently because of her disability. That was how the two of them became friends, Angela told me. 'Fifteen year back, that's how I met her, she was getting a lot of bullying in the street, calling her a "hunchback" and so on. I was going to the shops, and she asked me to come over, she said, "They are throwing

stones at me." I said, "Come along with me, I'll make you a cuppa." '
Soon they were seeing each other nearly every day. They came to
consider each other not only friends, but family. Christine had a spot
on the sofa, where she would always sit when she visited Angela's. It
was nearest the TV and she'd be round for her Christmas dinner every
year. They went on outings together, Angela remembered fondly.

'She was funny, outgoing, we used to go on family days out to
Scarborough and she'd have a paddle sometimes, though it would
depend what mood she was in. She had a good brain, though: she
won a quiz on the TV once, she rang me to say she'd won £800, I
didn't believe her. She said, "I'm getting the cheque, I haven't slept
all night," she got the money and came round here, she went to the
pawn shop and the next day we went to Middlesbrough. She picked
clothes out, we had our dinners in a cafe, she treated me and I said,
"Christine, you keep it, you need it," but she treated me. She was
generous and kind, she was a smoker, she always brought me ten tabs,
little presents, she bought me flowers just to show appreciation, you
couldn't get a better friend. She'd tell the kids to look after me.'

But the targeting never ceased, and it cast a shadow over the life
of a sunny personality. 'She was happy, but you'd know when sum-
mat had gone wrong, she'd come in with a face. She'd say, "I've been
down York Road and couple of lads have just shouted 'hunchback',
and I'm sick of them." It did used to get her down, sometimes. She
didn't want to talk about it. Some places we could go and there was
nothing said, but she did get a lot, when she was walking about. But
she used to shout back and I did too: "Leave her alone." '

Despite that, Angela told me, Christine was by nature an extrovert.
'She did go to the bingo and she had friends there, at the Mecca.'
But, she added: 'It was regular, the name calling, every week, all the
time we knew her. Sometimes we went into the town, people used to
look; fair enough, she was never scared to go out, she had guts. Some
people isolate themselves; Christine said, "I'll stick up for myself." '
But she never reported the mockery to the police, perhaps because it
happened so often that it was just part of everyday life to her.

Anthony Anderson moved into the street, opposite Christine, just a few months before the incident. The house soon became notorious, what Keith Groves called 'a party house'. Young people drifted in and out of the house, and there were complaints from neighbours in the quiet street, about the noise. Angela remembered: 'He only lived opposite. They must have known she was disabled. Plus she did used to go on about him, he was called Tripper, because of the drugs, he had got form. She said, "I'm sick of him, I can't get no sleep with his music, all night." She used to sleep here sometimes.'

But on that night she decided to go home, leaving Angela with a feeling of ineradicable guilt. 'I still say to myself, Why didn't I walk round that night, why didn't I go that way to come home, that way instead of this way, she might have been saved, that's what sticks in my mind.' I tell her she is not the one to feel guilty, but my words change nothing. 'But you do, don't you? I would have phoned the ambulance, chased him over the road. I couldn't understand why the neighbours didn't come out, chase them away.' Mark Lakinski, Christine's brother, thinks the same. He told me: 'If an ambulance had been called when Christine had collapsed, she might have died with dignity and with pain relief in hospital and not on a dirty pavement, violated at the moment of her death by a braying bunch of louts who, I firmly believe, saw her as an easy target because she was disabled.'

We will never know what was in Anderson's mind that night, but Keith Groves clearly felt that Anderson was intelligent enough to know the dangers of admitting he had targeted her because of her disability. 'I have no doubt, if he was thinking straight, he was never in a million years going to say, "I targeted that woman because she had a disability." We as a force never ever proved that that was a disability hate crime, because it is so difficult to prove what is in someone's mind. Unless they say something that is witnessed by people, they say, this is why we are doing this, otherwise we have got to prove what was in his mind at the time of doing it. And we never proved that. She did have a most obvious physical disability, curvature of the spine, very much hunched over, but regardless of that for me, he says he did it because she was a "smack head or a drunk". That's why he picked on her.' He added: 'It would have been nice for me to prove that he did this because she was disabled.'

He was also sceptical as to whether Anderson was ever truly remorseful. 'It's always difficult to work out whether someone is sorry for what they have done, or sorry for being caught. I know what I think, but again it's proving it. I think in the majority of circumstances like this they are sorry for being caught.'

And what about the neighbours? Groves hesitated. The area is a maze of quiet, small, neat Victorian terraced housing, now scheduled for demolition and so-called 'regeneration'.[3] Walking around the narrow streets, it certainly felt friendly enough, with people sitting outside their front doors, drinking tea and bidding me good morning. It seems unreal that in such a close-knit community there could have been such a death, on the doorstep.

Groves, too, found it hard to accept. 'The neighbours didn't want to get involved. They are all decent people but they keep themselves to themselves.' Groves described the area as tight-knit. 'Everybody knows everybody, and they will try and help each other as best they can but they are the sort of people on an evening that at nine o'clock will close the curtains, lock the doors and just don't bother going out any more.' There had been isolated reports about the noise from the house but no one had treated it as the beginning of a pattern of antisocial behaviour. If it had been seen as such by neighbours, Christine's humiliation might have been averted, Groves told me. 'If the neighbours had come forward, then Anderson might not have lived there for long. We work with private landlords, we work with the council and if somebody is breaching the tenancy agreement with noisy parties, whatever, we get them moved. That could have removed this, the whole situation could have been stopped. Would it have saved Christine's life? Probably not. As I understand it, she was going to die. But she could have died in a lot better circumstances.'

Angela, for her part, simply misses her best friend. Sitting in the corner of the sofa where Christine used to sit, she told me: 'I've got nobody to knock about with now. I've got my partner, but if I didn't have the kids I think I'd end up in the hospital. I've took bad now, I'm diabetic now . . . some days I have my bad days, Christmas when she would be round, I lost my own family that year, we lost me mam, my dad, my daughter's bairn. Christine came with us to the hospital, she was very good, all my family loved her. It feels strange without her, she always used to sit here, this was her place in the corner. I have my days when I burst out crying, although I try and hide it.' Anthony Anderson was released this year and lives in Hartlepool.[4] Angela has seen him a couple of times in the town with his friends. 'It's disgusting, how can he come back?'

Before I left Hartlepool police station, DI Groves told me: 'I think Christine's death disappointed me the most in my whole career in that it didn't need to happen. I was so disappointed that someone who was so vulnerable died like that. I've dealt with many other suspicious deaths, murders, manslaughters, none of which are good really. This one disappointed me most. It was so unusual. I hope I never deal with another.'

Sir Ken Macdonald, the former Director of Public Prosecutions, whom I asked to comment on the lack of verbal insults in such cases, believes that it and others like it should at least be laid before the jury to examine whether there was a disability hate element. 'You look at the circumstances and you draw inferences, we do that all the time in criminal law. People don't make confessions in many cases. You draw inferences from what they say. If prosecutors say they want verbalisation then is what they are saying they will only prosecute disability hate crime if there is a confession, "I'm doing this to you because you are a spastic"? If we took that approach to every area of crime there would be no prosecutions.'

Moreover, the inferences need to be drawn so the crime can be marked, investigated and prosecuted for what it is. So many crimes against disabled women are not seen as disability hate crimes. Often they are seen as domestic violence, or sexual abuse. A disabled woman might be targeted both as a woman and as a disabled person, yet this 'intersectional discrimination' is still not really recognised by the criminal justice system. In the case of a young Chinese woman with learning difficulties who died four years ago, this is particularly true.

In the cold March of 2006 a young Chinese woman, Shao Wei He, was found dead in the snow outside her husband's takeaway in Sheffield. A post-mortem found that she had been beaten with copper piping and with wood embedded with nails. These beatings, and another which was so hard that it snapped a broom handle, were committed by her husband's lover, Su Hua Liu, who then threw the dying woman out into the backyard. The temperature that night was minus four degrees.[5]

Liu, and Lun Xi Tan, Shao Wei's husband, were arrested on suspicion of murder a few days later. Tan became the first man in Britain to plead guilty to a charge of 'causing or allowing the death of a vulnerable person contrary to the Domestic Violence, Crime and Victims Act 2004', involving an adult victim. Liu pleaded guilty to manslaughter.

Sheffield Crown Court heard that Tan had travelled to China to marry and bring back Shao Wei He in 2005. Once she was in Britain, he treated her 'like a slave', according to neighbours, demanding that she pay back the £20,000 she allegedly owed him for bringing her to Britain. Then Tan took as his lover Su Hua Liu, and the three lived together. The Crown prosecutor told the court: 'There was a systematic, brutal abuse of a young vulnerable woman and eventually unlawful killing after weeks, if not months, of abject misery and suffering at the hands of Liu.' He continued: 'She became scruffy, very quiet and her hands were red raw and swollen and became infected. Her hair was hacked short and her face ballooned. She was seen with a badly bruised eye and it looked like she had been burned . . . there were 55 sites of injury on her body from multiple blunt trauma.'[6]

Despite the fact that Shao Wei He was identified to police and prosecutors as a disabled woman, no one thought to ask what had motivated the months of abuse she suffered – and why she had never complained about her treatment. Prosecutors were innovative in their use of a new law covering neglect and domestic violence, but they may well have missed the element of disability hate crime. I asked the South Yorkshire Constabulary about the case, and about what motivated a pregnant woman to kill another woman. They told me that the case had been archived and that they could not find any details about it on their system.

Shao Wei He's case is not an isolated one. Far too many other disabled women suffer similar experiences, invisibly and in silence. The 1995 British Crime Survey (BCS) found that disabled women were twice as likely to experience domestic violence as non-disabled women.[7] In 2008 the organisation for women's refuges, Women's Aid, published its first report looking at domestic violence against disabled women, backing up the BCS research with distressing stories from their disabled interviewees. They reported being raped, abused, starved for as long as twenty-four hours, robbed and attacked. One woman, a wheelchair user, was shut in her room and her husband refused to take her to the toilet. He also tipped her out of her wheelchair. Another husband used to take the battery out of his wife's wheelchair and others would put sanitary towels out of reach so women could not care for themselves. Disabled people, unlike most other hate crime victims, are not even safe in their own homes.[8]

Women with learning difficulties are even more likely to be at risk and the level of violence that they experience is also likely to be higher. The more dependent they are and the more complex their needs, the more likely it is that they will be at risk, as are women with mental health problems. As the Equality and Human Rights Commission (EHRC) concluded in 2009, in its first report on targeted violence against disabled people: 'There is not only an increased level of risk of targeted violence and hostility but also increased victimisation'. It went on to say that its review of research shows that more than 70 per cent of women with learning difficulties are sexually assaulted, a rate that is twice as high as for those in the general population.[9]

Disabled women are therefore more likely to experience domestic violence and sexual assault, and their assailants are also far more likely to get away with it than the assailants of non-disabled women. As the director of Bedlam discovered three hundred years ago, it is far too easy to rape and abuse disabled women and get away with it by terming them 'unreliable'.

We cannot really tackle violence against women and children if we do not challenge the use of the term 'unreliable witness' to refer to someone with a learning difficulty who is being routinely sexually assaulted. Louise Wallis, the policy officer of Respond, a charity working with survivors of sexual assault with learning difficulties, has discovered that such labelling is a routine occurrence. This is an account from one of her colleagues.

'I was recently told by a police officer that all they can really do is an intelligence-gathering exercise after one of my service users was threatened with a gun if she didn't engage in prostitution. The police accept that, because of her learning difficulty, her attention span is too short to give a coherent statement but say there is nothing they can do and a change in the law is needed for anything to change.

'The unfortunate thing is that, because I know her so well, I can get a coherent story out of her but the police won't let me "interfere" in the interview process to support her to stay on track.

'I have been told the same thing on three previous occasions about the same service user. She has been subjected to a long history of abuse from various individuals known to the police but each time she reports anything we are told she is not a reliable witness and so no action is taken. The most we've ever had is a harassment order preventing someone who had sexually abused her, given her crack and forced her into prostitution, from contacting her. It seems people are free to abuse the most vulnerable because they don't have access to police protection or to the justice system.'[10]

In another case that I featured in *Getting Away with Murder*, a Scottish woman with learning difficulties was allegedly raped over seven years by a number of attackers. Yet again, her attackers have not been charged because she is deemed an unreliable witness.[11] The Mental

Welfare Commission, which reviewed her case, concluded: 'Those who pose a known risk to her safety remain at large within her community, while Ms A continues to endure a protective regime that effectively deprives her of much of her liberty.'[12]

Sentences also lag behind sentences for rapes generally – which are usually inadequate enough anyway. In a case in Wood Green a young woman with learning difficulties was lured to a house, scarred with caustic soda and repeatedly raped by a gang of up to ten youths. They were originally given sentences of just two and three years, despite the violence shown in the attack[13] (although those sentences were later increased, after the intervention of the Attorney General).[14] At least that case came to court.

The casual sexual use and abuse of disabled women goes almost completely unchallenged. In the case of Fiona Pilkington and her disabled daughter, Frankie (which I discuss in detail in the next chapter), one of the most horrifying events was when a gang of eighteen youths gathered outside their house and encouraged Frankie to lift her nightshirt so that they could jeer at her exposed body.

That is why the involvement of disabled women like Ruth Bashall and Anne Novis in disability hate crime has been so important. I first met Ruth and Anne at a Metropolitan Police Authority meeting on a filthy winter evening in 2007. They did their job formidably well, acting as co-chairs of the Police Disability Independent Advisory Group for the Met. After the meeting I went up and introduced myself, rather nervously. But they have become two of my greatest allies and friends, and they advised on my report, *Getting Away with Murder*.

But despite the fact that we included a section on disabled women and hate crime in that report, it is clear that their experience is still largely invisible and untold. One of the most sobering reasons for this, Ruth believes, is that disabled women will put up with horrifying levels of domestic violence because they know that if they complain they are likely to be 'put away' into care homes, losing their independence and being exposed to abuse there as well. The perpetrators of these most intimate crimes of sexual violence, both at home and in institutions, know that they can act with almost total impunity.

Ruth, two years on from this work, has developed her thinking: 'Non-disabled people experience abuse as children, and might experience domestic violence as adults. So if you're black or Muslim you might get domestic violence in the private sphere and hate crime in the public sphere and there is the overlap when someone throws a brick through your window, but with disabled people, it's different. Our private sphere is public because we have so many members of the public coming into our homes, care workers, occupational therapists, physiotherapists, all assessing you for something. The opportunities for domestic violence are massive.'

The disability programmes director at the Equality and Human Rights Commission, Hilary McCollum, has worked for twenty years on violence against women and children, and comes at disability hate crime from that perspective. Both of us agree that understanding the links and similarities between such types of violence, particularly the intimacy involved, may help us tackle disability hate crime and also unearth the silent victims of this crime – women and children. McCollum observes: 'The most crucial thing for the women's movement was listening to the voices of survivors.' She pinpoints other key issues: identifying where the violence happened, how to avoid it in the future and how to recover from it.

But it is not going to be easy, McCollum believes. It was only after survivors (of domestic violence and rape) started to talk that services began to develop. Disabled women are often still afraid to speak out and so services have not developed for them. There is just one specialist refuge for women with learning difficulties in the UK, and it has hardly any funding and few places.[15] Although the Havens (specialist rape centres) are developing disability-specific services, they remain underfunded, and women's refuges have often not yet been adapted for disabled victims. Women facing domestic violence or rape who are disabled may want to escape their attackers, but this usually means leaving their own homes, which have often been specially adapted for them.[16] And, as Hilary McCollum notes, we know little or nothing about the perpetrators of violence against disabled women and children. 'Are people who sexually assault learning disabled girls the same as people who write graffiti and shove dog faeces through a wheelchair user's letterbox – are their motivations the same or not, and what difference would that make to the intervention that would be put in place?'

Despite the differences, I believe that the disability movement has much to learn from the women's movement and its focus on violence. Professor Betsy Stanko, for example, carried out an in-depth study of domestic violence for the Metropolitan Police between 2000 and 2003. Her analysis found that almost half of domestic sexual violence offenders had criminal records, and some had convictions for sexual assaults on other women, including stranger rapes. Her analysis also identified several risk factors for domestic violence victims in general, including pregnancy.[17]

Stanko's work has proved effective in saving lives and has revolutionised the support offered to victims. In 2003–4 around forty women were being killed in domestic violence in London each year. That figure has been cut almost in half, partly due to the risk assessment that is now done for victims and on offenders. If we understand the crime better, especially when it is repeated time and again, the police can intervene earlier. As Betsy Stanko asks: 'How do you get the police to act differently with the information they already have?'

Cocoon Watch, a scheme developed in Yorkshire, whereby friends and neighbours of a survivor of domestic violence act as a social support network before, during and after an attack, has also been shown to be effective. The survivor feels safer and, crucially, doesn't need to leave their own home because they are being supported to stay there and yet remain safe. This could be an excellent scheme to apply to victims of disability hate crime, who are often moved on while the perpetrator stays put and is free to attack the next disabled person who moves in.[18]

The risk-assessment conferences for survivors of domestic violence, involving many agencies, may also be a useful model to study in developing policy for victims of hate crime, but they will require reform if they are to work for disabled people. Far too often, at the moment, the victims of domestic violence are excluded from taking part or attending the conferences, leaving them feeling disempowered. They should surely be able to attend, and speak at, such meetings.

There has been some progress. In one case that came to court in 2009 the Crown Prosecution Service in Devon and Cornwall successfully prosecuted a minibus driver, James Watts, accused of sexual offences against four disabled women without speech who lived in a care home. Watts was jailed for twelve years for sexual assault after one of his victims gave evidence by blinking her eyes. He was convicted on six of the thirteen charges after the jury heard from his victims, three of whom have cerebral palsy and a fourth who has brain injuries.[19] Watts appealed but the conviction was upheld, although the sentence was reduced.[20]

But the CPS took the case despite the difficulties, with the Crown advocate for Devon and Cornwall, Ann Hampshire, saying: 'This case . . . raised many issues in terms of supporting the victims and witnesses through the difficult process of giving evidence in court. The victims' disabilities make it very difficult for them to communicate, and the Crown Prosecution Service worked hard to ensure that they could give the best evidence possible by using what we call "special measures".'[21] She continued: 'We . . . arranged for a video link to be installed at the residential home where the victims live, to enable them to remain in a familiar environment and to ensure that their individual care needs could be met. There was also considerable support from one dedicated volunteer of the witness service who spent many hours with the witnesses and the intermediary prior to the trial to explain the court process, how the video link would work and how the oath would be administered. The jury watched video of a police interview in which one of the women used a pointer on a computer screen to tell police what had happened to her . . . The woman then used symbols of body parts to describe what Watts had done to her.'

The judge, Graham Cottle, described it as the most difficult case he had heard. 'You used the opportunities that presented themselves to abuse the ladies in your care in a sexual way and you did so safe in the knowledge, you thought, that they would never have the capacity to complain.' Watts appealed against his sentence, and there was newspaper coverage suggesting that the conviction was unsafe because of the women's disabilities. However, it was unsuccessful. Thanks to the innovative approach shown by the CPS, the case was successful and justice had been done.

Chief Constable Steve Otter's force, in Devon, investigated the case, which he calls 'extraordinary'. He observes that the 'grounds for appeal were, "how can you rely on these people, because they can't communicate with the jury?". But they could, even if they couldn't speak. It was a prejudice.' And, he added, his employees in Witness Care learned a lot from the case: 'Those in Witness Care were very frank about the journey they went on, of their own prejudices, when they started, about the people they were dealing with. They didn't think they could have a relationship with those people, and they realised they could, that they were real people. That sort of journey, in a micro-sense, represents the journey the police service needs to go on.'

It was the first case where women without speech were believed and allowed to give evidence. Many other cases, says the charity Respond, are not even taken. Even if the police investigate, many juries simply do not believe disabled women when they say that they have been raped. The attrition rate for rape cases for non-disabled women is disturbingly high.[22] But the one for disabled women is likely to be even higher still.

But if the record of the criminal justice system towards women is patchy, it is even worse when it comes to disabled children. Disabled children are twice as likely to be abused as non-disabled children.

The rates of physical and sexual abuse for disabled children are also higher in comparison to non-disabled children.[23]

Certain groups are more likely to be bullied. In 1999, Mencap carried out an in-depth survey of 500 children and young people with a learning difficulty throughout England, Wales and Northern Ireland. They found that 80 per cent of children with a learning difficulty had been bullied and 60 per cent physically hurt. Twenty-seven per cent were bullied for three years or more. Half said that it affected where they went, and 80 per cent were scared to go out.[24]

In 2006 the National Autistic Society carried out the largest ever survey of autism and education. They received 1,400 responses and interviewed a further twenty-eight children in depth. That research found that 40 per cent of children on the autistic spectrum have been bullied at school. Children and parents interviewed recounted harrowing experiences. One child was found contemplating suicide, on a motorway bridge. Another used to bang her head against the wall before being taken to school. Another, just 13, tried to kill herself. Of those who said that their child had been bullied, 44 per cent said that no action had been taken by the school.[25]

Disabled children are bullied inside and outside school, in both mainstream and specialist institutions. As I documented in *Disability Now*'s Hate Crime Dossier, children are even targeted on the way to school, particularly in school minibuses (they are highly visible in such transport and are often called 'window-lickers'). In one case, a minibus carrying disabled students from Bridge College in Offerton had a stone hurled through the back window while on the motorway.[26] The Equality and Human Rights Commission also found, in their research study in 2009, that a number of their interviewees with learning difficulties and mental health conditions had referred to being 'bullied persistently when at school, involving both physical assaults and verbal abuse'. Some had even left school or college as a result.

In two of the worst cases I have looked at in this book, disabled young people were bullied at school. Because it was never properly challenged, things then escalated outside school, with tragic results.

Fiona Pilkington's son Anthony, who has severe dyslexia, was bullied at one school and was moved to another. But it was here that he met one of the alleged perpetrators – who thereafter made his life a misery. Indeed, at one point, Anthony was marched at knifepoint to a shed and locked in. He had to break his way out.[27] Later, in despair at the targeting of the family (which had started with Anthony), Fiona killed herself and her daughter, Frankie.

One of the saddest cases that I covered in *Getting Away with Murder* was that of Laura Milne, a 19-year-old woman with learning difficulties who was targeted at school in Aberdeen by bullies. One of them was later involved in her murder. In July 2008 Stuart Jack, 22, was jailed for eighteen years for murdering Laura Milne. Debbie Buchan, 19, and Leigh Mackinnon, 18, were both found guilty of attempted murder and sentenced to nine years.

Laura's throat was cut during the attack in December 2007 and she was then dismembered to prevent discovery. The gang wanted Laura to disappear for ever, even to be replaced by 'the new and improved Laura Milne', as one of her attackers termed it, pretending to be her just days after the attack. Forty-eight hours after the murder, Jack and Buchan were filmed gloating over the violent death. The video clip was recorded on a SIM card taken from the dead girl's phone, with Buchan asking: 'Did you enjoy cutting her throat, yes or no?'

'Aye,' Jack boasted.

Buchan finished the clip by saying: 'Thank you. Goodbye. You are the weakest link.'[28]

In a statement issued through Grampian Police, Laura Milne's family criticised the length of the sentences handed down to Buchan and Mackinnon. Laura's family pointed out that she had previously been bullied by Debbie Buchan at school and that the family had tried to prevent her seeing Buchan. But she assured them that Buchan was now her friend.[29] But her friends had turned against her, and had decided that her life was not worth living.

Disabled children can also be targeted outside of school by 'friends of the family'. In 2008 two teenagers who were supposed to be looking after a young disabled child, to give his family some respite, tortured him instead over a weekend. They burned him with a cigarette, suspended him by his ankles in filthy water and repeatedly pelted him with hard plastic balls. They, too, filmed their attack on a mobile phone. Brett Kitchin, 20, and Craig Hurst, 25, evaded a jail sentence. Although they were both found guilty of four charges of assault by magistrates in Newcastle, they walked free. Kitchin was sentenced to four months in jail but was bailed whilst he appealed against the sentence. Hurst was given a community order of 200 hours of unpaid work.[30]

When such insultingly light sentences like these are handed out to perpetrators of crimes of torture against disabled children and women in particular, it is easy to see why so many disabled people do not even bother to report the crimes. It is humiliating, distressing and exhausting to give evidence in court, the more so if you are a disabled person, as you are far less likely to be given the support that you need to get through the process. So, all too often, the crimes go unreported by the victims, the patterns of assault are not recognised because too few are reported, the crimes are not punished appropriately and the hate element is unmarked by society.

Small wonder that disabled women and children, who are subjected to some of the most humiliating and violating of disability hate crimes, frequently with a sexual element, are all too often the silenced and silent victims. Crimes against them are put in other categories, and the disability hate element overlooked. As a result we do not understand disability hate crime, because so many of the crimes are identified and sentenced as other crimes.

In Chapter 15 I will discuss the motivation for such crimes, but one factor stands out clearly. Crimes that have an intimate element are less likely to be prosecuted, because there are no witnesses and the victims fear the effects of reporting, such as institutionalisation and repeat victimisation. They are also less likely to be prosecuted because disabled women and children are often dismissed as unreliable – by police, prosecutors, juries and judges. Not one of the horrific crimes I have written about in this chapter was prosecuted or sentenced as a disability hate crime. Few of those responsible spent any time behind bars for their crimes. It appears as if those most at risk of harm are least likely to receive justice.

12

The Hounding of Fiona Pilkington:
the Hidden Victims of Hate Crime

Getting Away with Murder was published in the summer of 2008. Support for the report came from the Director of Public Prosecutions, Sir Ken Macdonald, the Home Office minister Vernon Coaker, Deputy Assistant Commissioner Alf Hitchcock from the Metropolitan Police, Brendan Barber, the secretary general of the TUC, and others, including Stephen Brookes, chair of the National Union of Journalists Disabled Members Council, who all endorsed the report with very supportive comments.[1] Since then the media have also been largely positive, with a number of television documentaries, radio programmes and articles in the mainstream press all bewailing the tide of violence against disabled people.

But the lack of data, academic research and good solid analysis about perpetrators, victims, locations and motivations has led to confusion when crimes are actually committed. This means that justice is still, all too often, not done. Social workers, benefit officers, housing workers and police officers all see disabled people differently. This explains, partly, why they are so often failed by the very systems that have been put in place to protect them – 'vulnerable adults' legislation and the criminal justice system in particular.

Disabled people, unlike other groups affected by hate crime (such as ethnic minorities or gay people), stand at the intersection between many different services. This means that when they are attacked it can be characterised in different ways. If they are robbed by a carer it might be logged as financial or carer abuse by a social worker; if they are exploited by a friend, perhaps viewed as a mate crime; or perhaps

151

dismissed by school or college as bullying, if they are a young person. If they are harassed by a neighbour it could be seen by a local police officer as a neighbour dispute or, if it becomes serious, as antisocial behaviour. Not that this means that anything will come of it, as the case of Fiona Pilkington illustrates.

Fiona Pilkington wanted to enjoy an ordinary family life and raise her children. She was a good friend, a good daughter and above all a wonderful mother. Instead of seeing her children reach adulthood, Fiona, aged 38, drove herself on 23 October 2007 to a lay-by near Earl Shilton, just a few miles from Barwell where she lived, and killed herself and her daughter, 18-year-old Frankie, who had learning difficulties, along with their much-loved pet rabbit.[2]

It followed several years of abuse, perhaps as many as eleven, during which a gang of youths terrorised her and her two children and drove her eventually to her tragic decision. The Pilkington family had become the 'best game in town' for these youths, who were largely unchallenged by social services, the council and the police. Fiona's case should have been the tipping point in disability hate crime consciousness. But those who drove a devoted mother to her death live unpunished in the same street today. And that street, and those around it, have been poisoned by the crime. I wonder whether Barwell will ever come to terms with what happened.

I lived near Barwell as a young child, in the small town of Hinkley and then in a village, Packington, dominated by the close-knit mining community nearby. All my early memories of Leicestershire reflect feelings of safety and happiness. I could walk out alone in the village as a child down to the village shop and feel safe. I played out with friends, walking round to their houses, alone, at the tender age of 7 or 8. I was looked after by a community with a purpose, and with nigh-on full employment. So I had found it hard to believe that Barwell could be so very different from an area that for me represented happiness, security and community.

I drove into Barwell on a rainy late summer's day in 2010, to visit Hazel Smith, a local parish councillor who had raised the alarm about Fiona's treatment time and time again. She lives with her disabled husband in the next street along from where Fiona was targeted. She has been open about her anger with those who targeted Fiona and about the lack of action by the council and the police. And, like Fiona, she has paid a high price for coming forward.

She told me, eyes filling with tears: 'A lot of people didn't bother to help, didn't believe her. So when I stuck up for her, they even tried to get me evicted. There's been a petition round. I've been ostracised and pushed out.' She claimed that she had even been threatened with arson and death threats. 'It was such a terrible tragedy,' she continued. 'I've been blamed, and everything has been thrown at me. There may be ten police officers under investigation, but I'm the one who's been abandoned in all of this. I know how that poor woman felt.'

Hazel Smith told me more about the harassment that Fiona endured for eleven years. She first heard about it when she founded a local Neighbourhood Watch scheme to support another resident with cancer, who was also being harassed. One evening, Fiona came calling. 'I'm Fiona Pilkington,' she said, 'I'm from Bardon Road.' 'I said to her, "I knew your mother, she was a lollipop lady, I know you," and I let her in.' It was 2005, and Fiona brought Frankie with her. '"Can you help me," she said, and she told me what was happening. I said, "I'll report them to the council and to the police."'

The abuse included urinating on Fiona's small, neat front garden, throwing stones at the windows, jumping in the hedge and damaging her car, all of which Hazel, Fiona and Fiona's mother Pam, at different times, reported to the police and council. 'But every weekend, that poor woman, on a Friday night, would phone me: "They're at it again, Hazel," Time after time I'd put my coat on, I'd go round to her and I'd get abuse: "Neighbourhood Watch bitch, copper's nark, get in your own road."'

Hazel believes that the family was targeted because of their multiple disabilities. Fiona had mild learning difficulties and her mental health deteriorated as both her children were targeted. Frankie, whose learning difficulty was more visible, was repeatedly insulted,

Hazel told me. 'They used to call her Frankie "Frankenstein", they used to call her "spastic","nutcase","spazzo", "lunatic".' Frankie liked to stand in the bay window of their front room, look out at the quiet street and wave to passers-by. The gang jeered at her, made obscene gestures and tried to persuade her to lift her nightdress. They imitated her walk. They taunted her. Anthony, Fiona's son, had dyslexia and was also bullied for his mild impairment.

A once-cheerful family was dragged down by the harassment, which intensified after Simon, Fiona's husband, left. Hazel Smith re-called: 'I saw her go downhill, she got terrible lines on her face, she more or less became a recluse. I saw Frankie go downhill as well. Fiona said to me, "Oh my God, I can't take it any more, what have I done to deserve this?"'

Being the local freak show for disaffected youths didn't only af-fect Fiona, it affected her children as well, Hazel remembered: 'Fiona rang me, one dark, rainy November night. I went round to her, and I knocked on the door and she quickly let me in. Frankie had a rab-bit, and cockatiel. She brought the rabbit to me, and put it on my lap. She asked what my glasses were for, and she was telling me about her rabbit, and saying, "You've got grey in your hair, why do you wear glasses?"Then she said, "I don't like my life, they keep picking on me, they are horrible to me." And Fiona heard, and she burst into tears, and said, "What can I do?" I said, "I'm reporting it, I'm here for you." But things never got any better.'

It emerged at the inquest that Fiona Pilkington had pleaded for help from the police on a total of thirty-three different occasions, thirteen of them in the year of her death. But both the police and the council had failed to link the calls and therefore notice the targeted nature of the repeat attacks. They also failed to act against the youths who were causing the family such misery. On one occasion the po-lice told her to draw her curtains and ignore the fact that the gang was destroying her back garden. Fiona discussed the case with social workers, antisocial behaviour officers and parish and local council-lors. But nothing was done.[3]

By 2006, things had got even worse, Hazel told me. 'In 2006, Fiona rung me and said they were here again, and I had stones thrown at me, they were f-ing and blinding at me, and I was more or less told I was a copper's nark again, you shouldn't be round here. I knocked on the door and she let me in, and I'd be in about an hour, and there was a mighty crash and they'd hit the window. Fiona shouted, "Oh my God please help me," Frankie ran away screaming, hysterical, and Anthony cowered in the corner. I was shocked myself, I was stunned. I couldn't believe what had happened. I telephoned the police but no one came out. It cracked and damaged the window, and all they asked was, "Is she insured?" ' Hazel continued, her eyes full of tears: 'Fiona herself had got learning difficulties but she cared for those children like gold-dust. They went without nothing, those two. But we got nowhere, we just got nowhere with nobody. That poor woman was crying out for help, all those years.'

A flavour of that constant harassment can be tasted from the 'harassment diary' that Fiona kept for a short period in the year of her death. In one entry, she writes about shouts outside from 11.30 p.m. until the early hours: 'Sat in the dark until 2.30 a.m., stressed out.' The harassment peaked around Hallowe'en and Bonfire Night. Fiona, after eleven years of harassment, had no panic alarm. The police could have, but didn't, fix unbreakable glass or acrylic in her doors and windows. She was not given an emergency mobile phone, nor did the police or council suggest installing CCTV to gain evidence. The harassment diaries the council gave her were never even collected.

Fiona took to sleeping downstairs on the sofa, on guard twenty-four hours a day, so that she could drag her children out if the house was firebombed – a bitter irony, given the manner of her death. The day of her death, her neighbour Ann Jones popped round to give the family some Bakewell tarts. Ann told me: 'Frankie opened the door and Fiona came to the door and said "thank you". I didn't go in, I was that tired, I'd been working all day. I had no idea what was going to happen. If I'd have known, I would have taken that petrol off her.'

Later, Fiona put Frankie in the car and drove a few miles to put a letter through the door of her mother, Pam, to say goodbye. Then she disappeared. Pam phoned a close friend of Fiona's, Brian, and the police. The police said they could do nothing to help. Brian drove around the streets, in a desperate attempt to find her. Their blue Austin Maestro was found, still on fire, late on the night of 23 October 2007, in a lay-by at the side of the A47 in Barwell, just a few miles from the home that Fiona was too afraid to live in any longer.

Hazel received a phone call the next day. 'I got a phone call from her mum, in a hysterical state: "Frankie and Fiona are dead, they've been found burnt to death in the car." It felt like an axe went straight through my heart. I cried, I felt bloody useless, like a failure, I know people said, "You couldn't do any more," but I kept thinking, Why couldn't I help her, why has she died? I carried terrible guilt because of it.'

Like many others, Hazel attended the funeral. 'To see Fiona's mum, dad and son stood up at the front, it was horrible, to see two lovely people who had done no harm in their lives come in that like that in their coffins. I cried.'

Later that day, I walked round to Fiona's house. A neighbour accosted me, and I told her why I was there. She said, bitterly: 'I can't stand all this trouble. It's brought the neighbourhood down, we can't sell our houses. I'm sick of that Fiona Pilkington.' As for Hazel Smith, she said, she should 'keep her nose out of our street'.

This bore out what Hazel Smith had told me. 'There's been two petitions got up for us to leave – they don't like me. One person came up to me, and said, "It's your f-ing fault. You've caused bad publicity for Barwell, you've painted Barwell that black, nobody can sell their houses or exchange or move because of you." ' Ann Jones, Fiona's neighbour, agreed about the bad publicity. 'Down the bottom end where the houses are, a lot of people have put their houses up for sale because of what's gone on.'

Fiona's house was sold after her death. From the outside, it's just an ordinary semi-detached house, on an ordinary street, in an ordinary neighbourhood. It should be a place where nothing really happens, where you raise your children in peace and live out your life. As Hazel, who was born and bred here, said, 'This is a lovely place to live, it's quiet.' But what happened to Fiona and her family was extraordinary. It's not as if Barwell is rife with antisocial behaviour or that the place completely lacks community, although it is very deprived on a number of indices.[4] No, the lesson of Barwell is not just about a lack of respect, or about lack of community, as politicians claim. It's about the community not wanting disabled people to live in it.

There were exceptions. Ann Jones, who lived opposite, considered Fiona to be a very close and wonderful friend. 'Fiona tried to help me, you know, after my son died in Holland,' she said, showing me a letter that Fiona wrote to her as comfort after his death. She was a kind woman, Ann observed, willing to drive neighbours to the doctor or take in parcels. She helped others, but nobody helped her, Ann added: 'She needed help, she were begging for help, and the police and the council did sod all. It got worse because no one topped them. They've shown no remorse, none at all.' She looks over the road to where Fiona once lived and added, simply: 'She would be here today if they had done something. I'm that gutted. I miss her. She never got justice.'

After Fiona's death, the wheels of the justice system started to turn, at last. The inquest, held at Hinkley Town Hall, found that Fiona was driven to kill Frankie and herself partly because the police did not heed her pleas for help. The jury also criticised a failure to share information between the police and the local council as one of the reasons why they did not respond to the calls for help. The jury found that Pilkington killed herself and her daughter 'due to the stress and anxiety regarding her daughter's future, and ongoing antisocial behaviour'. The foreman of the jury said the police's failure had an impact on Pilkington's decision to unlawfully kill her daughter and commit suicide.[5] He added that Hinckley and Bosworth Borough Council's response to complaints of antisocial behaviour also contributed to the deaths.

The jury also found that the county council failed to help the family, as they never assessed Fiona Pilkington's mental health. Although the main culprits were known to both police and council officials, their criminal harassment of the Pilkington family was never dealt with. The police, too, failed to recognise it as hate crime, and called it antisocial behaviour instead. The findings of a serious case review by Leicestershire County Council, also issued after the verdict, made a series of recommendations, including better communication between different agencies and more recognition of hate crimes against disabled people.[6] The Independent Police Complaints Commission (IPCC) has launched an investigation into the way that the case was treated, with particular emphasis on how seriously the police responded to the thirty-three calls for help.[7] Pam Cassell, Fiona's mother, has taken the difficult decision to sue the police. Her action is ongoing.[8]

Politicians, too, wrung their hands over the case, with the then Home Secretary, Alan Johnson, calling it 'shocking', saying that police and councils had to learn from such failures.[9] The Conservative Shadow Home Secretary, Chris Grayling, called for action to stamp out antisocial behaviour.[10]

Shortly after the inquest, one of the boys responsible for the hounding of Fiona and her family was taken to Hinkley Youth Court after allegedly abusing Hazel Smith and calling her a 'grass' and saying that Fiona and her daughter were 'freaks' who deserved the abuse.[11] Hazel Smith gave evidence that the boy had called her a 'copper's nark' and a 'Neighbourhood Watch bitch' as well as calling Frankie 'Frankenstein'. The case collapsed after Hazel was taken ill in court.

District judge David Meredith declared he was unhappy about the decision by the Crown Prosecution Service to abort the trial, after the prosecutor said it was in the public interest to drop the case. He said: 'I am backed into a corner from which I have no escape. There are particular aspects of this case that have caused me grave concern by the alleged response to Fiona Pilkington and her daughter's death. I should also add that the suggestion that a person [Mrs Smith] who is involved in Neighbourhood Watch is somehow an irritant to society is something I view as reprehensible.'[12]

No one has therefore spent a single day in jail for the hounding of Fiona, her family and those who attempted to bring their case to trial. The lives of a loving family have been destroyed, those of their friends and supporters damaged and the reputation of Barwell is in tatters and the atmosphere is poisoned. Barwell is stained by the aftermath of a hate crime, not the nuisance of low-level antisocial behaviour. Indeed, visiting Barwell, strangely, felt a little like reporting from East Berlin, before and shortly after the Wall came down. Post-war German writers such as Heinrich Böll wrote about the importance of the *Bewältigung der Vergangenheit* – how without coming to terms with painful history, the present remains poisoned. In East Germany, where that process was delayed by Communist dictatorship, the atmosphere in the 1980s was brutal, with ordinary social relationships soured by suspicion. The same is true of places poisoned by disability hate crime. Those living there need to understand why it happened, accept it happened and look at their own responsibility. Otherwise nothing really will change, and another disabled person, or a person from another group, will be targeted. And the cycle of hate will start again.

The minimising of disability targeted harassment, by dubbing it antisocial behaviour, is not confined to the Pilkington case. In March 2010, 64-year-old David Askew, who had learning difficulties and whose family had faced seventeen years of abuse, bullying and harassment at the hands of local youths, collapsed and died soon after Greater Manchester Police received the latest report of harassment outside his home. His mother, Rose, a wheelchair user, and brother Brian, who lived with her, had also been targeted. Rose said of her son: 'He had been put through hell over the years. It was not just one incident – it went on for years. Sometimes he would cry and ask me if I could move people out of our garden because they would call him very hurtful names.' Only one person, Kial Cottingham, received a sentence for his part in the harassment – of just sixteen weeks in a young offenders' institution. Another youth was given an ASBO.[13]

Greater Manchester Police (GMP) admitted that David Askew and his family 'had been subjected to prolonged antisocial behaviour and harassment for a number of years before his death' and that Askew 'had severe learning difficulties and because of this he was a regular target for youths'. A GMP spokesman said: 'We have had contact with the Askew family for several years, with several different generations of offenders who have been after this family.'[14] But, although the Crown Prosecution Service later flagged the case as a potential disability hate crime, the police had not gathered the evidence to prove that Cottingham's harassment was motivated by hostility or prejudice. A CPS spokesman refused to comment on what the police may nor may not have done, but he said the Crown prosecutor did provide details of Askew's 'vulnerable situation', which magistrates took into account in sentencing.[15]

Like Leicestershire, Greater Manchester Police is now facing an IPCC investigation into whether the police could have done more to save him.[16] Neither case is isolated – nearly a third of people who have contacted the police about antisocial behaviour are disabled, according to a major national report. The *Stop the Rot* report by Her Majesty's Inspectorate of Constabulary says antisocial behaviour (ASB) across England and Wales is a blight on the lives of millions of people, and calls for police to make a new start in tackling it.[17]

Disabled people are disproportionately victims of antisocial behaviour, suggesting strongly that targeted disability violence is far too often being wrongly termed ASB. Many disabled people also report being stalked. This glossing-over of a serious crime can have fatal consequences – as it did for Fiona Pilkington, her daughter Frankie and the Askew family. More than a third who had been repeat victims were disabled. The report says that of forty-three police forces across England and Wales, only twenty-two have IT systems that help them identify and prioritise repeat callers, with just sixteen of them able to identify those most at risk of harm.[18]

All of this suggests that what happened to David Askew, and to Fiona Pilkington, was not unusual and that it could happen again. It is a daily fact of life for a very large proportion of disabled people living in England today. It is not only Barwell, or Manchester, that is the problem. It is happening everywhere in our community, and only the community as a whole can tackle it. No one should have to live in fear like this. It is impossible to live an ordinary life in the face of unpredictable, unquantifiable and ultimately unchallenged behaviour. The terminology that surrounded the Pilkington and the Askew families, at the time of their deaths – harassment and antisocial behaviour – served only to disguise the offence, which was disability targeted violence. It brings shame on all of us that we condone both the behaviour and the official terminology that hides its roots from view.

13

Multi-Agency Chaos: Michael Gilbert and the Failure of Safeguarding

Fear, that's what almost all disabled people will feel if they are attacked in the community. They fear that if they report an attack they face the risk of being put back into an institution. 'Adult safeguarding', as it is called, is not working, partly because of this justifiable fear. No one can blame disabled people for not wanting to be shut away again, given the history of institutional care and the abusive situation still persisting in some residential homes today. This leaves too many disabled people, particularly women, facing the choice of being attacked in the community or attacked in institutions. But there are other reasons why safeguarding doesn't make disabled people safe.

One reason is that tighter criteria for social care means that fewer disabled people living in the community are qualifying for the support they need to avoid social isolation and live the ordinary life that so many of us take for granted – access to work, entertainment, shops and citizenship.[1] In particular, those who have no formal diagnosis of disability, even if they are identified as vulnerable, are very unlikely to be given any support. Many high-functioning disabled people are never known to social services – even though they can be at high risk of harm if they are targeted by unscrupulous individuals. So, despite the local authority parlance of 'multi-agency working' and 'protecting vulnerable adults' through 'safeguarding', disabled and vulnerable adults in many places simply do not have the protection they deserve, as equal citizens, to lead an ordinary life.

The *No Secrets* protection guidelines published in 2000 gave social care agencies in England and Wales the lead in responding to, and ultimately monitoring, crimes against vulnerable people.[2] This has led to confusion, arising from the blurring of duties between social care agencies and the criminal justice sector and, in some instances, a vacuum of responsibility. The current review of *No Secrets* by the Government is an opportunity to bring those two sectors together.

Those who live in the community who are deemed 'vulnerable adults' are supposed to get support, if they need it, from what are called 'adult safeguarding' teams in each local authority, which should report concerns to the police, as well as to multi-agency safeguarding boards. It all sounds great on paper. But few of these agencies seem to understand that disabled people might be targeted by unscrupulous individuals seeking to harm them. They do not understand disability hate crime, and disabled people are falling through the gap. Incidents can be both safeguarding and hate crime issues at one and the same time and should be treated as such.

One case that shows how badly multi-agency working functions is that of Michael Gilbert, who was dubbed vulnerable from an early age when he went into care – but was released into the 'care' of a criminal family that robbed him, mocked him, tortured him and eventually murdered him. Having heard one highly placed official from Bedfordshire Council speak about safeguarding generally, it is hard to believe that they have understood the implications of Michael's case – both for Luton and for local authorities generally.

On 10 May 2009 parts of Michael Gilbert's dismembered body were found by men walking dogs by the Blue Lagoon, a lake near Luton. (His head was found later, in the same lake.)[3] Michael was just 26 when he was killed. He had been abused, tortured, filmed for entertainment and stolen from by members of the Watt family, who were known to police and other agencies, for around ten years.

James Watt, 27, together with his girlfriend Natasha Oldfield, 29, and Nichola Roberts, 21, were all found guilty of murdering Michael Gilbert on or about 21 January 2009. James Watt's mother, Jennifer Smith-Dennis, 70, was found guilty of familial homicide, as was another brother, Robert Watt.* The family will serve nearly 90 years in prison in total. Antonio Watt, the father, was cleared.[4]

Police and Luton Council provided me with detailed information about Michael Gilbert, including the opening statement from the prosecutor in the case, Stuart Trimmer. I have also sourced material from the family and friends, as well as further facts from the local authority and police in this important case.

Michael Gilbert tried hard to escape the Watt family. I have discovered that he, and the few friends he had, reported their concerns about the family and his own safety on at least eight (and possibly more than ten) occasions to different officials between 2002 and 2009. Friends reported three alleged abductions to three different police forces (Bedfordshire, Cambridgeshire and Lancashire). On other occasions a GP and two housing workers recorded serious allegations that Michael Gilbert had made against the Watt family. Michael was also hospitalised following a stabbing by the Watt family. Officials heard Michael allege that he had been abducted, assaulted and beaten up by people he knew in Luton. But these allegations, it seems, were never properly investigated, followed up or linked. No official action against the Watt family was taken in connection with their treatment of Michael Gilbert until they were accused of murdering him.

Michael Gilbert first came into contact with the Watt family after his own family put him in a children's home, the Brambles, in Luton, when he was about 15 (following a false allegation of rape). Michael's sister Patricia later joined him at the children's home, where they met James Watt. Despite the fact that staff at the home described him as vulnerable and suggested that he had a mental health problem and doubted his ability to live independently, a formal diagnosis of his disability and his support needs was never carried out. No one ques-

---

* An offence under the Domestic Violence, Crime and Victims Act 2004. It allows prosecutors to prosecute a number of adults in contact with a child or vulnerable adult for not preventing serious harm to that person, closing a legal loophole in which each accused adult blames another for the crime.

tioned Michael's 'transition', as it is known in social care, into the Watt family, despite the fact that James Watt had ended up in the children's home because he had threatened his mother with a knife.

A statement from Bedfordshire Police to me confirmed that nobody was looking out for Michael. Although the prosecutor, Stuart Trimmer, described Michael in court as a vulnerable adult who was kept as a 'slave' by the Watt family, the police concluded that he was only 'vulnerable in an emotional context', going on to explain that this meant that 'once he was out of the care system he was not therefore on the radar of agencies/authorities etc.'[5]

Over ten years, Stuart Trimmer said in court, Michael was threatened and viciously assaulted. The violence mounted over the years. 'They used his benefits and the various loans he had from the DSS as their own. He was their dogsbody and their slave.' Mr Trimmer added that he was 'abused and assaulted for entertainment. Some of the beatings were filmed on mobile phones.'

Michael had first tried to escape in 2002, but he was brought back by James Watt. A friend of the family, Phillip Budd, recalled him being put against a wall and used as target practice, to be shot with an air rifle, as a punishment. The same witness recalled Michael being dragged around the room by metal grips attached to his genitals. Budd also saw Michael being struck by a lizard with a six-foot tail for sport. Zoe Smith, a one-time girlfriend to another brother, Colin Watt, said in court that Michael was treated 'as a slave about the house' and kept prisoner, handcuffed at night to the bed of James Watt.

In 2008 another friend of the Watt family, Daniel Saunders, witnessed Michael being brought back from another failed escape. He was encouraged to punch Michael full in the face, an incident that was also filmed for sport and a video of which was played in court. Another witness, Amanda Chapman, saw Michael just before Christmas 2008 and witnessed his severe bruising and the fact he had not been fed. He was forced to drink his own urine. And Michael was used as a freak show too. Natasha Oldfield, the girlfriend of James, devised a game show with various sums of money linked to different assaults on Michael. In one scenario, Michael ended up dead.

Colin Watt eventually moved out because he says he could not bear to see the violence meted out to Michael. The torture game that may well have killed Michael was to jump up and down on his stomach. By the time Colin left, Michael could no longer control his bowels and his stomach was distended. On one occasion Colin, who gave evidence against his family in court, asked Michael why he put up with it. He replied: 'Because I love you, you are my family.'

Despite that tie, Michael tried hard to alert the authorities. Some time around 2002, according to his mother, Rosalie White, Michael first made a complaint to police about his treatment at the hands of the Watt family after he turned up at her house having been beaten with a sledgehammer. But no action was taken, despite the fact that around the same time Michael was stabbed and taken to hospital. (On that occasion two of the brothers stayed with him to make sure he said nothing to the doctors.)

A year later Michael raised very serious concerns about his treatment to a health professional in Norfolk. As far as I have been able to establish, this information was not passed on to the police. In 2006, when Michael was abducted from Dunstable, his girlfriend, Tina Garner, reported to police that he had been taken away. Again, no action was taken. In January 2007 Michael signed on at a job centre in Cambridgeshire, after escaping from the Watt family. He told a homeless key worker that he was in fear of his life and had to leave Luton.

In March 2007 he moved to a hostel in Cambridge, where he was confirmed as a 'vulnerable person' and was in fear of his life. On 29 June 2007 another friend, Darryl Everest, reported to Cambridgeshire Police that Michael had been abducted from outside the job centre where he was due to sign on. Again, this was never followed up properly.

Just one month later, in July, Michael was arrested with James Watt in Luton (on an unrelated issue) and was accompanied by what is known as an 'appropriate adult', to support him as a 'vulnerable adult'. The investigating officer was told that Michael had been allegedly abducted from Cambridge. Michael confirmed the story, but he refused to press charges. Instead, he asked for a travel warrant to Cambridge. The abduction was not pursued as an investigation.

In September 2007 Michael again managed to escape, this time to Blackburn. Yet again, on 28 January 2008, he was abducted from a job centre. The Iddon family, who had housed him, reported the incident to police in Blackburn. Lancashire Police confirmed in an email to me that police were called on 1 February 2008, reporting 'a concern for safety of Michael Gilbert'. The informant, the police spokeswoman told me, 'reported Gilbert was driven away in a car against his will. Officers went to seek further information and after reviewing the case there was no indication that Gilbert had got into the car under duress . . . It seems from the log we are satisfied he left of his own accord.' Lancashire Police were not aware, they told me, if this information had been passed on at the time to Bedfordshire Police and were unaware of the previous abductions.

At least three abductions in two years, but no one asked questions, talked to Michael about why he was in fear of his life and why he had been abducted. Nobody joined the dots, partly because Michael was never given a diagnosis or extra support. Doctors, housing workers, police and job-centre workers all saw him, but none of them raised the alarm. No one wanted to take the responsibility for saving Michael.

Members of the public tried to – Scott Iddon and his family, Tina Garner and Darryl Everest all reported to police that Michael had been abducted by the Watt family (in Blackburn, Dunstable and Cambridge). But their complaints were not followed up. Nobody looked at the pattern of events. So the Watt family were free to torture him, rob him and finally murder him.

On 16 January 2009 Michael was seen by a job-centre worker in Luton, Anthony Marshall. He was so concerned about Michael's health that he made a note in the file and offered to get Michael medical assistance, but Michael refused. His giro was cashed by the Watt family. Five days later Michael was dead.

I spent a number of days in court, following the trial of the Watt family. Antonio Watt, the only member of the family to be cleared of any offence, sat motionless much of the time, impassive and unsmiling behind his dark glasses. But the other defendants talked to each other, smiled, asked for water and looked relaxed, even during the most devastating descriptions of the evil done to Michael. Around this time Nichola Roberts complained to friends about how disruptive the trial was to her life. She wanted to move away and start over, she said – as if it is possible to put torture and murder behind you. She, like the others, was found guilty and sentenced to well over a decade in jail.

Rosalie White, Michael's mother, who has a mobility impairment herself, still struggles to understand what happened to her son. Despite a severe lung infection, she attended court every day, leaning heavily on her crutches. She readily admitted to me that she had found life with her young children difficult. But she has steadfastly argued that Michael hasn't had justice, and wants to understand why so many cries for help were not heard by the authorities.

'Michael was always the fall guy,' she explained to me, over coffee in a small cafe near the court. 'He always took the blame, he was so gentle. He was bullied at school, and he just took it.' 'Was he vulnerable, or disabled, do you think?' I asked her. She shrugged. 'I don't know. He would just do anything for anybody. He had the build and the height, but he didn't have it in him to hit back.' Michael's life was a mystery, even to his own family. Chrissie, Michael's brother, broke in: 'You see, he went into foster care for a while, so I didn't see him, but he would come and see Mum sometimes.' Indeed, Rosalie remembered, he came to see her in 2002. 'His head was like a sponge. He said they had hit him with a sledgehammer.' They went to Luton Police together, she said, and did a twenty-six-page statement, over six and a half hours. This was never raised at the trial and I asked her whether anybody had ever followed it up. She shook her head. 'Nothing happened. We did try.'

On 12 May 2009, when Rosalie was driving with her son Chrissie, her daughter Patricia phoned and told her to stop the car. Then Patricia told her that Michael's body had been found, and her world changed for ever. Before we said goodbye, Rosalie, leaning on her crutches, said to me: 'Someone must have known about Michael.' She was right. Lots of people knew about Michael, but nobody in authority lifted a hand to help him.

On yet another trip to Luton, on a beautiful autumn day, I walked to the road where Michael was held captive for months, tortured and murdered. I was expecting it to be a grim housing estate, like so many of the other cases I have investigated. But the street was calm and bourgeois, with clean driveways and pots of flowers outside well-scrubbed doors. The house where Michael was attacked, killed and then dismembered is not far from the middle of the street and is semi-detached. Did no one hear the screams? Why didn't anyone intervene?

Luton Council, which took Michael into care as a teenager, is conducting a serious case review that will establish whether his death was preventable. The IPCC is investigating his mother's claims about the 2002 incident. They are also investigating the abductions, and whether or not the police forces involved investigated them thoroughly.[6]

Luton, like many other councils, seems largely unaware of the links between so-called vulnerability and hate crime. Indeed, a Luton Council official I heard speak at a conference in 2010 outlined a case that they had treated as a 'safeguarding' case, in which a disabled man had had disability motivated graffiti scrawled on his property. The council did not see this as a hate crime and never passed it on to the police. They got that wrong. I believe they got Michael Gilbert's case wrong too, from the moment he left care and was released, by a children's home, into the hands of his eventual killers.

My understanding is that the Coalition Government is unlikely to give local authorities a clear national mandate to link hate crime, mate crime and safeguarding together. Crucially, too, serious case reviews relating to the serious harm or death of a so-called vulnerable adult and what lessons can be learned from such incidents are not compulsory for local authorities. A study of adult serious case reviews, carried out by Jill Manthorpe and Stephen Martineau of King's College London, found that many local authorities contacted did not know about serious case reviews carried out by their councils in the past, and records of them had been lost. The researchers found that local authorities would like centrally collected data and were in favour of the reviews being compulsory, as they are when a child dies in similar circumstances.[7] Without the data being available centrally, we are almost completely unable to learn lessons from previous cases where 'vulnerable adults' – almost always disabled people – have died. Local authorities don't even have to publish the reviews in full (in practice almost all are heavily edited) and they are, understandably, reluctant to publicise them.

The safeguarding 'system' is, in effect, a plethora of unconnected units and officers, none of which necessarily speaks to each other: antisocial behaviour units, housing units, safeguarding or vulnerable adults officers, the police, fire service and A & E. Public protection units, operated by the police, can also get involved when a safeguarding issue has criminal overtones. But few safeguarding referrals (which increased during the recession, with some areas reporting over 1,000 a year) ever get handed to police and even fewer reach trial.[8]

Three main reasons are advanced for not taking cases forward: that disabled people want to be treated as independent, and that therefore local authorities have no right to intervene; that if the person in question does not have a diagnosis, or meet the criteria for care, there is no budget for intervening; and that the Data Protection Act does not allow agencies to share information. Therefore no one agency takes responsibility for reporting and, even if exploitation is spotted, nobody thinks its their responsibility to stop it.

It is certainly true that a number of cases in this book demonstrate that disabled victims of hate crime refused intervention. One is the case of Raymond Atherton, in Warrington. Steven Hoskin, similarly, refused social care support. But another less well-known one illustrates an all too common practice: blaming the victim, rather than taking responsibility. A Leicester man, Steven Gale, was starved and beaten so badly by his self-styled carer, Andrew Green, that he died in 2006.[9] His case was never subject to a serious case review and Leicester Council has not been forthcoming about their missed opportunities to intervene, although I have obtained some information about the case through a number of freedom of information requests.

Although the council says that a sudden death report and a management report have been written, they have not disclosed them, and my request to see them has not yet been processed. The council has confirmed that a team social worker who visited Steven Gale, after he jumped from a third-floor window to escape what was said to be a domestic row, found him 'to be very capable, apparently happy, and he was adamant he didn't want any help or services from us'.[10] Further information I have obtained denies, however, that the council had decided not to intervene, saying instead, in double-speak: 'No decision had therefore been made not to give Mr Gale any extra support.' Steven Gale starved to death a few months after he threw himself from the window. He was described by a social worker as 'reluctant to engage'. I suspect that if a woman had thrown herself out of a window after a domestic row, police and social workers would not describe her as 'reluctant to engage' but would conclude, instead, that she was living in fear of her life and was a 'vulnerable and intimidated witness'.

Councils must not hide behind independent living and so-called 'reluctance to engage' in this way. They have a duty of care to all who live in their area. If Leicester City Council had commissioned and published an adult serious case review into his death, it might well have shed light on disability targeted violence in the Leicestershire area. This might well have helped Fiona Pilkington and her family.

There is also a very limited understanding of the Mental Capacity Act, behind which councils and police also prevaricate, saying they can't intervene if someone 'has capacity' (i.e. is considered able to think and act independently). But many disability campaigners, myself included, believe the whole concept of capacity needs looking at again. A disabled person may have 'capacity' to live alone and function, but that doesn't mean that they can do that if they are targeted by an unscrupulous person. It doesn't necessarily mean they can consent to an intimate relationship that becomes abusive. It doesn't mean that they understand what it means to refuse support when they are being targeted, as was the case, for instance, with Steven Gale, Steven Hoskin and Raymond Atherton.

DI Hemingway, who investigated the Atherton case, now works as a senior officer in Cheshire's public protection unit. She says: 'We are now trying to put in intervention earlier and earlier, and make sure that crimes like that don't happen in the future.' She sees that everyone now needs to be far more proactive: 'Everyone should feel responsible. Everyone should be wearing that hat, when they see someone, and making sure if something is wrong, that they report it. I don't mean statutory bodies alone, I mean housing officers, anyone. If they have concerns they should report it to us.' But they don't. There seems to be an institutional disengagement between the so-called 'adult safeguarding' work that local authorities do, and the agenda of police forces, which investigate crimes. The two systems do not speak to each other often enough.

David Congdon, who is head of policy at the learning disability charity Mencap, is also concerned about balancing out the lip service that local authorities pay to independent living with assessing and addressing risks: 'Statutory agencies hide behind independent living. It is too convenient for them to say that a vulnerable person refused help. I think in terms of human rights "proportionate" is a very useful term. The alternatives are not either to do nothing or to stick someone in institutional care. They should ask the question, is the person at risk, as Steven Hoskin was? If they are at risk, then support should be provided. It might mean intervening. Because the net result of not getting involved, in Steven Hoskin's case, meant that he ended up dead. But I acknowledge that intervening is a draconian step.'

And David Congdon makes another point, which is uncomfortable for some in the disability rights movement, but does deserve debate: 'There is no doubt that the physical disability lobby was right to argue aggressively for independent living. But for people with a learning disability it's different. It is right to argue for independent living, but they need support. We have to face up to the fact that they have a learning disability, they don't have the armoury to look after themselves, we need to recognise that. We need to say, "We are not going to constrain your life to the extent that you will be locked up in an institution, that is quite wrong, we will create opportunities for you to live in the community but we will provide a supportive environment." To pretend that some people with learning disabilities don't need support is frankly immoral. I can think of people I know, with a moderate disability, they can survive well, but if someone targeted them, I think they could be in trouble.'

Sergeant Nigel Bolton, who has been instrumental in developing an innovative information-sharing system, the Multi-Agency Safeguarding Hub (MASH), in Devon and Cornwall, is also forthright about the flaws in the system:[11] 'We hide behind data protection. It is about data sharing and usage. We are protecting people from harm. I have heard far too many lectures about human rights, and the right to a private life. But it blends into insignificance when you look at Article 2, the right to life. That should be paramount, shouldn't it?' And, he adds, in one recent serious case review that he has read (not from his own region), information sharing yet again was all but absent: 'I added up the number of contacts with the family, from partnership agencies, the system. There were 300 points of concern before the person died. We, as agencies, let a person die.'

Life back inside should not be an option for most disabled people, and appropriate 'safeguarding' is crucial if we are to tackle disability hate crime. But ignoring the problems connected with independent living, and local authorities hiding behind them when things go wrong, is not right either. That said, disabled people are right to distrust institutional care. A surprising number of disabled people remain in the care system – some 57,000 at least, in residential homes, local authority homes or in what remains of the NHS long-stay system. They live in over 6,500 residential homes. Some, even very young people, are still placed in homes with older people.[12] A much larger number, perhaps around 120,000 people with learning disabilities, access care in settings like day-care centres. Old habits die hard and institutional abuse has not been eradicated.

John Pring has written a series of articles in which he has un-picked allegations of serious abuse at the Solar Daycare Centre in Doncaster.[13] A report into the care there, initially leaked to the *Doncaster Free Press*, described how staff allegedly hit disabled people vis-iting the centre and used 'inappropriate force', as well as detailing other allegations of ill treatment between 2005 and 2007. There were forty-four allegations of abuse. Staff had allegedly threatened and hu-miliated disabled visitors, withheld food and drink and even locked them in cupboards. Following concerns raised by other members of staff in early 2007, South Yorkshire Police investigated allegations that staff were physically assaulting some of the disabled visitors, but failed to obtain enough evidence to press any charges.

Rotherham Doncaster and South Humber Mental Health NHS Foundation Trust (RDaSH) then carried out its own investigation, which ended in September 2008. Its subsequent report described incidents involving eighteen people with learning difficulties, high support needs, and physical and sensory impairments. The Trust said the majority of the allegations made against four members of staff were proven, although all four are said to have denied all the allega-tions. But the Trust failed to pass a copy of its report to the police, despite the nature of the allegations. They included one person being pricked with needles around their eyes, and a wheelchair user being propelled, with force, from one side of a room to another, crashing into other visitors as a result.

The regulator failed to pick up on the allegations as well. Indeed, despite the regulator being told about the allegations in 2007, the Trust was given an 'excellent' rating that year and the next two. The Care Quality Commission (CQC), which became the regulator of residential and at home care in 2009, even described the Trust as 'high performing' that year.[14]

The Solar Centre is not an isolated case of abuse. In September 2010 the CQC announced that it had closed thirty-four care homes and eight agencies providing care in people's homes. (*Private Eye* and the BBC, however, have questioned the CQC's figures on closures, and questioned whether the regulator is robust enough.)[15] The regulator documented verbal and psychological abuse of residents, medicines not being managed safely, and poor nursing, medical care and sanitary conditions.[16]

The CQC provided me with a breakdown of the care homes and agencies where enforcement action has been taken. Those specialising in dementia and learning difficulty are over-represented in the figures.[17] There have also been recent investigations, by the CQC's predecessor body, into services for people with learning difficulties in Cornwall and Sutton and Merton.[18] Indeed, so poor is the state of care at the moment that the CQC has launched a strategic plan to tackle the many 'inequalities' facing disabled people using care.[19]

Dame Jo Williams, who chairs the CQC and is a former social worker, is aware of the dangers of institutional care: 'I just believe passionately that if you work in an institution you have to be extraordinary mindful of the potential for subcultures to develop.' She adds: 'Before I started as a social worker, I read Erving Goffman's *Asylums*, where he talked about institutions robbing us of our humanity. I've always felt that where institutions are isolated, subcultures can develop and staff can lose sight of what they are there for. If they are within that subculture, they will misuse power and it can cascade very quickly.' She readily acknowledges that there is an 'imbalance of power' in institutions, especially where residents have learning difficulties and dementia.

It is unlikely that all disabled people could ever live fully independently. A small number, particularly of those with learning disabilities, will always require extra support. A strong regulatory and inspection system for institutions is therefore essential – and disabled people should be involved. Jo Williams says that she would like disabled people to play a part in inspecting homes. They are the experts, she says – and can ask the right questions. And the doors of institutions must be open: 'I'd be looking for places where residents have a strong voice, where they are involved in selecting the work-force, where each resident has an individual work programme, and where the institution is connected to the community and has an open-door policy.' With an eye on history, she notes: 'It's those isolated closed-door institutions where, for generations now, we have seen problems developing.'

Institutionalisation is clearly not going to protect disabled people from harm. Living in the community is the right answer for almost all. Therefore the links between social care, safeguarding and hate crime need to be made more explicit. And disabled people must not be threatened with institutionalisation if they complain. The Law Commission, which recommends law reform in England and Wales, has suggested shifting the focus of adult safeguarding from 'vulnerable adult' to a 'person at risk of harm'. This is welcome, because it acknowledges that people can be in risky situations at certain times, but can be made safe, with support, and stay in the community. Its other proposed change, that adult social care will be provided on the basis of need, without a diagnosis of disability, is also welcome. It might have saved Michael Gilbert's life, and might save other lives in the future. Having a diagnosis should not be the only criterion for support. It allows councils to get away with substandard services.[20]

But the bigger picture is ending the social isolation in which so many disabled people live and which puts them at risk of harm, where the only people with whom they come into contact are paid workers – or those who want to prey on them. What we need to do instead, as we discuss in the next chapter, is to create real friendships and tear down the walls between 'us' and 'them'.

14

Mate Crime: the Importance of Friendship

Independent living, laudable as it is, is not a panacea. It was, and clearly remains, the right model for disabled people, particularly those with mobility or sensory impairments, who can lead an ordinary life, go to work, go out at night – with a bit of extra support that they can choose and fund themselves.

But it has not been adjusted so that it works for all people with learning difficulties and mental health problems. In many of the cases I have looked at, people with those conditions were assessed as not needing extra support, because their disabilities were not considered serious. They were living on their own, or with very limited support. They had money to spend and were in charge of their own medication. This should have been all well and good. But they were also socially isolated. The old networks that were in place when institutional care was more common, imperfect as they were, had been swept away by the rhetoric of 'independence' and 'choice'. The level of social isolation in which some people live, at the margins of society, and the risks that it creates, has not until recently been thought to be important. That's wrong.

The worst murders, many of which I had investigated over the last three years, were all of socially isolated people with learning difficulties or mental health conditions – Keith Philpott, Sean Miles, Michael Gilbert, Barrie-John Horrell, Raymond Atherton, Steven Hoskin, Steven Gale – the list goes on and on. All tortured, many of them killed, by friends. And, crucially, my analysis also shows that the safety net that most of us take for granted – our families – was not there for these victims. It is possible to create a new proxy family,

177

of course, with friendship. But what if the new family, as in Michael Gilbert's case, only wants you for your money and the sport they can have with you? Then the ordinary, desperate need for human contact proved fatal.

What happened to these individuals in the run-up to the killings was eerily similar. Their deaths were preceded by 'grooming', by people approaching them and offering friendship. Then problems started to crop up. Medication and money went missing. The victim was blamed for something, often a sexual offence. (All but one of the victims above were falsely accused of paedophilia.) The assaults started and were not effectively challenged by those officials who did come into contact with them. The victim, intimidated, refused help anyway. Eventually, many were attacked so badly that they died. This sub-set of disability hate crime is often called 'mate crime'.

Mate crime is an aspect of hate crime, not separate from it. However, anecdotal evidence (and my report, *Getting Away with Murder*) shows that mate crime is particularly problematic, especially for people with learning difficulties. If they do not have good family or social networks to support them, the risks are greater. The Safety Net project, which is working in two pilot areas, North Devon and Calderdale in West Yorkshire, tries to reduce mate crime by working with people with learning difficulties, training them to understand what true friendship is and raising awareness of the risks of mate crime with families, police officers, adult safeguarding teams and front-line staff.[1]

David Grundy, who runs the Safety Net project in Calderdale, says that knowing the difference between real and false friendship is a key protective factor. Independent living support concentrates on help with shopping, cooking and budgeting, rather than on showing people how to create appropriate friendships. 'There is a sense', Grundy observes, 'for many people with learning disabilities that any kind of friendship is better than no friendship at all. We are having to teach people to recognise the difference between friendship and exploitation.'

Coruscating loneliness exposes too many people to risk. As the Dutch theologian Hans Reinders points out, many people with learning difficulties only come into contact with paid workers. 'Many people with intellectual disabilities are, for most of their lives, surrounded by people or professional caregivers and support workers. This means that relationships in their lives are either a matter of natural necessity or – as in the case of professionals – of contractual obligation . . . both of these kinds of relationship are very important for the disabled person, but neither can establish the crucial good that disabled people long for: being chosen as a friend . . . Friendship is special because it is freely chosen. Our friends want us as their friend for our own sake. No other relationship, either professional or kinship, can give what friendship gives.'[2] He goes on to observe that although disabled people have made great strides in achieving their rights, friendship has lagged behind. 'Despite the success they have found in strengthening their status in the public sphere, people with disabilities – particularly intellectual disabilities – experience loneliness in the sphere of their personal lives.'[3]

These observations are not new. The criminologist Nils Christie made similar observations about deinstitutionalisation in Norway, in 1989: 'Through deinstitutionalization some of the people in need of help are back to ordinary society, but in a special way. They are, but they are not. It is as if an invisible wall of glass exists between them and us. They are in our streets, our buses, our schools, our houses and places of work. Close but distant, among us but lonely.'[4] Research by Keith McVilly in Australia and Angela Amado in the US has also shown that despite progress in employment and education, people with learning difficulties are largely friendless.[5]

Professor Tom Shakespeare, a disabled academic, believes that deinstitutionalisation, like slum clearances, has had unintended consequences. 'It's like people living in slums and they know their neighbours. Then you put them in a tower block and it's all atomised. And it's potentially the same with deinstitutionalisation. Unless you build networks and you have staff who are dedicated, not just to make sure that people are fed, but connected as well, there are dangers. We want "the village idiot", to some extent, let's go back to that. It's a good image, in some ways. That's John, for instance, we are all his mates and we understand that we have to look out for him. Otherwise what are we going to do? Shut him up again in protective conditions?' And he adds: 'I don't think that independent living is freedom to be screwed, to be lonely or, at worst, the freedom to be murdered.'

This de facto segregation from ordinary life is not only true of people with learning difficulties, it's something many disabled people experience. A recent poll from the charity Scope found that nearly 40 per cent of people who are not disabled and do not have a disabled family member do not know any disabled people. Only one in ten British people has ever invited a disabled person to their house for a social occasion, and only one in five has had a disabled work colleague.[6]

Family and friends protect all of us from harm. The lack of real friendship, and the false friendships that flourish in their place, have proved fatal to far too many disabled people, particularly those with learning difficulties. Linked to this is ignorance and inexperience about how to make appropriate friendships and how to behave appropriately. If you don't know the etiquette of everyday life (even when to shake hands, when it's okay to kiss someone, when touching isn't appropriate), you can be vulnerable to unfounded accusations. This lack of knowledge lies behind the frequent vicious accusations against many people with learning difficulties, that they have sexually assaulted someone or that they are guilty of paedophilia.

Michael Bayley, the author of *What Price Friendship?*, explains that many disabled people encounter a 'friendship barrier' with non-disabled people, leaving them in a 'relationship vacuum'. This is an apt description for what happened to many of the people who were killed. He quotes the example of Mark, a man with learning difficulties, who misread the casual friendship of a non-disabled woman, pushed for an intimate relationship and was then disappointed:

'All too often people in Mark's situation have been excluded from learning the almost imperceptible signals which govern social behaviour. Thus intellectual disability is exacerbated by lack of social experience. Fundamentally where someone has a vacuum in his or her own range of relationships, especially at the "belonging and attachment" level, other relationships may be sucked into that vacuum. The result is inappropriate social behaviour.'[7]

In a recent case, three people attacked a man with learning difficulties who thought he was among friends. It started with an innocent kiss, the *Northern Echo* reported.[8] 'The assault began after he innocently kissed Davey on the cheek and she cried rape. The victim, a 44-year-old Darlington man, was persistently beaten and had tape put over his mouth to stop his shouts being heard during the ordeal – described as torture by a judge. He was left with seven marks from blows, at least one cigarette burn, bruising, a swollen eye, cuts to his arm and scratches to his back before they relented and apologised.'

It is hardly surprising that people with learning difficulties, isolated as they are, sometimes over-interpret, or misinterpret, friendship. And the stereotypes about disabled people and their sexual proclivities, much discussed in the nineteenth and twentieth centuries in particular, as I described earlier, don't help. They linger in folk memory, exposing people to more harm.

This invisible segregation is not what anyone intended when the institutions closed. But until these walls in our society between 'us' and 'them' are torn down, disabled people will continue to be targeted by so-called friends. Some will even pay the ultimate price, and end up dead.

15

Motivations

'I'm not going down for a muppet,' said one of the three murderers of Brent Martin.[1] Those words have remained with me for the last few years. Yet Brent's death, like so many others, was seen as 'motiveless'. As I have argued in other chapters, all kinds of terminology obscure disability hatred from view – with 'vulnerability' and 'motiveless' perhaps the most pernicious. These crimes are not, despite newspaper reports and handwringing by police and prosecutors, 'motiveless' acts carried out on 'vulnerable' people who should be tucked away at home or in institutions. But they are far too often described as such.

The judge called the murder of the 'vulnerable and defenceless' Barrie-John Horrell, who was abducted from his house by people he considered to be friends, hit with a brick, robbed, called a paedophile and strangled, 'senseless'.[2] Detective Inspector Geoff Brookes, who investigated the torture and death of Kevin Davies, observed that only the guilty trio could say 'exactly what motivated them', with the judge dubbing Kevin 'vulnerable, gullible and naïve'.[3] The judges sentencing those responsible for the murder of Rikki Judkins and the manslaughter of Raymond Atherton also called both men 'vulnerable'.[4]

I have investigated, in greater or lesser detail, around a hundred cases of disability hate crime. These range from nasty, low-level abuse and property-related attacks, right through to rape, torture and murder. A number of motivations and patterns can be identified. There are striking similarities in many of them. The motives are varied, but there are common threads that join many of them together.

Historical attitudes towards disabled people run deep and dark. Some disabled people have been treated as slaves, similarly to the way they were in classical times – Kevin Davies, Michael Gilbert and Steven Hoskin, to name just a few. Others, including Kevin and Brent, were singled out as scapegoats. As Brent's mother said, Brent was blamed for the misdeeds of others, from early schooldays onwards. A significant number of victims were identified as 'grasses' who should have known better than to talk to the police (among them Kevin Davies, Michael Gilbert and Barrie-John Horrell) and who were attacked to punish that 'crime'. All too often disabled people are seen as 'sinners'. Far too many have been called paedophiles or accused of other sexual assaults to give the perpetrators an excuse to subject them to overwhelming violence.

And then, of course, there is 'killing for kicks', where the murder of a disabled person is seen, as one prosecutor said, as a 'game show', a modern version of a classical, medieval or Victorian freak show. Brent Martin was beaten to death for a £5 bet and Michael Gilbert shot, beaten, stabbed and tortured in an ongoing 'game show'. Christine Lakinski was urinated on and filmed, suggesting that it was done for fun. In the Fiona Pilkington case, the family was also tormented, over years, because it was 'fun' and 'the best game in town'. (Disturbingly, urination appears in a number of high-profile cases, which suggests it is part of the denigration and ritual humiliation of disabled people, depriving them of their humanity before a vicious attack.)

There are newer prejudices too, which dovetail neatly with older attitudes, creating a toxic mix of hatred and jealousy. Disabled people are seen as undeserving 'scroungers', with unjustifiable benefits – they have become, in many people's eyes, what used to be known as the 'undeserving poor'. Because disabled people get slightly higher benefits than non-disabled people (to reflect their higher living costs), and often have what is perceived as superior, specialist housing and parking spaces, they often become targets for jealousy and exploitation. Craig Robins, for example, a wheelchair user from Birmingham, was left with a severe brain injury when he challenged a gang of youths he believed were responsible for repeated vandalism to his adapted car. I was flooded with similar stories when I wrote about his case in 2007 in *Disability Now*.[5]

Neighbours are often jealous of the 'privileges' that go with disability, punishing disabled people for them, creating disputes that police often term neighbour problems or antisocial behaviour but which are in fact incidents of targeted hostility. My colleague on the Disability Hate Crime Network, Anne Novis, has recently found that mobility scooters are often targeted by arsonists, who in one tragic case caused the death of an elderly couple unable to leave their house when their mobility scooters were set on fire.[6] All this targeted violence against adapted housing, car parking and equipment chimes with the findings of academics, who describe disability-related violence as a reflection of growing hostility to those who require such equipment so they can live an ordinary life.[7] Long-held beliefs, together with more recent prejudices, are part of what one American psychologist, Professor Dick Sobsey, calls the 'cultural exosystem, the cultural and social beliefs about disability – that has contributed to the differential treatment of people with disabilities, as well as patterned and predictable violence against those with disabilities for centuries'.[8]

So how do these cultural attitudes relate to what we know about hate crime offender theory generally? Barbara Perry, a professor of criminology and a leading American hate crime specialist, explains that certain groups are 'potential victims because of their subordinate status. They are already deemed inferior, deviant, and therefore deserving of whatever hostility and persecution comes their way. In sum, they are "damned if they do, and damned if they don't" . . . If they perform their identities on the basis of what is expected of them, they are vulnerable. If they perform in ways that challenge those expectations they are equally vulnerable.'[9]

Those who are seen to be demanding their rights are resented, she says, which can motivate a backlash: 'Increasingly, as those who have historically been advantaged relative to the poor and marginalized members of society continue to be pressured to relinquish power, wealth and control, intergroup resentment and bigotry is likely to continue. Although most people endorse principles of equality at an abstract level, challenges to the status quo are vehemently protested.'[10] Economic downturns, for example, are often linked to a surge in rates of hate crime. This explanation has led to what has been called 'scapegoat theory', where one group is picked out and blamed for financial problems in society generally.

The American psychologist Jeanine C. Cogan writes: 'The scapegoat is then held responsible for causing the current frustration and often becomes the target of violence. A notable example of such scapegoating occurred between 1882 and 1930, a time of great economic frustration. Statistics show that the lynching of black people in the US South was higher during this period, when very low cotton prices resulted in economic hardship.'[11] Cogan goes on to explore what happens in scapegoating: 'Scapegoating results in an "us" versus "them" distinction . . . this also leads people to exaggerate the differences between groups . . . Common stereotypes of lesbians and gay men, blacks and Jews have emerged within our US history. Each of these groups characterized as the outsider has been categorized as animalistic, hypersexual, overvisible, heretical and conspiratorial.' She concludes: 'Clearly, this is a fragile common thread that connects people from these various marginalized groups; each is easily targeted as a scapegoat.'[12]

Tragically, scapegoating of disabled people seems to be on the increase, mainly because many are blamed – by government, the media and society at large – for increasing benefit bills. Many of those who already dislike disabled people have found the perfect excuse for targeting them – they are benefit cheats and scroungers. This was seen most clearly when the Chancellor solicited ideas from the general population on 9 July 2010 about making welfare cuts. The public comments on the Treasury website spilled over into downright abuse and incitement to violence (which I discuss further in Chapter

18). There is a similarity between such attacks and the lynching of black people during the crisis in cotton prices. Disabled people are clearly being targeted, right now.

Other explanations for hate crime have been suggested by American academics. One is psychological, and is linked to pure hostility to the group in question. Another theory argues that people in small groups can infect each other with extreme attitudes and that a yearning for group acceptance can push someone to commit a hate crime.

Jack Levin and Jack McDevitt carried out ground-breaking research in the early 1990s into what motivates offenders. They suggested that hate crime offenders can be grouped into three major categories. Based on interviews with police officials, victims and several hate crime offenders, Levin and McDevitt identified three primary motivations: offenders who commit their crimes for the excitement or the thrill, offenders who view themselves as defending their turf, and a small group of offenders whose life's mission is to rid the world of groups they consider evil or inferior.[13]

They expanded their analysis later, because they felt that it was incomplete, looking in detail at what motivated offenders in 169 hate crime cases investigated by the Boston Police Department in 1991–2: 'The findings indicate that the most common type of hate crime was an attack committed for the thrill or excitement experienced by the offender. The youthful offenders often told police they were just bored and looking for some fun.' They also identified a further motivation, retaliatory attacks for supposed slights, but concluded that the underlying factor for all attacks was bigotry.[14]

These insights into hate crime, along with the historical attitudes we have examined, throw light on why disabled people are routinely targeted, for a variety of reasons, in different locations by different sorts of offenders. The thrill-seeking factor appears similar to the freak shows of the past. Antisocial behaviour and neighbourhood dispute start to look like a defence of territory, and retaliatory attacks might become more common if disabled people continue to be seen as scroungers, sponging off the state. The violent murders of Laura Milne and Michael Gilbert, among others, look much like 'mission hate' crimes, where the overwhelming desire of the perpetrators seems to be to eradicate the victim from the face of the earth, through violence.

And what of offenders themselves? Although no one has yet carried out an analysis of what motivates perpetrators of disability hate crime in particular, I have been able to analyse some of the cases and they exhibit interesting similarities – and differences – with what we know about hate crime offenders generally.

Home Office research on other forms of hate crime has found that offenders tend to be poor, white and male. Most homophobic offenders are aged between 16 and 20 and most race hate offenders are under 30.[15] This is confirmed by academic research. Hate crime offenders are 'ordinary members of the public. Often, those convicted of hate crimes are male, from deprived backgrounds and with a history of criminal or violent behaviour. They frequently act in groups when carrying out their offending, creating a dynamic that may exacerbate.'[16] Studies of perpetrators from abroad confirm these findings. A substantial German study into hate crime found that the perpetrators were mainly teenage boys with low academic achievement, that they committed their crimes in groups and felt justified by the general attitudes in the community.[17]

There is much discussion at the moment about whether, and to what extent, those who commit hate crimes know their victims. The Home Office says that that almost all hate crime perpetrators are either strangers or casual acquaintances of those they target. This chimes with most American academic work in this area. But British research is increasingly questioning that assumption. As Paul Iganski argues in *Hate Crime and the City*, the evidence suggests that disability targeted crimes are more similar to race crimes than had previously been thought. Iganski says that many crimes (both disability and race) are ones of ongoing harassment and are carried out by those known to their victims, contrary to previous research. (However, he too says that 'mate crime', the most intimate of hate crimes, is a completely different phenomenon.) Another influential study, taken from complaints of harassment recorded by the Metropolitan Police Service of homophobic and racist crime in 2005, found that the victim and assailant were strangers in less than a fifth of such incidents. (The author, Gail Mason, counsels caution in interpreting the results, saying that they know each other because they use similar locations, rather than anything necessarily more intimate.)[18]

So there may well be some level of acquaintance between perpetrator and victim in other hate crimes too. However, the most vicious homophobic and racist attacks – the ones that end in murder – tend to be stranger attacks. For instance, the murder of Stephen Lawrence in 1993 is thought to have been committed by strangers and Anthony Walker, who was murdered by two young men in 2005, did not know his attackers; nor did Mohammed Pervaiz, murdered in 2006, nor Lee Phipps, nor Kris Donald. In the first case in which Section 146 of the Criminal Justice Act was applied to a homophobic murder, two strangers were convicted of murdering a young gay man, Jody Dobrowski, in an unprovoked attack in 2005.[19]

Compare the perpetrators of these vicious murders with the equally vicious killers of disabled men and women, and you find a different pattern. In most of the killings I have investigated the victims were killed by so-called friends and only a tiny minority by strangers. And most were also killed by a group, rather than an individual – usually between two and four people were involved.

Kevin Davies was captured and tortured by friends before he died in their so-called care, as was Raymond Atherton. Barrie-John Horrell, Steven Hoskin, Steven Gale, Sean Miles and Albert Adams were all murdered by friends or neighbours, as was Keith Philpott. William Ripsher was murdered in July 2007 by acquaintances, as was Brent Martin. Steven Gale and Albert Adams were murdered by people who even described themselves as their 'carers'. Just two disabled men, Rikki Judkins and Colin Greenwood, died at the hands of strangers.

Chief Constable Steve Otter, who represents the Association of

Chief Police Officers on equality and diversity, sees 'some similarities with domestic abuse: it often happens in the home, it's done by people closest to you, or by those who befriend you, like boyfriends. Boyfriends, too, live off women, so there is quite a similarity there.' But he also says that there are many motivations for disability hate crimes: 'People have different motivations. Some crimes are committed out of pure ignorance, prejudice, name-calling, some of those who would name-call against a disabled person would also call a Muslim names. Then there are different motivations for somebody who is apt to go to some lengths to attack someone, using their disability as a route in. They don't even always have to befriend them, as in the case of the bus driver in Devon, who assaulted women who couldn't speak.'

Mike Smith, from the Equality Commission, agrees that the motivation seems to vary from crime to crime: 'Sometimes it can seem closer to domestic violence, and it can be more about power. There are different motives for different sorts of hate crime. Some of them are opportunistic and some are about the way society views disabled people. There are also power dynamics involved in dysfunctional social settings. You kind of imagine that there is more of this going on in very poor areas.' And, he adds, 'We are perceived as different, treated differently, in some way less deserving of equality, which is of course taken to an extreme with the murder cases. There you see that the person has stopped being a person, a human being, they are attacked for fun, in the same way that people torture your dogs.'

Women seem to be much more likely to commit disability hate crimes than any other form of hate crime. Disturbingly, they initiated the attacks in a significant number of the investigated crimes. Amanda Baggus, for instance, was instrumental in the decision to hold Kevin Davies hostage. It was her meticulously recorded entries in her diary about his torture that helped to convict the trio. In the case of Steven Hoskin, Sarah Bullock took part willingly in his torture and delivered the killing blow. And in the case of Laura Milne, Debbie Buchan claimed after the murder that she was the 'new and improved Laura Milne because the bitch is dead'. Leigh Mackinnon, an escort girl, also admitted being party to Laura's murder. In the Andrew Gardner case, his partner (and mother of his child), Clare Nicholls, tortured and starved him for months before murdering him. In the Steven Gale case two women, Lisa Smith and Claudette Green, were convicted of perverting the course of justice in a trial where Green's husband was convicted of starving, beating and murdering Mr Gale. In the Shao Wei He case, her husband, Lun Xi Tan, looked the other way as his pregnant mistress, Su Hua Liu, subjected the young woman to overwhelming violence and cruelty. In the Sean Miles case, Karen Fathers inspired the crime, by crying that he had molested her, and was a willing 'follower' of the instigator, Edward Doyle. (Another woman, Tracey Fathers, was charged but not convicted.) In the Keith Philpott case, a young woman, Gemma Swindon, befriended him before he was murdered by her brother. In the Albert Adams case, his self-styled carer, Jennifer Henry, stabbed him seventeen times and then hid his body from view for three weeks. In the Michael Gilbert case, two women, Natasha Oldfield and Nichola Roberts, were found guilty of his murder, and a third woman, Jennifer Smith-Dennis, convicted of familial homicide.

Most disability hate crime offenders are young, as are offenders in other hate crimes. Of the murders I have analysed in detail, the age ranges from just 15 to the mid-twenties for some of the most violent crimes. However, in some cases where there is a domestic violence element – Steven Gale, Michael Gilbert, Shao Wei He, Andrew Gardner and Jennifer Henry – some older people are involved (up to the mid-fifties). Only one murder I have examined here was committed by a single person. All the others acted together, some in larger groups (as many as six in the case of Michael Gilbert).

The perpetrators in all the cases except Shao Wei He's were either unemployed or engaged in light casual labour, often on the black market. Few had any sort of qualification. In a number of cases disabled people turned on other disabled people and attacked them. We need to know why we are seeing these patterns. All, except Shao Wei He's killer, were white.

In three significant cases (Raymond Atherton, Christine Lakinski and Brent Martin) the victim was urinated on either leading up to the death or at the point of death. Michael Gilbert was forced to drink his own urine. Perpetrators also urinated on Fiona Pilkington's property and garden, a behaviour that seems to mark disability hate crime, as noted in a report by the charity Mind. Steve Otter is much struck by this, as well as other common factors, in a number of cases put together by the Association of Chief Police Officers: 'What is fascinating, horrifying, is the nature of the crimes and how many of them involved urinating or burning, with hot knives and cigarettes. That is different from other crimes, it's even different from domestic abuse. You think back to the Nazis, when they were torturing the Jews, it's quite extraordinary. It seems to be about seeing the victims suffer: a large proportion of the more serious cases have this sort of torture element, urinating, burning, and certainly it's about not treating the person as human, not like yourself.' As Otter and others observe, the level of violence, which often turns into torture, is far higher than in many other forms of hate crime. It would be interesting to look at whether historical 'remedies' for disability and sin, such as ducking in water for witchcraft and branding for criminals, are reappearing in today's crimes, as are pernicious images of disabled people's sexuality.

My analysis, modest as it is, suggests that disability hate crime offenders are different in some aspects to other hate crime offenders and are more likely to act in groups. The motives may be similar in other forms of hate crime, but what is also clear is that the prejudices shown by perpetrators can often be found in the general society. The level of violence is higher and, unusually, women and even children are involved in many disability hate crimes (research shows that children and young people are overwhelmingly involved in antisocial behaviour around disabled people's homes, on the buses and on the streets). So why are so disability hate crimes missed, or categorised as something else?

One of the key reasons has to be that the victim is labelled as vulnerable. This labelling does not happen with other forms of hate crime. By failing to see the motivations for disability hate crime, the attitudes that underpin it, and by putting the responsibility onto the victim by describing him or her as 'vulnerable', we are letting those responsible for hate crimes continue to get away with it.

The assumption that every disabled person is vulnerable is similar to saying that a woman who is raped was 'asking for it' by being in the wrong place at the wrong time. We are all vulnerable at certain times in certain situations. By confusing vulnerability with targeted hostility towards the victim – we do not see the crime for what it is. As Sir Ken Macdonald conceded, when I interviewed him in 2007, 'the question of vulnerability clouds the issue' when prosecuting disability hate crimes, unlike other sorts of hate crime, such as racially motivated or homophobic violence. He also agreed that, because lesser crimes against a disabled person remain unreported and unchallenged, they often escalate to alarming levels of violence. As Sir Ken admitted: 'I think that prosecutors would do well to bear in mind the scenario you have suggested, that something can start off as one crime and continue as another.'[20]

Professor Alan Roulstone and others, in a recent paper ('Hate is a Strong Word: Unpicking UK Constructions of Disablist Crime'), have argued similarly: 'The motivation to commit a crime may well deliberately take the form of targeting disabled people for their vulnerability; whilst hatred cannot be discounted from such targeted abuse.' The authors go on to say: 'it seems concerning that vulnerability should weaken disabled people's right to legal redress, especially where institutional practices have helped cement notions of difference and where their categorical status is seen to weaken rather than strengthen such rights'.[21]

This is not to deny that vulnerability can awaken violence, hatred and contempt in some people. As Professor Barbara Perry, the leading American criminologist, suggests in an interview for this book, some hate crimes might be motivated by fear: 'This would be the fear that the perpetrator could just as easily become that person in the wheel-chair, or that person with a brain injury, and thus it presents as prey-ing on those perceived to be "vulnerable" rather than threatening, as in racial violence.' This analysis takes us back to classical times, where a disabled person might be feared and hated, powerful and powerless at the same time because their impairment was seen as 'contagious'.

The criminologist Professor Betsy Stanko, whose work on violence against women has revolutionised action on rape and domestic viol-ence in the Metropolitan Police, also has a useful perspective, writing: 'Violence is often targeted at vulnerability. Women – young or old – are still most at risk from known men. The youngest targets of hom-icide – babies under one year old – are most at risk from their carers. It is therefore important when dealing with the impact of violence to understand as best possible the context within which it takes place . . . We must continue to ask why the contexts of violence are invis-ible to social service[s] and other statutory agencies and demand that the context of violence is known as much as is possible. Recognis-ing inequality can assist in exploring long-term solutions rather than short-term responses which neglect structural or policy change.'[22]

Vulnerability (in a child, a woman or a disabled person, for exam-ple) provides an opportunity for an underlying (perhaps even uncon-scious) hatred to manifest itself. As the late disabled feminist Barbara Faye Waxman has persuasively argued: 'the contention that vulner-ability is the primary explanation for disability-related violence is too superficial. Hatred is the primary cause, and vulnerability only pro-vides an opportunity for offenders to express their hatred. Indeed, people who are respected and considered equal are not generally abused.'[23] It is hard to disagree with this analysis. We can surely ac-knowledge that if we are weaker physically, we are easier to attack. I might, for instance, hate a man, but I am unlikely to be able to harm him. A man, conversely, might be able to harm me. The same is true of children, and of some disabled people. There is nothing wrong in acknowledging this fact. It does not put the blame on us and it does not excuse the latent hostility in the act.

We know little about why some disability hate crimes look different from other hate crimes and why some of them are carried out by different sorts of perpetrators – friends and family rather than mythical stranger danger, women as well as men, children as well as adults, disabled as well as non-disabled people and, often, mobs that stand around and watch a gang attack, effectively condoning the crime. But we do know that perpetrator analysis can cut crime levels, identify risks and triggers for attack and, later, can address what is known as 'offending behaviour'.

The work done by Professor Betsy Stanko profiling rape offenders for the Metropolitan Police has revolutionised the way in which the force understands and investigates rape. It has also helped the Met understand domestic violence, cutting the homicide figures considerably because rapists, according to Stanko, often 'start at home'. We need perpetrator analysis like this for disability hate crime. Such research helps police to identify potential offenders and victims so that when the alarm is raised, patterns can be spotted quickly. If we don't detect the crime early enough, and stop it happening again, we will continue to fail the victims. As Stanko asks: 'How do you get the police to act differently with the information they already have?'[24]

Steve Otter, for his part, as the lead officer for the Association of Chief Police Officers on equality and diversity, agrees. A new, common risk-assessment tool, across all police forces, should shed light on victims, perpetrators and locations, he says. But now at last he wants to go further and commission perpetrator analysis. 'You realise how little the authorities still know about the motivation that leads people to do such horrible things to other human beings.' It is long overdue. It could save lives.

16

Locations

Professor Tom Shakespeare, a person of restricted growth, had long been sceptical of the concept of disability hate crime. But when he was attacked twice on public transport in the Newcastle area a couple of years ago, his thinking changed.

'I had always been stared at, photographed; drunken people would have a go at me,' he told me in an interview, but this was not something that he thought of as hate crime. 'Then I was on the metro system, coming back from Newcastle, and it was seven o'clock and a bunch of girls, 14 and 15, abused me, really, in a sustained and unpleasant manner. I was very upset, it was a mob thing, physically I was vulnerable, and I was worried I would be mugged. I ignored them; I asked them what school they went to. I told them, "I will write to your school, this is unacceptable." They were disinhibited, because they were high, or perhaps because they were in a mob. It was very unpleasant. Finally they got off the train before I did.' He wrote to the head teacher to complain, but he did not report the incident to the transport operator.

Soon afterwards, he was targeted again. 'There was another attack, in a car park near the metro, before I was a wheelchair user, and I parked in the car park, and I was going to my car. The car park was a hang-out for Neets [not in education, employment or training], and a number of them ran over to me. They were taking photographs, and competing to say more and more insulting things. Again it was horrible. I got into the car, shut the door and got out quickly. It was a mobbing scenario. They were preying on me, perhaps because they were bored. And I learned, as I asked around, that this is what happens to people with learning difficulties every day.'

He adds that his experience, as someone of restricted growth, is mirrored by others with the same impairment. 'What's interesting is when we researched why cars were so important to people of restricted growth, it was because they didn't have to use public transport because they didn't like it. We feel vulnerable, stared at. And after these events I did not go on the metro again, I avoided it. And every time I got on I sat next to people.'[1]

Tom Shakespeare is not alone in this humiliating and upsetting experience. When I started investigating disability hate crime, particularly when I was collecting cases for *Disability Now*'s Hate Crime Dossier in 2007, it was difficult to make sense of the data. It seemed as if disabled people were being attacked wherever they went. But the truth is far more nuanced. My analysis in this book suggests that disabled people are targeted in five key physical locations, and that where they are targeted depends, to some extent, on their impairment. The sixth location is a virtual one – disabled people are increasingly targeted on the Internet.

My friend Stephen Brookes, who coordinates the online forum, the Disability Hate Crime Network, walks with a stick and has a heart condition. In 2009, shortly after a heart operation, he boarded a bus for home. The seats for disabled people were occupied by two teenage girls. After realising that he needed to sit down, he asked them politely to make way. They stood up, and one said loudly, 'I'd better get up for a fucking cripple.' There were about twelve people on the bus. All of them took sides and the atmosphere became heated. The bus driver did not intervene. Steven got off the bus, before his stop. He said, looking back on it: 'It was total embarrassment to the point of demeaning me, the situation was so hostile that it was going to get to a point of physical violence if I didn't get off. But when we look at hostility on public transport as an issue, it's all about us apparently having special treatment. Of course we aren't, we are just being given access to the same transport as anybody else but this is not how it is seen.'

Ruth Bashall, a friend who advises numerous statutory agencies on disability and is a wheelchair user, has also experienced numerous incidents of disability targeted hostility on the buses, including one bus driver refusing to lower a ramp and another refusing to come in to the kerb so that she could get on the bus, saying that she shouldn't be out at that time of night (10 p.m. on a weekday, after working). Other people I have interviewed have given up on using public transport, such is the level of abuse that they experience.

These cases are only anecdotal evidence, but academic research also suggests that public transport (and attacks on people's private mobility equipment) is a hot spot for disability targeted violence. As one interviewee told the Equality Commission: 'Transport is a key area where abuse is experienced, compounded by a modern culture of not getting involved. This leads victims to believe that it is tolerated, possibly encouraged, by society.'[2]

People with learning difficulties are less likely to have driving licences, so in order not to be socially isolated they have to use public transport. But so bad is the abuse that many will not use buses, particularly when schools are coming out. This limits their potential working hours at a time when more are being forced out to work or else facing cuts to their benefits. Another point of conflict, say wheelchair users, is with parents with pushchairs, who are vying for the same space on buses.

This tolerance of abuse on public transport will only end if transport operators get involved. Unfortunately funding cuts mean that conductors are unlikely to be brought back on most buses, but CCTV, better training for drivers and the automatic ejection of those responsible for such abuse and, in the case of children, curtailment of their free bus passes, might go some way to help.

Will Bee, who serves on the Disabled Persons Transport Advisory Committee, has been investigating how disabled people report incidents on public transport and whether or not they are recorded. He cites a Department for Transport study, published in 2008, *Experiences and Perceptions of Antisocial Behaviour and Crime on Public Transport,* which found that: 'A quarter of respondents with a limiting health condition said that they would feel unsafe travelling on public transport. This compares with 12 per cent with a non-limiting health condition and 14 per cent with no health condition.'[3]

Bus, coach and train operators are mostly extremely lax about recording incidents on public transport, Bee observes. 'I was astonished how little evidence there was, given the level of background noise I hear from people who feel uncomfortable about using public transport, or even at the idea of using public transport. I couldn't nail down anything. I was surprised by the reaction of the industry. They were saying, effectively, this is not an issue and we don't want it to be an issue.' He argues that it is in the interests of transport companies to document incidents because if they don't, disabled people will continue to stay away from public transport in large numbers. But, he notes, as private companies they are not covered by the Disability Equality Duty, so they mostly don't record incidents. He thinks there is an argument for putting pressure on them to do so, perhaps by making it a condition of any subsidy they receive from the public purse.

Crimes on public transport are all but invisible in official statistics. Yet again, people are getting away with criminal and antisocial behaviour – in this case because both public bodies (such as Transport for London) and private companies providing transport (trains and buses outside London) are not taking their duties, moral or otherwise, to protect disabled citizens seriously enough.

So transport is one hot spot. But there are a number of others, which mean that far too many disabled people neither feel safe out on the streets nor, tragically, in or around their own homes. Research for hate crime locations by the Home Office demonstrates that much happens on the streets. Most hate crime offences occur near victims' homes (but, crucially, not in them), and between 3 p.m. and midnight.[4] But the research analyses race, homophobic and religious hot spots. Disability hate crime happens in a wider selection of locations (and, as I have said before, different kinds of people are responsible for it).

Those who attack disabled people on streets appear as perpetrators in other hate crimes too. They attack anyone who is different from them. The Equality and Human Rights Commission found that people with learning difficulties, especially, were attacked on the streets, mostly by children and young people, and that the attacks were both physical and verbal.[5]

Disabled people are also routinely attacked near or in their own homes, mostly by neighbours and acquaintances. This is often viewed by the police as antisocial behaviour or vandalism, but the targeted nature of the offence (damage to adapted cars or specialist equipment, arguments over disabled car-parking spaces) suggests that there is an element of hostility in many of them. They are often similar to targeted attacks on minority ethnic citizens and religious groups, but unlike those attacks, they are in the main not viewed as hate crimes. The motivation is often similar to race attacks. As a Home Office researcher, Rae Sibbit, argued in an analysis of racial violence in two London boroughs, resentment on housing estates of such groups was often 'fuelled by the (unsubstantiated) suspicion that these groups were "stealing" their jobs, housing and other resources'.[6]

The fact that disabled people are attacked inside or near their homes, and that the perpetrators are so rarely challenged, has a devastating effect on their lives. They live under siege – the most famous example, of course, being Fiona Pilkington. Far too often it is the victim who has to make changes to their life, including moving, rather than the offender. Mind, Mencap, the Disability Rights Commission and Capability Scotland have all documented the effects of ongoing harassment. Mind's report found that most people who were targeted didn't feel safe in their own homes. They were the targets of appalling campaigns of violence, including urination, graffiti, hate mail and even death threats.[7] Some were physically assaulted and most were called names, often by young people and neighbours.[8] The Equality Commission (EHRC) confirmed these trends in 2009, finding that disabled people (particularly those with learning difficulties and mental health conditions) were targeted in or near their own homes, by people they knew, at least by sight.[9]

Another form of disability hate crime, as I argued earlier, is intimate violence at home by friends, families and carers, which is rarely, if ever, recorded as such.

Additionally, institutional violence against disabled people is rampant, but is rarely viewed as a police matter because of an unpardonable lack of communication between local authorities, their safeguarding boards, police and other agencies dealing with 'vulnerable adults'. As the EHRC concluded: 'The wider evidence base suggests that "victimisation by caregivers and peers" [in institutions] may be more common in comparison to those who live in the community.'[10]

These five physical locations for violence – public transport, the streets, neighbourhood crime, crimes inside the home and in institutions – are joined by an emerging virtual one: harassment and bullying on the Internet.

When I was drawing up recommendations for *Getting Away with Murder*, I talked to police officers and politicians about whether the law on incitement – particularly relating to inciting hatred using the Internet – should be broadened to include crimes against disabled people. At that time I was unable to find evidence that the Internet was being used routinely to mock, taunt, bully or harass disabled children and adults or to incite others to similar acts or to physical violence.

This isn't true any more. Three years on, there is increasing evidence that the Internet (and, to a lesser extent, television) is being used as a very modern freak show where disabled people can be mocked, as well as being a place where disabled children are being bullied and disabled people harassed with virtual impunity. As in the past, when disabled men and women were exploited for the amusement of society, they are now being used as the unwilling stars of virtual reality shows, then transmitted to millions without any regulation. Disabled people who themselves use chat rooms,

Facebook and other social networks are often targeted for the amusement of others.

In November 2010 I came across a website, based in the US, on which anonymous users were encouraged to add to a so-called 'torture thread' about disabled people. The webmaster asked for 'stories how you maltreated, bullied or tortured your retarded friends, classmates, children'. Contributors came back with accounts of theft, assaults, putting faeces in milk for a schoolmate and throwing rocks at disabled people. Some contributors boasted of serially raping other classmates with learning difficulties. The police are now investigating this site, as well as another, which had encouraged attacks on deaf people.

In another case, Jane Williams,* a deaf woman who is confined to her house, has reported a two-year campaign of harassment conducted through a well-known social network. She was targeted by a fellow user. He had created a website in her name, captured her account details and started to spread rumours about her. These included naming her husband as a paedophile (a baseless accusation) on the Internet (complete with their address), mailing threatening letters to her doctor and sending her death threats. Tim McSharry, head of disability at the charity Access Committee for Leeds, which has supported her, says that although the man was convicted of harassment, he did not stop: 'The perpetrator then took action to report Jane to the DWP for fraudulently claiming benefits (of which she was completely cleared).'

In another example, the charity Index on Censorship expressed its alarm and horror when three executives for the Internet service provider Google were convicted in February 2010 of violation of privacy laws in Italy. The charity denounced the court's 'flagrant disregard for free expression'. The case had been brought by a disability charity, which claimed that Google was culpable for not gaining the consent of all parties in a video before it was uploaded to Google

---

* Not her real name.

Video. The video showed a young boy with autism being beaten, humiliated and insulted by a group of youths at school in Turin, Italy. The charity also claimed that Google had been slow to react when asked to remove the clip. The video was, briefly, rated as the funniest video on Google Italia, and was one of the most downloaded before it was removed.[11] In another recent UK case, a young man with Asperger's was bullied so badly, first at school, then on the Internet by the same people, that he hanged himself.

It is very difficult, though not impossible, to regulate Internet service providers.[12] Google, YouTube (also owned by Google), Facebook and other sites have, in the last two years, become major broadcasters and publishers, with unmoderated content being uploaded by the public every day – videos, audio, animations, and blogs. But they are almost completely unregulated, unlike terrestrial broadcasters and publishers. This lack of regulation allows broadcasts of attacks on disabled people without serious fear of prosecution.

Christine Lakinski, for instance, was filmed as she was urinated on and covered with shaving foam. The man who filmed it yelled: 'This is YouTube material!' He was arrested before the film could be uploaded. The phone has never been found. In another incident, in Melbourne, Australia, around the same time, a group of high-school students assaulted a disabled girl, urinated on her, set her hair on fire, sexually assaulted her and then posted their exploits on YouTube.[13] In another case, a group was created on Italian Facebook, suggesting that children with Down syndrome should be used for target practice.[14]

Online harassment is pernicious and can be long-lasting, and many police forces are still playing catch-up in their knowledge and training of how to tackle it. However, if the online evidence trail is preserved, it can be investigated and prosecuted. In the past it has been difficult to get Internet service providers and social networking sites to act when abuse is alleged. This is partly because many are based in America, and UK court orders have to be dealt with there, causing delay. But it is far from impossible, and the CPS has recently published new guidance on harassment, including cyber-stalking.[15]

And the Government is consulting on whether it needs to make it clearer that 'vulnerable' victims of cyber-harassment (and harassment generally) have the right to ask for reporting restrictions if a case comes to court.[16]

More academic research is on the way too. The Electronic Communication Harassment Observation study was commissioned by the charity Network for Surviving Stalking and will be carried out in partnership with the University of Bedfordshire. Project leader Dr Emma Short expects the research findings to change public attitudes towards cyber-stalking. As Dr Short says, people are operating in a world where there is little regulation. 'On-line – at the moment – anything goes.'[17]

Regulation is key. It's imperfect, but it helps, as the regulation of television shows clearly. In 2010, on Channel 4's *Big Brother's Big Mouth*, ex-footballer and actor Vinnie Jones mocked presenter Davina McCall, saying that she walked like a 'retard'. Channel 4 was initially unrepentant, claiming that participants had the right to freedom of expression 'without censure'. However, after numerous complaints by disabled people and charities, the broadcaster eventually apologised, admitted its initial stance was a mistake and cut the offending item from its recorded programme. Vinnie Jones also saw the error of his ways, with his spokesman saying: 'On behalf of Vinnie Jones I'd like to apologise for any offence caused by comments made on *Big Brother's Big Mouth* on January 29th 2010. While the show was live and the conversation was unscripted and off the cuff, Vinnie in no way meant to upset anyone and fully appreciates the choice of word was inappropriate.'[18]

The complaints also went to the broadcasting regulator, Ofcom. It ruled against the first complaint by Nicky Clark, a mother of two disabled children and a promoter of disabled talent on-screen. Ofcom said that although the matter was 'sensitive' the word was not aimed against people with a learning disability. But the matter didn't end there. Undeterred by the ruling, Louise Wallis, from a charity for people with learning difficulties, Respond, and a group of disabled people, demonstrated outside Ofcom's headquarters. Backed up with an energetic online campaign by Mencap, Ofcom eventually backtracked and ruled against Channel 4.[19]

One triumph, of course, doesn't change general attitudes. Indeed, just a few months later the so-called comedian Frankie Boyle devoted a large part of his show *Tramadol Nights*, also on Channel 4, to taking potshots at a number of disabled targets, including the disabled son of the model Katie Price, wheelchair users, and people with cancer and mental health conditions. Yet again Channel 4 has chosen not to apologise and yet again Ofcom is investigating.[20]

Reality and talent shows also have a questionable role to play in the way in which disabled people are treated and viewed. Susan Boyle, who was born with a mild learning difficulty and has said in a number of interviews that she was routinely targeted both at school and at home by young people, succeeded against the odds on *Britain's Got Talent*.[21] But the strain on her mental health was enormous, and she is reported to have had a nervous breakdown.[22] Another contestant, Alyn James, has talked since about his mental health problems and the effect of the show on his condition.[23] As the *Observer* concluded in the summer of 2010: 'The early rounds of *Britain's Got Talent* and *The X Factor* are a circus fairground where we're invited to laugh at the freaks and clowns.'[24]

The situation in the mainstream media is better, because of regulation. Broadcasters can be, and are, censured, both by the regulator and the mainstream media. But this is not so on the Internet. The new de facto broadcasters and publishers are hiding behind the 'right to free expression' when anyone challenges them about violent content on their sites. This is wrong. Most people now accept that real children get hurt in online pornography and that it is just as bad as pornographic films. Viewing online child pornography is a criminal offence, and rightly so. It is also an offence to incite violence against racial or religious groups online. The same should be true when disabled people are attacked to provide material for online freak shows.

Clearly online harassment and bullying is a new tool deployed by those committing hate crimes. It's an international problem, and will require an international focus. President Obama is concerned about it and in December 2010 he issued a Presidential Proclamation during US Stalking Awareness Month, saying: 'Increasingly, stalkers use modern technology to monitor and torment their victims, and one in four victims report some form of cyberstalking – such as threatening emails or instant messaging – as part of their harassment.'[25] The Internet needs to be seen as an important and growing location of disability hate crime, and treated as such by politicians, the media and the criminal justice system.

There are some geographical similarities between most of the crimes I have looked at, with many happening in rural towns or in cities, rather than deep in the country (with the exception of institutional violence). They happened in places where both antisocial behaviour and deprivation are present. So, for instance, the general area of St Austell, where Steven Hoskin was murdered, is full of owner-occupied houses, many of them relatively prosperous or at least comfortably off. But we are able to look even closer, using what are called the 'super output areas', which are a geographical measure of very small areas of equal size.

When we examine these statistics the cluster of housing where Steven Hoskin was killed, known as Restormel, emerges clearly as a pocket of poverty.[26] This is also true of the area in which Kevin Davies was tortured and died, despite the fact that Gloucestershire is one of the most affluent areas of the country.[27] A similar pattern emerges from a close analysis of Town End Farm, where Brent Martin was murdered,[28] and the area of Hartlepool where Christine Lakinski was attacked,[29] and it also holds true for the Mowmacre area of Leicester, where Steven Gale was murdered.[30]

During my research I have been very struck by the high number of extremely violent crimes against disabled people in the North East. In March 2005 Keith Philpott, a man with learning difficulties from High Grange, Teesside, was murdered by acquaintances who falsely accused him of being a paedophile. They disembowelled him and stabbed him to death.[31] Then came three crimes in quick succession. In early August 2007 in nearby Newcastle, two boys tortured a disabled 12-year-old over a weekend.[32] Just twenty-three days later and a few miles away, Brent Martin was tortured, lynched and murdered in Sunderland.[33] In the same month, just seventeen miles away, Christine Lakinski was urinated on whilst dying.[34] Three crimes within twenty miles of each other, within one month. In 2009, in Chilton, Teesside, very near to where Keith Philpott was murdered, around twenty-five miles from Sunderland and just seven miles from Hartlepool, Andrew Gardner was held captive, tortured, starved and murdered by his common-law wife and her brother.[35] Other crimes against disabled people in the area include a man in Middlesbrough being murdered by his half-brother,[36] and many cases of robberies with violence.

None of these crimes was recorded as a disability hate crime, and recording in the North East is very poor. In a piece of research funded by the Equality and Human Rights Commission in the North East across three counties, Cleveland, Sunderland and Northumbria, researchers from a local organisation of disabled people, VisionSense, found that whilst the region had a larger than average population of disabled people, the numbers of recorded disability hate crimes were very low. There was also a significant disparity in reporting between the three counties.[37] Race hate crime was most recorded, with disability hate crime a very distant second. Susie Balderston, the report's author, also points out that this ranking 'is not reflected proportionately in the number of successful prosecutions' – that, again, as in the CPS data nationally, disability hate crime is not as successfully prosecuted as other forms of hate crime. Despite the fact that there were far more disability hate crimes reported to police than homophobic crimes, less than 3 per cent of the former went to trial compared to 20 per cent of the latter. This attrition rate between reporting and prosecution is, Susie Balderston observes with some understatement, 'disappointing'.

The apparent crime pattern in the North East may be a result of good local papers with a track record in crime reporting (the North East Press group was very helpful in researching the Brent Martin murder, in particular). But it might well be an indication that some disability hate crimes are linked to poverty and deprivation. The poverty statistics for the area show that the North East is one of the two poorest regions in England.[38] And as the pressure on scant resources grows in poor areas, and the drive to find a scapegoat increases, we may be likely to see more such crimes, rather than fewer.

Understanding where disability hate crime is happening is crucial, as it will help us with what one criminologist, Marcus Felson, calls 'situational crime prevention'.[39] If we don't identify where crimes are happening, and who is doing what to whom, we will not be able to identify or prosecute them as hate crimes. And we won't know enough about why people are committing such crimes, or be able to divert them from committing more crimes in the future.

17

Leading the World?

On 28 October 2009 President Obama signed the Matthew Shepard and James Byrd Jr Hate Crimes Prevention Act.[1] This expanded existing US federal hate crime law to include crimes motivated by a victim's actual or perceived gender, sexual orientation or disability. Obama declared: 'No one in America should be forced to look over their shoulder because of who they are or because they live with a disability,' adding: 'We must stand against crimes that are meant not only to break bones, but to break spirits, not only to inflict harm, but to instil fear.'[2]

The Act was named after a gay teenager, Matthew Shepard, who was murdered by two teenagers who clubbed him with a gun and tortured him in 1998, and after a black father of three, James Byrd, who in the same year was tied to a pickup truck by two white men and dragged along until he died.[3] No disabled person was named specifically in the title of the law (although James Byrd had seizures and a physical impairment, the media has focused on his racial background).

America has seen its fair share of disability hate crimes, but until now they have been largely hidden because of the lack of federal laws to challenge them (just a few states had hate crime laws and they were mostly not used) and a lack of lobbying by disability groups to raise the profile of such crimes. Almost exactly a year before President Obama's speech, a young man with learning difficulties, Justin Hamilton, was lured from his home in South Dakota by a former classmate and others whom he considered to be his friends. On two consecutive nights they took him to a remote area and tortured him.

He was tied to a tree, beaten, burned with cigarettes, then tied to a motorbike and dragged for sixty metres. They threatened to set him on fire. He was left for dead on the second day. A county attorney filed charges against those responsible, including that of 'assault motivated by bias'. One attacker, John Maxwell Maniglia, got eight years for kidnapping and other charges – but not for disability hate crime. This attack did not make national news, as such an attack would have done in the UK, and no politician commented on it, as they have done here.[4]

The Hamilton case, and other cases in the US, support the argument that disability hate crimes, wherever they happen, look different from other forms of hate crime, are less likely to be reported, and are less likely to be investigated and convicted as such. And, as in the UK, women are also involved as perpetrators. In the Hamilton case, the instigator of the crime was reported to be Maniglia's girlfriend, Natasha Dahn, who initiated the crime by saying that Mr Hamilton had hit her (later admitting she had lied).[5] Moreover, as in the UK, it is often groups that attack victims – five in Mr Hamilton's case and as many as eleven in the case of Eric Krochmaluk, below.

In the first ever disability hate crime to come to court in the US (in a state jurisdiction, New Jersey), a gang of men and women invited Eric Krochmaluk, a man with learning difficulties, to a party and then tormented him for hours. They shaved him, whipped him and dragged him to the woods to be beaten. They were indicted for hate crimes.[6] But this case was highly unusual. Although the US Government makes much of its hate crime enforcement, until recently attention has focused on race, homophobic and religious hate.[7]

The issue can be confused if a victim of hate crime is targeted for more than one reason. James Byrd's impairment was rarely mentioned by the media (and, in fairness, it appears that he was targeted out of racial hatred).[8] In the case of Megan Williams, a young black disabled woman who in 2007 was allegedly kidnapped, raped and tortured by six so-called friends, men and women, the media and activists focused on her colour rather than her disability. Her disability only became an issue when Ms Williams recanted her statement. At that point the prosecutor said, somewhat negatively, that he had not relied on her testimony, because of her learning difficulty, but on confessions instead.[9]

As the criminologists Ryken Grattet and Valerie Jeness have pointed out in *Hate and Bias Crime: A Reader*, reporting of disability targeted crimes in the US lags behind that of other crimes and police training is very poor. They conclude: 'Disabilities provisions remain less embedded in hate crime law than do the race, religion, ethnicity, sex orientation and gender provisions.'[10] This is clearly borne out by hate crime statistics gathered by the Department of Justice and the Federal Bureau of Investigation. The figures for 2008 showed that 51.3 per cent were racially motivated, 19.5 per cent religiously, 16.7 per cent stemmed from sexual-orientation bias, 11.5 per cent from ethnicity/national origin bias and 1 per cent were motivated by disability bias.[11] In 2009 the disability percentage had increased slightly, but only to 1.5 per cent of the total (just ninety-seven offences in all).[12] Three-quarters of these offences related to victims with learning difficulties or mental health conditions and the rest to people with physical impairments.

Institutional abuse in the US is still rife, as it is in the UK. In 2009 it emerged that at least eighty-six cases of sexual violence had been investigated against older and disabled people in Chicago institutions, but only one of these had resulted in an arrest. The *Chicago Tribune* reported on the 'terror endured by elderly and disabled women in some city nursing facilities where predatory males stroll through common areas and unlocked bedrooms with little supervision'. Almost all of the eighty-six cases the *Tribune* examined involved residents attacking other residents. This is partly because the state of Illinois, incredibly, houses psychiatric patients, many with criminal records, with older and disobled people.[13] As in the UK, experts point to the hidden nature of such institutional abuse and note that it is difficult to secure a conviction where the victims have mental health conditions and age-related impairments such as dementia. And of course some die before being able to give evidence.

In another case, not treated as a hate crime, a group of men were treated as defacto slaves by a Texas labour broker, who for over forty years sent men with learning difficulties to 'labour camps'. At West Liberty Foods in Texas, the men were forced to live on-site in a bunkhouse, were paid less than the minimum wage, and money for food, fuel and lodging was deducted from their pay packets. (One employer justified this by saying that the 'boys' could not take care of themselves, in language reminiscent of that used about black people a hundred years earlier.) They were treated only a little better than slaves and, according to an Iowa senator, Tom Harkin, were routinely taunted, beaten and kicked.[14]

Professor Barbara Perry, the leading American hate crime expert, says that disability hate crime has been the least researched of the hate crime strands in the United States. The focus in North America, she notes, has been on race, sexual orientation and, more recently, Islamophobia. She argues that disability hate crime victims remain second-class citizens under hate crime law. She explains that while the crime is now recognised in federal law, 'it is not typically enforced or counted. There are several reasons for this. Like violence against women, I think that much of the violence against people with disabilities tends to be interpreted as "domestic" to the extent that it is perpetrated by "care-givers". Thus, it is considered of a different order, not encompassed by legal or intuitive understanding of what constitutes hate crime. There is also the broader problem of the justice system's inability to effectively serve the needs of people with disabilities generally.' And she adds: 'Evidence seems to suggest that few victims are willing to report their victimisation. Indeed, for those with developmental disabilities, they may be unaware of the significance of their victimisation.'

Disability groups have not campaigned strongly on this issue, Perry observes. Andy Imparato, who until winter 2010 headed the largest American pan-disability organisation, the American Association of People with Disabilities, acknowledges that this has been the case. But, he says, that is now changing because of the new federal law: 'Although much of the hate crime debate in the United States has been driven by high-profile cases involving race and sexual orientation, there is an increasing recognition that children and adults with disabilities get targeted for abuse and assault in part because of their disability status, and that many of these crimes go unreported. We view the new federal hate crimes law in the US as an important tool to combat these kinds of crimes.' Mr Imparato is now advising the influential US Senate Health, Education, Labor and Pensions Committee on disability issues, taking hate crime and other issues such as employment to the heart of the American administration. And, he points out, progress has been relatively fast. The Department of Justice has issued an indictment against three men accused of targeting a man with learning difficulties of Navajo descent in New Mexico. The indictment alleges that they 'branded the victim by heating a wire hanger on a stove and burning the victim's flesh, causing a permanent swastika-shaped scar on his arm. It is alleged that as part of the plan and purpose of their conspiracy, the defendants further defaced the victim's body with white supremacist and anti-Native American symbols, including shaving a swastika in the back of the victim's head and using marker to write the words "KKK" and "White Power" within the lines of the swastika. The indictment also alleges that the defendants took advantage of the victim's developmental disability to induce him to make a cell phone video in which he purportedly consents to the branding.'[15]

If America is at last prosecuting such crimes, change elsewhere is slow. Indeed the US, UK and Germany are among the few countries in the Organisation for Security and Cooperation in Europe (OSCE) (which includes the US and Canada as member states) that record disability hate crimes. Because OSCE member states collect data in different ways, it is difficult to compare the incidence of disability hate crime internationally. In 2008, ten countries indicated that they recorded such crimes, but only the UK and Germany had identified any. The UK had recorded 800 cases and Germany 47. (The US collected data but was unable to return it in time to be included in the report.)[16] A year later (the last for which figures are available), the countries tracking such crimes had increased to eleven and the UK, again, recorded by far the most. It reported 1,476 cases as being recorded by the police. Germany reported just twenty-six and Belgium just one. (The US, again, failed to return data in time to be included in the report.)[17] This does not mean that people in the UK commit more hate crimes. It means that police and prosecutors have been put under more pressure, to which they have responded, to record and prosecute possible hate crimes, rather than ignore the disability aspect completely.

Such myopia was clearly evident in a case in France where a bus driver, Emile Louis, eventually pleaded guilty and was jailed for life in 2004, for murdering seven young women with learning difficulties in the 1970s. The original investigation was bungled and the police have been accused of covering up evidence. Indeed, in March 2002, the Government punished three magistrates for failing in their duties by allowing Louis to avoid prosecution for more than twenty years. Many of the victims had severe learning difficulties, yet the local authorities had recorded them as runaways, despite the fact that many of them could not live independently. The French police had appeared to show little interest. Only one local *gendarme* pursued evidence against Louis. But the gendarme was found dead in mysterious circumstances, inquiries were halted and a damning report was lost until 1996.[18]

In Australia too, where there are state but no national disability hate crime laws, there has been a series of horrific crimes.[19] In a recent case, a young Canadian wheelchair user, Heath Proden, was attacked whilst on holiday in Sydney. He was set upon as he left a concert by two teenagers, punched, hauled out of his wheelchair and beaten with iron bars.[20] In another recent case, a young man with learning difficulties was abducted, punched and raped in Rosedale, in the Latrobe Valley.[21]

The UK is leading the world in identifying, prosecuting and challenging all forms of hate crime, including disability-related ones. The 1,400 or so crimes reported in 2009 throughout England, Wales and Northern Ireland (Scotland has just started collecting figures and reporting remains almost non-existent) represent a 75 per cent rise in recorded cases in just one year.[22] Chief Constable Steve Otter welcomes the rise: 'Recording is going up sharply. That mirrors our experience with race and gay crimes, that more police officers are aware of the problem and are asking the right questions. Before, we would have missed the fact it was a hate crime. You can expect to keep seeing an upsurge in numbers.'

The Stop Hate UK information and action line,[23] a national charity that works with the police to increase reporting of hate crime, is taking an increasing number of calls on disability hate crime – from just a handful two years ago to 187 in 2009–10 – outstripping in numbers all but race calls.[24] Its chief executive, Rose Simkins, says that the calls come from people with a range of impairments, and that most complain about verbal attacks. But many are also reporting being called 'paedophiles' and others report being exploited.

Similarly, we have also seen a sustained and encouraging change in prosecutions. Prosecutions for disability hate crimes more than doubled in a year, to 393 prosecutions in 2008–9.[25] The numbers nearly doubled again in 2009–10, with 638 prosecutions. This all looks good. A closer scrutiny of the figures is less encouraging. The conviction rate for racist and religious crimes is 82 per cent, and 80 per cent for homophobic crimes. The conviction rate for disability hate crimes is significantly lower, at 75 per cent, and has actually fallen slightly for two years in a row. These crimes also only represent less than 5 per cent of the total number of hate crimes.[26] The refusal by the CPS of my request to see prosecutor statements and charging decisions for key cases in this book is also disappointing. I have appealed to the Information Commissioner's office.

Dale Simon, Director of Diversity and Equality for the Crown Prosecution Service, readily admits that there is room for improvement, although she points to areas where progress has been made. Almost all regional hate crime scrutiny panels (which analyse whether cases have been prosecuted correctly) now have disabled members. Training on disability for prosecutors is much better, but the CPS is still missing – and dropping – key cases. In January 2009 the CPS was found by the High Court to be in breach of the Human Rights Act after deciding not to pursue the case of a man whose ear was bitten off, in front of witnesses, on the ground that he had a mental health condition. The case was dropped on the morning of the trial, with the CPS claiming that the witness could not give credible evidence because of his impairment.[27]

The problem now, Dale Simon maintains, is to raise awareness in society at large: 'My view is that you don't simply raise awareness by implementing laws. Before you get to that, something happens that raises awareness. With race crime we had the murder of Stephen Lawrence and the Macpherson Report. But in terms of disability there hasn't been that catalyst, that event that changes everything.' She adds: 'We are prosecutors, we are dependent on victims and witnesses coming forward, we are relying on cases being identified as possible hate crimes by the police and the courts sentencing appropriately.' So perhaps it is now the judiciary that needs to be questioned on why so many offenders are getting light sentences. As Dale Simon notes: 'The evidence suggests that we are getting cases to court. Sentencing is a different debate, that's not in our control.'

I know from my own experience that the scrutiny panels are holding prosecutors to account, and that some regions of the CPS are analysing and re-analysing to see if they are missing disability hate crimes. In the London area, for instance, the CPS is scrutinising every single crime involving a disabled person (around twenty every week), to see if a hate crime motivation has been missed. The CPS is also using the online forum on Facebook, the Disability Hate Crime Network (of which I am an active member), which publishes cases on a daily basis from around the country, to see if local prosecutors are missing a hate crime element.

Another welcome development is the Equality Commission's decision to launch a formal inquiry into disability-targeted harassment, because we still understand far too little about the issue – in terms of prevalence, perpetrators, victims, locations and solutions.[28]

Recent studies suggest that disability hate crime remains a serious problem, however. One recent study in Lancashire, by the Crown Prosecution Service, the county council and the police, points this out starkly, with nearly half of the respondents saying they had been the victim of a crime or incident because of their disability. Some were being attacked more than once a week, and 10 per cent of those polled had even moved home to avoid the harassment.[29]

Anne Novis, from the Disability Hate Crime Network, collected media articles relating to disability violence and analysed them on a monthly basis in 2010.[30] In the first sixth months of the year she identified 317 attacks (and 23 killings, although she included assisted suicide). These included attempted murder, torture, rape and abuse in care homes, as well as grooming and six online threats. In the previous year she identified fifteen murders and ninety-six attacks, with the same pattern as 2010, but also including damage to mobility equipment and arson and with the same disproportion of people with learning difficulties to physical impairments. She found roughly the same number for 2008 (fourteen killings and seventy-six attacks, again with the same proportion of physical disabilities to learning disabilities).[31]

These pieces of research, however, do not provide a clear picture of disability hate crime because they are not comparing like with like. As the EHRC said in its 2009 report, the methodologies of data collection are not robust, there is limited systematic reporting and a preponderance of anecdotal and small-scale, non-representative evidence.

Moreover, disabled people remain largely unimpressed by the criminal justice system and have little confidence in it. If we analyse the British Crime Survey over three years, the picture is clear. Disabled people don't have as much confidence in the police as non-disabled people, they fear crime more, and worry disproportionately about antisocial behaviour.[32] There is clearly a long way to go before disabled people will believe that they are getting a fair and just deal from a system that is pledged to protect all equally.

We cannot be complacent about the increase in reported cases. Disabled people are clearly the focus of horrendous crimes. But we can be proud that the police, prosecutors and the media in the UK are likely to ask themselves 'Is this a hate crime?' when they come across an attack against a disabled person. This is not yet the case in many other countries. The hard work by many charities, disabled people's organisations and individual activists is paying off. This is at least some cause for celebration.

18

Not Them But Us: Society's Challenge

On a wet and windy winter's evening in 2010 I travelled north of London to give a talk on disability at a hate crime forum. There was another speaker there, a young man called Michael.* Michael, like other people with learning difficulties, had been encouraged to come off benefits and go back to work in a large supermarket, one of the biggest chains in the country. He was, like many disabled people, put to work on collecting trolleys. His place of work was in a parade of shops, and bored local youths gather there. On one occasion, the youths identified a man with Down syndrome who was shopping, and targeted him, verbally abusing him. Nobody stepped in – except Michael. Then the gang turned on him. Over the next few months the gang verbally abused him, kicked him, punched him and burned him with cigarettes.

He, of course, told his employer. The store manager was having none of it, telling him: 'You're a grown man. Deal with it.' He complained to the job centre. They told the store to have someone accompany him at work. After a few days the store stopped doing it. He reported it to the police, who referred him back to the store. By now Michael wasn't sleeping at night and was very anxious. Eventually he quit his job. He is now unemployed.

No one – shoppers, his employer, the job centre or the police – took responsibility for what happened to Michael. This may be because their attitudes towards him were not much better than those of the perpetrators. Understanding the negative attitudes of many in

---

* Not his real name.

society towards disabled people is critical. Without confronting those attitudes, and discrimination against disabled people, we will never be able to challenge those who attack them.

A poll in June 2010 by the leading social care organisation Turning Point of over 1,000 members of the public found that nearly a quarter of those polled believed that disabled people should live in institutions, and nearly one in ten that they should be cared for out of town, in a secure hospital. One-third of those surveyed believed that disabled people could not live independently or undertake employment. The general stereotype of a person with a learning difficulty, held by those polled, was of someone with poor social skills, who is likely to be aggressive and have slurred speech.[1]

Mark Dale, a research scientist, reviewing existing evidence on this subject in 2006, as well as carrying out his own polling for the disability charity Enham, concluded that: 'Attitudes toward disabled people are predominantly negative.'[2] His own research, with both disabled and non-disabled people, found that both groups held broadly similar attitudes towards impairment groups and that people with learning difficulties and schizophrenia were the least tolerated. And he found that disabled people themselves held similar views, also having most prejudice against those groups. The attitudes of the general population towards disabled people, and certain impairment groups in particular, mirror to some extent those of the perpetrators of disability hate crime.

Discrimination starts before birth for a disabled person, and continues right up to the point of death. Expectant mothers are offered an increasing array of pre-natal testing and if there is the possibility of giving birth to a disabled child they are offered, quite rightly, counselling and advice on which steps to take. As a feminist, I do believe in the right to choice whether or not to continue with any pregnancy, but this does not take place in a framework of neutrality towards disability. I can see the point of view of many disabled people who argue that unconscious attitudes towards disability create difficulty for those who continue with a pregnancy of a disabled baby – not only for the parents, who are seen by some as bringing an expensive 'burden' into the world, but for the child itself later, when he or she realises that many believe he or she should not have been born, as the leading British psychotherapist, Valerie Sinason, has written eloquently.[3]

The legacy of eugenics, here in the UK, in the US and in Germany, hangs over public discourse and influences it, albeit unconsciously. Hitler ordered the murder of disabled people, who he believed were 'useless eaters' and 'life unworthy of life'. Many people make a similar judgement today about the lives of disabled people. The journalist and cultural commentator Virginia Ironside said in 2010 that it could be 'merciful' to kill disabled children.[4] The conscious or unconscious assumption that a disabled life is not worth living inevitably affects disabled people's self-esteem. Some people, particularly those with learning difficulties, internalise that prejudice – and expect to be treated without respect, and even to be abused. It is no surprise then that they don't bother reporting their everyday experiences of abuse.

Many parents, Valerie Sinason has observed, experience something akin to grief for the 'perfect child' who was expected, when they have a disabled child. As a result, recent studies of the effects on attachment of an early diagnosis of learning disability suggest that attachment is more likely to be insecure.[5] This can be particularly tragic when parents reject a disabled child, and have the child adopted.[6] But it can go further still, when parents decide to murder their own children. The case of Naomi Hill is one of the saddest I have covered, and shows just how parents of disabled children can internalise society's hostility to their offspring, with murderous results.[7]

Joanne Hill killed her 4-year-old daughter Naomi, who had cerebral palsy, by drowning her in a bubble bath, in November 2007. Witnesses testified in court that she was ashamed of her daughter's impairment, and wanted to have her adopted. Michael Chambers, the prosecutor, said: 'Witnesses will describe how Hill, an advertising saleswoman, was "embarrassed" by her daughter, who wore callipers and had hearing difficulties, and was irritated by some of the effects of her medication.'[8]

DCI Simon Price, who was the senior investigating officer on the case, interviewed Joanne Hill. Tragically, he says, she was the only one in her family who felt so negative towards Naomi. 'Naomi's father was devastated, he doted on her, and her family were devastated, the head teacher was too. She had friends. The only person who saw it differently was her mum. She was the only person from whose perspective it would be a mercy killing. There was nothing to be merciful about. I have no doubt in my mind that Naomi would have made a serious contribution to society. It's such a tragedy.'

There are other problems of perception, particularly around the time when disabled people become sexual beings. Several pernicious myths have sprung up around disabled people's sexual appetites, which feed into attacks where disabled men are described as paedophiles and disabled women routinely sexually abused. Nor are disabled people seen as credible sexual partners by many – the stigma is too powerful.

Conversely, in some sections of our multicultural society marriage and children are seen as a 'normalising' procedure by which a disabled person can be brought back into the mainstream of their culture. In a number of African, Middle Eastern and Asian cultures disability is still largely seen as a stigma. Two major problems are being uncovered because of this: an explosion in so-called 'healing', and the growth of forced marriage.

Another belief has also gained traction in certain communities – that disabled children are witches or cursed and possessed by evil spirits. Some children are attacked by church leaders trying to cast out demons, particularly in African communities. In Asian communities, a parallel practice has developed, in which unscrupulous quacks have set up as 'healers', promising to remove the stigma of disability both from the person and the family. Mandy Sanghera, an Asian community activist who has uncovered the extent of this practice in the Sikh, Muslim and Hindu communities, says that it is a major, heartbreaking and expensive problem. 'I've been to temples and other places of worship and discovered just how big a problem this is. I talk to families, telling them that however much you pray, your child will still have a learning disability or be without a limb. I tell them that they have to promote their child's independence instead, but their faith is often so powerful that it overrides common sense.'

As the *Eastern Eye*, a leading newspaper for the Asian community in Britain, reported in July 2010, some healers are carrying out spells using black magic, or beating children to rid them of evil spirits. One young man with learning disabilities, Jiaz, told the newspaper: 'My family sent me to an expert in black magic in Birmingham. He did like an exorcism where he pressed his hands on my face and chest to try and cure me. He was doing religious chants and gave me religious verses to keep in contact with my body. It did not work, and my family were devastated.'[9]

Many families, observed Mandy Sanghera, even when they have been robbed of several hundred pounds, don't want to report it because of pressure from the community not to be shamed in public: 'It's very widespread. In temples, they will charge you up to £300 to talk to you, then another prayer for £300. Muslims will do it with sheikhs. They say to people, "You've got a disabled son because one of your neighbours has put a spell on you." They don't understand about the genetic factors. They put it down to stigma or bad karma.'

Forced marriage is also having a devastating effect on a growing number of disabled men and women. Here in Britain the Government's Forced Marriage Unit (FMU) deals with around four hundred cases a year, although there are thought to be far more unreported ones. Evidence that I assembled in 2008, when I was working at *Disability Now* magazine, suggests that a significant number of those marriages involve disabled people. Victims of forced marriage are often subjected to violence by family members to make them marry. Some are kidnapped if they resist. Many are either sexually assaulted, or even raped, once married. A number of forced marriages have ended in murder. Most cases involve people from the Indian subcontinent but others have involved Eastern European, Middle Eastern and African victims. Most of the victims are young, and a growing number are thought to be disabled. A spokeswoman for the FMU acknowledges that it has 'handled many cases involving men and women with mental health needs or learning disabilities'.

Saghir Alam, a lawyer and member of the disability committee at the Equality and Human Rights Commission, is concerned about the rising number of such cases. As parents age, he says, they fear leaving their disabled children behind to fend for themselves. Many are isolated and know little about the model of independent living championed by the wider disability movement, so they try and find another solution through forced marriage. 'It is a caring decision, but by the wrong means . . . they are trying to get the best for their children, but when I look at the decisions they have made I am quite shocked.' Mandy Sanghera agrees: 'Asian people with learning difficulties are being abused by family, friends and the community.' And the problem is on the increase, because funding is getting tighter, and young people are losing the support they need during their transition between children's and adult services. Social services, she says, tend to turn a blind eye to forced marriage because it relieves pressure on their stretched budgets.

A number of Members of Parliament have raised this issue over the last few years, as have the learning disability charities Voice UK, the Ann Craft Trust and Respond, which consider it a 'serious, but largely hidden problem'. Voice UK identifies another trend, in which people with learning difficulties are 'forced into marriage as a means of assisting a claim for residency or citizenship and the people with learning disabilities may then be divorced after such a claim is successful'. The Director of UK Visas, Mark Sedwill, confirmed this trend when he gave evidence to the Home Affairs Select Committee in March 2008.[10] He said that 452 visas for Pakistani applicants were refused in 2007 on the ground of family abuse, most because of fears of forced marriage. Nearly a quarter of the cases involved vulnerable adults, including people who were 'severely disabled'. In a study of people with learning difficulties in Tower Hamlets who were either married, parents or pregnant, the authors found that all of the Bangladeshi women were married (compared to less than half of those from other groups). This indicates the scale of the problem, given that the authors noted that it was questionable whether the women would have been able to give consent to marriage, given their disability.[11] The government, along with the charity Respond, has now developed practice guidelines for social workers working with young people and vulnerable adults facing forced marriage, as well as an easy-to-read leaflet for those who might experience forced marriage.[12]

The world can be a very hostile place for families with a disabled member. Parents of disabled children often say that they are either avoided or even attacked for bringing them into the world. The writer Ian Birrell recently described people turning away from them in the park.[13] As Valerie Sinason puts it, many people either look through, or stare at, disabled people, even disabled children: 'sometimes the curiosity is excited and voyeuristic, like the curiosity that can accompany a disaster. The sight of damage, of something gone wrong, induces an excited disturbance in such onlookers. Sometimes there is a turning away, a fear and a hostility, a sometimes spoken wish that such sights should be hidden from public view; there is a fear of catching the damage, or having to recognise that such an event is possible.' She continues: 'At the root there is unresolved anger and fear in some societies that the sexual and procreative connection between a man and a woman could lead to a damaged offspring . . . the mentally handicapped carry, stamped on their features, the mark of what is feared bad sexuality.'[14]

But it is often worse than that. Disabled people who have children are often attacked for their chutzpah, daring to pass on their 'genetic impairment' to the next generation (a clear throwback to eugenics). One prominent disability rights campaigner, who is married to a wheelchair user with whom he has a son, at that time just a toddler, still remembers the time he was accosted by two well-spoken women in Marks & Spencer. They were castigated for marrying, and were told that they should have had a dog instead of a child. In 2006 the Social Care Institute for Excellence reviewed existing research and found that social workers and local authorities were less interested in supporting families with disabled members to stay together than in 'safeguarding children'.[15] Disabled parents are constantly put on their guard about their parenting capacity, rather than being supported to be good parents.[16] Indeed many disabled parents (particularly those with learning difficulties) who have children lose them to social services, even as soon as they are born, before being given an opportunity to prove themselves.[17]

There is also the vexed question of disability benefits, much debated under successive governments, but never more so than now. Language about benefit 'scroungers' is bandied about by politicians and tabloid journalists. As the minister Iain Duncan Smith says, eagerly, work is 'good' for you.[18] And so it is, in most circumstances, but it should not define our humanity. Not all disabled people can hold down a full-time job, but that does not mean that they do not contribute to society in other ways. As Sir Bert Massie, the former head of the Disability Rights Commission, observes: 'I think there is a strong argument to be made that there is an obligation to support those who need support and that should be unconditional; you can do what you want to the scroungers, but by and large, there are some people who cannot work, it is fanciful that everyone can work – you support them and you do it with magnanimity, this should be a right.'

Sophie Corlett from Mind says that many people on their advice lines are talking about changed attitudes towards them since the Government launched its crackdown. One person with a mental health condition told the charity: 'Tabloids . . . are actively . . . encouraging people to shop the apparent easy-to-spot cheats directly to the paper. With mental illness, it is not that easy and this targeting feels unacceptable. I fear this will increase hate crime and further alienate those with mental illness who are on benefits.' Another said, movingly, that life was now barely tolerable and added that they felt like an 'object of hate and derision with no escape. I worked for as long as my body could stand it and I do not need someone with no comprehension of my daily life, telling me that I am a "scrounger" and languishing on benefits', adding that many with hidden disabilities now find themselves 'the victims of an orchestrated hate campaign and what I can only describe as institutional bullying'. As Mind's submission to the EHRC inquiry puts it: 'People with mental health problems already face disproportionate levels of crime and discrimination and now appear to be the scapegoats for the Government's welfare reform programme.'

When the Treasury website invited comments from the general public on how to reduce welfare spending, the comments about disabled people (which were not moderated) were vicious. One argued that all disabled people should be sterilised. Another said: 'depression is not a disability, neither is stupidity'. Many suggested that disabled people got too many perks and were particularly exercised about disabled car-parking spaces.[19] Another suggested that disabled people should be used as weapons of war: 'Those who can work that upon rigorous medical examination turn out to be just thick or bone idle to undertake intesnive [sic] course in employability, where they will learn to be punctual, meticulous, smartly dressed, articulate, and gain working attitude. Those who repeatedly fail the course to be deployed in Afghanistan as IED deterrents.'

After repeated requests, the website was closed down and the comments removed, but they shed light on attitudes among many in society.[20] Disabled people are not seen as equal citizens. They are seen as a useless burden. Small wonder, then, that so many of them are attacked – the perpetrators are merely acting out the unconscious wishes and desires of many in society.[21]

The arguments about disabled people and their place in society pursue them right to the point of death. Many disabled people complain that they are put under pressure to end their lives, and fear that pressure to legalise assisted suicide is only going to make things worse. Many conflate assisted suicide with euthanasia, which reminds them of what happened to disabled people during the Holocaust.

New Crown Prosecution Service guidelines on those who assist people wishing to commit suicide were issued in February 2010, after Debbie Purdy, who has multiple sclerosis, asked the courts to clarify whether her husband would be prosecuted if the couple travelled to Dignitas, a clinic in Switzerland, to end her life. The DPP has stressed that the guidelines do not decriminalise assisted dying, that no case would be guaranteed immunity from prosecution, and that it did not 'open the door to euthanasia'.[22] But the pressure for legalisation has continued. Indeed, a Commission on Assisted Dying has just been established, with campaigners against it warning that it might be biased in favour of euthanasia.[23] And the campaigning group Dignity in Dying is vocal and well organised.

Jane Campbell, a disabled peer who chairs the group Not Dead Yet UK, an organisation which campaigns against legalisation, doesn't think we are ready for it. She argues that disabled people and those with terminal illness are not seen as equal members of society, but rather as a 'burden' that costs the NHS scarce resources. A professor of palliative medicine and a fellow peer, Ilora Finlay, agrees. She argues that better care at the end of life, including advances in pain relief, could and should allow more people to die naturally.

In another recent case, the General Medical Council, the body that regulates doctors, has struck Dr Howard Martin off the medical register after he admitted that he had hastened the death of a number of older and disabled patients by injecting them with morphine. Mr Martin has said that he did not always seek the consent of patients or families before doing so. The case may be reopened by police.[24] Such cases appear to add weight to the argument that disabled people feel that their right to life is constantly being questioned.

From the moment they are born, as the psychotherapist Valerie Sinason has eloquently argued, disabled people are told that their lives are not worth living – they face what she calls an 'internal and external death wish'.[25] If they want to have sex, marry or have children, their decisions are seen as controversial, and their children are more likely to be taken away from them than from non-disabled families. Then they are told that they should not have benefits wasted on them. That they should go into a home, or if they can't work have their benefits cut. If they can work they should also have their benefits cut, as they clearly don't require extra support. As they get older, they are told that they are a burden on society and should die for the sake of others. If we do not take seriously these widely held views, which are part of the mood of our times in which hate crime has flourished in our society, we are never going to be able to understand it and we won't be able to find solutions.

19

Ways Forward

Hugh Gallagher, a disabled American academic, writes about the land of the 'crippled'. 'The usual rights and privileges of citizenship do not apply here . . . a great wall surrounds this place, and most of what goes on within the wall is unknown to those outside it. What follows is a message from over the wall.'[1] We have to read that message from over the wall, and take the wall down, brick by brick.

For Mike Smith at the Equality and Human Rights Commission, it will require 'something fundamental, a paradigm shift in the way that disabled people are viewed in society. Most people have a discomfort talking about disability. As a disabled person you are still perceived as different, treated differently and in some way seen as less deserving of equality.' This doesn't mean, however, that he is totally pessimistic: 'I'm very optimistic, but it will require an inter-agency approach, a re-think on vulnerable adults, more of a focus on changing environments before something happens, rather than sorting things out afterwards, as well as addressing my reservation that the criminal justice system is designed to be effective if the worst does happen.'

David Grundy, of Action for Real Change, also sees it as being about a 'huge cultural shift', similar to the move against racism in the 1970s: 'We won't be fighting on the streets, but it's just as challenging. We need disabled people to live alongside non-disabled people, not to be segregated. That means shopping at the same times, swimming at the same times, working in the same places. That just isn't happening at the moment. By early afternoon most people with learning difficulties will be tucked up at home, curtains drawn, hoping they won't be targeted.'

The time to change, everyone agrees, is now. And change will have to happen everywhere – in schools, hospitals, workplaces, on the streets, in people's minds. Disabled people are human beings like any others, not a race set apart. What I have taken from my conversations with so many of those bereaved by this crime is simply that those who were targeted, and died, are missed as friends and relatives. Angela Shotton misses Christine Lakinski, who came to see her nearly every day, and has 'nobody to knock about with now' at the bingo. Christmas isn't the same without her. Ann Jones has lost the friend, Fiona Pilkington, who lived opposite, who took in parcels for her, drove her to the doctor and was there for her when her son died abroad. In a world where so many turn aside from disabled people, some decent, ordinary people didn't. But that simple act is harder than you think. Go to a pub with disabled friends or travel on the Tube with a visibly impaired friend and you watch the world watching you, avidly at times, sucking in the spectacle and then turning away. The ordinary, decent people who befriended Fiona Pilkington and Christine Lakinski simply gave the gift of friendship, and it was reciprocated, as friendship is. Everyone gained, and we could all learn a lot from them. Befriending projects, such as the one run by Disability Action Waltham Forest, where disabled and non-disabled people socialise together and support each other, are crucial in this. The Outsiders Club, which offers dating opportunities, friendship and peer support to disabled people, is also a wonderful resource. We need more initiatives like this.

This emphasis on friendship and mutual support resonates with many in the disability movement, as they refine their ideas about independent living – and how it has meant isolation for some. Jane Campbell, who pioneered independent living in the UK, puts it thus: 'Independent living shouldn't mean being on your own. All the people who were killed did not have the peer support that I eventually had in my life, and without that I don't know the meaning of independent living. It is not about living on your own, it is about having choices and control over your life which is what those individuals did not have.' And she continues: 'I think we have to understand that we are interdependent and unless we create an environment where we are mutually supportive of one another you will have people who are killed because it is survival of the fittest, and they will be isolated and they will be targeted and that is our darkest side as human beings.'

Campbell ends by observing: 'We will pick on people who make us feel uncomfortable and scared. And it's all about transference, about our own feelings of inadequacy and anger. A lot of young people are angry because they haven't been given anything to do, no structure in their own lives; if you don't have that mutually support-ive structure then that is what will happen. So independent living is for everybody, not just for disabled people – it is interdependent living. That is the next stage, for us to all ask, what do we all need from each other to feel safe?'

Bert Massie, for his part, believes it's about winning hearts and minds and it's about the stick too – giving some hate crime perpet-rators really hefty sentences. But above all it is about disabled peo-ple being in society, being accepted, whether or not they can work. 'There are some people with learning disabilities who have an awful lot to offer, people with Down syndrome have so much to offer, we could do with that in the world. If somebody comes into the world and gives so much pleasure, is that such a bad thing? It shouldn't all be about work.'

Rachel Hurst, who has spent thirty years campaigning for human rights for disabled people, believes it's going to take time: 'I think we have to have friends from a wide circle, because you can make friends tire of you very easily, so you need an awful lot of them. And it's important that people with learning difficulties, and children gen-erally, learn more about life than reading and writing, that they are taught how to be friends. If we are taught to segregate at school, and be nasty, we will do it as adults. It all starts in classroom. We're after Utopia, but really it's a gradual change, implementation of rights, un-derstanding what rights really are, it's a hefty journey. I'm not sure it will end in my lifetime.'

I also believe that the disability movement now needs to look out-wards – and spend time identifying allies in the fight against disability hate crime, as well as eschewing the in-fighting that has, at times, characterised the movement. As Liz Crow, a disabled filmmaker and artist, says: 'There are further divisions that make us vulnerable, not least within disability. There's a still a sense of "us" and "them" (dis-abled and non-) and, historically, impairment groups have also been very divided, with people with physical impairments disassociating themselves from anyone with learning difficulties, mental health issues or illness.'

Rose Simkins, the director of Stop Hate UK, welcomes disabil-ity hate crime being seen as part of the hate crime spectrum, rather than being treated as something separate. 'We believe that people's immediate needs are the same, but their longer-term support needs are different. We deal with the different strands all day long. There is no difference to what people are wanting, and what they are feel-ing. They have all been attacked, and their initial support needs are the same.' She adds: 'I would have a concern if there was too much separation from the wider hate crime agenda, because we shouldn't divide people up. None of the strands are getting a good deal, we need to tackle bigotry and discrimination everywhere. One form of bigotry is as bad as another.'

Gary Bourlet, the founder of People First, the leading organisation in the UK for people with learning difficulties, agrees. He trains ad-vocates for disabled people, and no longer minds whether they have impairments themselves or not. 'We need all types of advocacy to improve. They are all feeling the pinch, family advocacy, peer advo-cacy, and we are working with families and carers on this. I am hoping that more people will come together instead of having in-fighting between the two groups. We want them to be our allies, not our enemies. We have to get away from "them" and "us" – we had that separate identity and I think it created problems; we just need to get together and we should have advocacy meetings that in-clude everybody. When we were younger we wanted separatism. If you want to make changes, you need to work together. That is hard, but it's right too.' I feel this movement towards inclusion, towards building alliances – and breaking down the separatism that has often defined the disability movement – is right, and long overdue. Working together with carers and families, who also experience discrimination and harassment, is crucial too.

Public attitudes can shift, as the alliance Time to Change has shown with attitudes towards mental health conditions.[2] Sophie Corlett says that there has been 'a 2.2 per cent improvement in public attitudes to mental health between 2008 to 2010 – with a 1.3 per cent improvement in attitudes from 2009 to 2010, following the start of the Time to Change campaign'. It's a small change, but at least it's a start.

The more that disabled people are seen as leaders who see beyond their own concerns, the more they will be respected within society generally. Radar's empowerment programme, which I discuss in the appendix on Best Practice below, gets disabled people ready to be leaders in society.[3] This promotion of what is called 'active citizenship' is essential. When disabled people are in positions where they are not only seen as taking, but also contributing to society, some of those pernicious myths will lose their strength.

For Professor Tom Shakespeare, in a new role at the World Health Organisation, violence should be treated as a 'preventable disease'. Once the data is available, perhaps interventions could be devised that might well work. 'We see violence as a preventable disease. Violence against people with disabilities can be reduced, and if we understand it better and intervene, and we can test interventions and see if they work, then we can reduce it. The first step is to establish the magnitude and nature of the problem. That's very difficult. Then devise some interventions. Then evaluate them to see if they work.'

While I agree with Tom Shakespeare that we need better and more systematic data, I don't think we can wait that long. We already know, for instance, that leadership from Sir Ken Macdonald (as well as pressure from disabled people) has had a real and measurable effect on Crown prosecutors and the CPS as a whole. When Sir Ken declared that disability hate crime was a 'scar on the conscience of the criminal justice system',[4] prosecutors listened, policy changed, training improved. This must be at least one of the reasons why prosecutions and convictions are going up.

We need to encourage similar responses from other parts of the criminal justice system, Government and social care. Government, police, prosecutors, judges and journalists need to tackle the attitudes and practices in general society that lie at the foundations of disability hate crime. A clear political lead, from the Prime Minister himself, speaking about the scar of disability hate crime on our society, would do much to bind disabled people back into a society where they feel they are disliked, sneered at, feared and hated. Parliamentarians, and religious leaders too, should speak out about this problem and give a clear moral lead on it.

We also know that early intervention, in terms of education, can challenge negative attitudes in classrooms. Too many disabled young people are bullied at school. Some have been targeted, violently, by their former classmates, such as Laura Milne and Anthony Hardwick. Circles of Friends projects in schools, where disabled people's organisations train both disabled and non-disabled children and young people how to support each other in class, have been shown to work and to reap dividends in terms of decreasing bullying and increasing self-esteem. Given that we know that hate crime perpetrators (and, indeed, many victims) are young, early intervention like this could save lives.[5]

And disabled people, and their organisations, are key to this. Disabled people are, often, equal citizens only in name. They need to be councillors, nurses, doctors, politicians, teachers, as well as shop assistants and refuse collectors.

Redress is important too. Hate crime victims don't necessarily need to have their day in court. For some of them it can be extremely traumatic, to have to relive the experience in front of the perpetrator and be questioned by a hostile barrister. Many families of victims, and victims themselves, have spoken movingly to me of how difficult it was to see the perpetrator so close, often smiling and waving at others in the court. Court reporting can even increase the risk of copycat attacks and repeat victimisation, if it is done salaciously and insensitively. But a sense of justice being done is extremely important. Mediation can work in some cases, where the perpetrator has to explain why they did what they did, and make amends for it. It might be particularly useful in neighbourhood disputes, or with very young offenders – but only if the victim agrees.

We also need perpetrator analysis, and fast, because it could save lives. Similarly, the Government should fund a behaviour programme for offenders, so that they don't reoffend when they are released from prison. This happens with those convicted of racial and sexual violence, and it should happen with disability hate crime offenders too. Paul Iganski, the leading British hate crime expert, advises that the programme should be led by disabled people and include ex-offenders too. We also need more information, so the British Crime Survey should include a question on disability hate crime in its next report.

Social workers and housing officers should be trained to recognise the early warning signs of disability hate crimes. The Government must also send out a clear lead on information sharing. Local authorities must not hide behind the Data Protection Act when it comes to saving lives. Information sharing between different agencies, such as social care, police and housing, is permissible and it should be made far more clear when and how it should be done.

If Internet service providers and social networking organisations continue to be unwilling to act against cyber-stalkers targeting disabled people, they should be regulated at an international level and forced to do so. ISPs operating here should respond promptly to court order requests for information on IP addresses and other information for court cases from the CPS. It is unacceptable that British citizens are targeted here by other British citizens, but that court orders for evidence in such cases have to go to the US headquarters, leading to delay and extra cost.

20

Conclusion

The targeting of disabled people has happened while society has looked the other way. Disability hate crime was the invisible crime, the crime that people looked straight through because they could not recognise it for what it was. Now it is coming into focus, and we can ignore it no longer.

Because the crime is, at the same time, both ancient and modern, it has been difficult for us to accept that it exists. Disabled people have been maliciously stereotyped for centuries. This has meant that they have never been accepted as equal citizens even when such equality is enshrined in law. So when they are attacked, they are seen, on some level, as 'fair game' or as 'asking for it' – and many disabled people, tragically, even internalise those feelings.

Despite all the best intentions of the disability rights movement, disabled citizens are mostly not seen as ordinary people wanting to live ordinary lives. The long-held prejudices I have explored in this book have successfully dehumanised disabled people. And it doesn't end, because such prejudices make it all too easy to create new, malicious stereotypes of disabled people, such as the scrounger, fuelling new hatred against them.

This is not to say that there hasn't been progress. Disabled politicians, journalists, artists and athletes are growing in number. The battle for the right to independent living, to employment and to access to shops, hotels, restaurants and transport has largely been won. But the war isn't over. Hearts and minds take longer to change than regulation and legislation. The moves to set disabled people free from centuries of institutionalisation – virtual imprisonment – have not unchained the minds of many in society who resent what are seen as perks that privilege disabled people.

Disability hate crimes are not motiveless crimes against 'vulnerable people'. They are reactive, angry crimes against disabled people who are demanding equal rights. Not everyone thinks that disabled people should socialise, work, marry and have children. Some don't even believe they have the right to life itself. Some hate crime specialists even believe that hate crimes happen because society, to some extent, condones those crimes – a condition known as 'collective culpability'. In the Holocaust, for example, hate crime specialists would argue that the heinous acts of the few were condoned by the many, who looked on and did nothing. And that has happened here too, as I have so often found in my investigations. Mobs of ordinary people looked on, did nothing, laughed or joined in, as disabled victims were humiliated, or even died, in front of them. That is a form of collective culpability.

I don't believe that means that society, in general, hates disabled people. But I think there is an underlying feeling that disabled people have not earned the equality they enjoy in name. This is why so many are attacked in our community, because some people believe that they should still be shut away. They are infuriated by disabled people demanding that they too should have the freedoms that non-disabled people take for granted. Some criminologists argue that hate crimes are about maintaining society's hierarchies – keeping certain groups in their place – which seems convincing, given the growing resentment against 'special treatment' for disabled people. Nobody knows, because reporting has been so inadequate, whether the numbers of disability hate crimes have increased in recent years as a reaction to the new freedoms. What we do know is that they are distressingly high. But disabled people aren't going to shut themselves away in institutions for protection. If segregation is over, however, there must be a quid pro quo. The separatist and sometimes hostile attitudes towards non-disabled people by a small number in the disability movement must be challenged. It takes two sides to make peace.

So what do we do now? Everywhere I have been over the last year, in my journey around England, I have seen the terrible aftermath of disability hate crime. Almost every disabled person I've interviewed, or even encountered socially, has experienced discrimination, or harassment, or worse. And their families and friends suffer too. This can't be allowed to go on. It shames our society.

The solution lies with all of us – to look within our hearts, and question whether we, too, are responsible, and to what extent. I believe we can combat disability hate crime and other hate crimes too. But those who commit them are not, mostly, isolated individuals on a mission to create a perfect state where nobody dares to be different. The uncomfortable truth is that hate crime perpetrators are a bit like the rest of us.

We have been here before. G.K. Chesterton called the fake science of eugenics a poison, almost a hundred years ago. Similarly, the atmosphere in which we live today is poisoned, by discrimination and violence against disabled people, and the fear and contempt in which so many hold them. We have to drain this poison from our society. That means being clear-headed and confronting our own prejudices about disabled people, for it is all of us who must make the change, not just some of us.

We need to understand other ugly truths about our society too. The obsession with the body beautiful, which puts such pressure on young people to self-harm and stop eating, and on people of all ages to have risky cosmetic surgery, is as damaging now as it was in classical times, if not more so. But it is even more harmful for most disabled people, who cannot even try to keep up with the impossible drive towards the perfect body. Perhaps one of the saddest consequences of this is the choice that some parents of disabled children make, to mask the obvious signs of their child's impairment (particularly children with Down syndrome) with cosmetic surgery, so that they can avoid the mockery that they would otherwise face.

So where do we start to make the change? It has to start with an acknowledgement that none of us is perfect – that's what makes us human. Most of us, in fact, live with minor impairments, such as short-sightedness and back pain. But more obvious disabilities discomfort us because they confront us with our human frailties, our inevitable mortality, writ large. We all grow old and infirm, and die. But at those times of vulnerability, we still believe our humanity should be recognised, beyond our looks, our ability to work or our intellect. Disability, therefore, is part of our human condition and cannot be set apart. So acknowledging what we want for ourselves – a respect for our innate humanity, irrespective of the state of our minds or bodies – is fundamental if we are to confront this crime. Because what we want for ourselves, we should demand for everybody in our society. Friendship, kindness, respect and humanity. It shouldn't be too much to ask.

Appendix

Best Practice

In some areas of England and Wales, disabled people's organisations, charities and statutory agencies, including the police and the Crown Prosecution Service, have developed projects to challenge disability hate crime and its roots. Although we need the same services everywhere, these projects do give us a sense of what works locally.

One of the most innovative organisations I have come across is called PIP Pack in Action, based in Hertfordshire and led by people with learning difficulties. Working with local police, they provide training and have developed a Keep Safe scheme where shops, pubs, libraries and other public places can display a sticker in their window to show they are a place of refuge where someone with a learning difficulty can seek help in an emergency. People can choose to carry a Keep Safe card or key ring to record contact telephone numbers. The Keep Safe stickers, cards and key rings are available free and are being used to set up a Keep Safe scheme across the country.

PIP Pack in Action has also developed the easy-to-use Disability Hate Crime Reporting Pack to aid direct and third-party reporting of hate crimes and incidents to police. This pack has been made available through the True Vision online hate crime reporting scheme to police forces across the country and for them to make suitably available to local people.
[www.pippack.org; www.keep-safe.info]
[http://www.report-it.org.uk/home]

Another initiative, called the Learning Together project, run by the self-advocacy learning groups Better Days, Coast 2 Coast and

Inclusion North, has developed a training pack (with Home Office funding) that people with learning difficulties can use to train others about disability hate crime.
[http://www.inclusionnorth.org/documents/Hate%20Crime%20 Learning%20Together %20Training%20Pack.pdf]

Values Into Action (VIA), which works to support and promote the rights of people with learning difficulties, has been running hate crime workshops for people with learning difficulties for several years. VIA produced the first national accessible guide to taking action against hate crime (the A–Z books *Let's Keep Safe* and *Let's Report It* in 2001). VIA still has a national programme of workshops on hate crime run by and for people with learning difficulties, and their current work includes an in-depth look at the phrase 'hate crime' and how it is being used by the criminal justice system and people with learning difficulties themselves. VIA also acts as an adviser to the CPS and many other local and regional hate crime projects.
[http://www.viauk.org/]

Other projects are equally inspiring: Redcar and Cleveland Mind invite police officers to come and spend time at the day centres to talk to people who have mental health conditions. A similar scheme is running in Dorset by Mind, which also runs a scheme for gay and lesbian people with experience of mental distress.
[http://www.mind.org.uk/news/3730_minding_our_community]

The Greenwich Association of Disabled People (GAD) was the first group in the UK to set up a third-party reporting site and a disability hate crime and domestic violence advocacy project in 2002. More disabled people's organisations have followed suit and set up their own third-party reporting schemes, though many still struggle to find sustainable funding. Anne Novis, a former chair of GAD, says that the project has increased reporting in Greenwich. GAD is now developing multi-agency risk conferences (similar to those used in domestic violence cases) for victims of disability hate crimes.
[http://www.gad.org.uk/]

In Blackpool my friend and colleague from the Disability Hate

Crime Network, Stephen Brookes, has been involved in an innovative project to tackle disability hate crime. Twenty partners from the council, police, health and charity sector, as well as disabled people themselves, have joined forces to work on disability hate crime. People with learning difficulties involved in the project joined together with young people from a local college to develop a DVD called *Hate Hurts*, which shows just how big the barrier is between disabled and non-disabled people. It is being used with Key Stage 3 pupils in schools to reduce bullying when it starts and to help prevent bullying in schools become a more serious issue for both the bully and those who have been targeted later in life.

[http://www.blackpool.gov.uk/Services/G-L/HateCrime/ HateCrimeReportingSystemLaunch.htm?&enable=false]

Disability Action Waltham Forest is introducing a pilot scheme called Stay Safe, which is partially funded through a grant from the Equality and Human Rights Commission. Its aim is to work with police to prevent violent crimes against disabled people, after staff identified a large number of 'unresolved cases' in the borough. Its chair, Ruth Bashall, said: 'It's taken a long time to change the system but we've been working to change the way police record hate crime against disabled people. Most disabled people do experience harassment or bullying and we also know that many disabled people are victims of domestic violence.' The organisation also runs an innovative befriending scheme for both disabled and non-disabled people.

[http://www.iwalthamforest.co.uk/profile/charities-and-voluntary-organisations/6020/Disability-Action-Waltham-Forest.html]

In Lancashire the police run an e-card scheme that helps police officers identify people who may need extra support if in contact with the criminal justice system. The Multi-Agency Data Exchange (MADE) project was set up to share data, with the aim of reducing crime and disorder throughout Lancashire. It is funded and run by the statutory authorities (fire and police services, local and health authorities). To create a more reliable picture of hate incidents and

hate crime in Lancashire, all organisations are encouraged to forward their recorded data to the project, including an incident reference number, date and time, details of the location of the incident, motivation, and victim and offender details.
[http://www3.lancashire.gov.uk/corporate/atoz/a_to_z/service.asp?u_id=1060&tab=1]

The Multi-Agency Safeguarding Hub (MASH) in Devon and Cornwall has also just started work. Nigel Bolton, who developed the information-sharing model, explains the reason for it: 'My real drive for the last nine years was that I had seen far too many women dead on the slab because of domestic violence. I wanted to develop a vision for harm reduction.' He recognised that it had to involve everybody, from fire fighters to paediatricians. 'It is possible, but you need leadership. It doesn't cost a lot of money.' The key ingredient, Bolton says, is 'information sharing. It's the chunky bit that's been missing, about keeping the partners in the room. The barriers that stop people talking to each other must be broken down.'
[http://www.devonlmc.org/uploads/File/2010/LSCB/multi-agency_safeguarding_hub.pdf]

The Metropolitan Police, too, have been extremely innovative in their approach to all forms of hate crime. They work closely with the CPS in London, looking at cases where the victim has a disability on a random basis to see if there was a hate crime element. They have found that a large number have been misidentified.
[http://www.met.police.uk/dcf/strands/disability.htm]

In Liverpool a witness profiling scheme, run by the city council's Investigations Support Unit, provides witness support to people with learning difficulties who want to give evidence in court. The unit has worked with over thirty witnesses in twenty-eight trials and many have been successful. It is now being considered for national roll-out.
[http://www.nationalworkinggroup.org/services/government-office-north-west/6-investigations-support-unit-isu-liverpool-city-council]

As I argued earlier, transport authorities are clearly not doing enough to promote safe travel for disabled people. However, the example of Merseytravel, covering the Liverpool area (which is now teaming up with Greater Manchester Travel), stands out as an example of how to change attitudes right through the transport system – on buses, trains and taxis, as well as among children. Merseytravel first set up a transport access panel, a forum for disabled people, twenty years ago, in an accessible venue and has offered free travel to disabled and older people since then. Eight years ago it also set up a fund for independent-travel training, run in conjunction with user groups and charities. Merseytravel also provides a Changing Place facility in the city centre, so that people can use accessible toilet and showering facilities, as well as a hoist.

Merseytravel is working with several partners including Merseyside Police, Oakfield Day Centre and Hate Crime UK to produce a DVD on hate crime and how to report it, which will be used by transport operators in training. It also wants to train bus drivers, in a similar way to its training programme for taxi drivers, who take compulsory disability training on issues such as carrying assistance dogs and treating disabled customers with respect. It is, in my view, the most systematic approach to disability equality in transport anywhere in Britain. If Merseytravel can also improve its reporting mechanisms, it will be a shining beacon of good practice.
[http://www.merseytravel.gov.uk/information_access-guide.asp]

The charity Respond offers a number of interventions to people with learning difficulties who have been sexually abused, including psychotherapy, support if they want to give evidence, and training in schools and colleges. People with learning difficulties are involved in the training. They also offer bereavement counselling.
[http://www.respond.org.uk/index.html]

A number of charities are working on reducing the barriers disabled people face in being leaders in public life, as well as active citizens.

The charity Scope ran a successful campaign called 'Polls Apart' during the last general election, to highlight physical barriers to voting for disabled people. It launched a website with information about voting rights and about how accessible the individual 25,000 polling stations were. It is also pushing for more disabled people to become elected representatives at all levels of public life. Ruth Scott, Director of Campaigns and Policy, said: 'Disabled people have an important and valuable contribution to make to the political process and make up approximately 20 per cent of the population and approximately 15 per cent of the working-age population.' The charity recommends an 'access to public life' fund to support disabled parliamentary candidates. [http://www.pollsapart.org.uk/pages/history.php]

The charity Radar's empowerment programme is also impressive. Radar runs a regional and national leadership programme, with coaching, peer supporting and networking sessions to encourage people with injury, ill health or disability to influence public life. [http://www.radar.org.uk/leadership/empproject.aspx]

Acknowledgements

I would like to thank the families, friends and survivors of disability hate crime who have so generously shared experiences of this terrible crime. Thank you, in particular, to the families and friends of Kevin Davies, Michael Gilbert, Steven Hoskin, Rikki Judkins, Christine Lakinski, Brent Martin, Keith Philpott and Fiona Pilkington, all of whom have talked to me over the last four years. Your painful testimonies are vital to our understanding of hate crime.

I'd also like to thank my many other interviewees, drawn from a very wide field, for taking the time and trouble to talk to me at such length, often more than once.

I would like to thank my wonderful friends in the disability movement, who have accompanied me on this dark journey into the heart of disability hate crime. Many of them, and allies of the movement, have also read and discussed particular chapters with me, and supported me during the writing of *Scapegoat*. I'd like to extend a particular thanks to Susie Balderston, Ruth Bashall, Will Bee, Stephen Brookes, Jane Campbell, Liz Crow, Paul Giannasi, David Grundy, Rachel Hurst, Paul Iganski, Dave Macnaghten, Ann Macfarlane, Bert Massie, Anne Novis, Barbara Perry, John Pring, Alan Roulstone, Mandy Sanghera, Rose Simkins, Betsy Stanko and Louise Wallis.

Many individuals in disabled people's organisations and advocacy groups have helped me. Thank you. Many people in disability charities, including ARC, Mencap, Mind, the National Autistic Society, Pip Pack, the RNIB, the RNID, Radar, Respond and Scope, have also been generous with their information and support. And a huge thank you to my friends and colleagues on the Disability Hate Crime

Network, as well as to all my dear friends at *Disability Now* magazine, who phone-bashed for evidence, right at the beginning of all this.

I'd like to thank many police officers for sharing their expertise, in particular Nigel Bolton, Geoff Brookes, Keith Groves, Christine Hemingway, Alfred Hitchcock, Steve Otter, Simon Price and Paul Richardson. I'd also like to pay tribute to the behind-the-scenes work of Nadine Tilbury and Joanna Perry to change the Crown Prosecution Service, as well as Sir Ken Macdonald, the former Director of Public Prosecutions, who did so much to catalyse essential reform. Thanks to Brian Cathcart for the kind gift of his brilliant book, *The Case of Stephen Lawrence*, and guidance in the very early stages.

Thanks to Saghir Alam, Jackie Driver, Hilary McCollum, Mike Smith and other individuals at the Equality and Human Rights Commission, as well as my colleagues on the Advisory Committee on Disability Targeted Violence inquiry.

Thanks, of course, to my agent, Andrew Lownie, and Tasja Dorkofikis, Benjamin Buchan, Aidan O'Neill and Christine Lo at my publishers, Portobello Books.

Last of all, I would like to thank my loyal and loving family (not least my late grandmother Isobel Božić, who taught me the classics as a thankless child and whose knowledge I have drawn on in this book) and my dear friends, who have been endlessly supportive in so many ways.

Note on terminology

The accepted terms used to refer to disability have varied much over the years and still vary from country to country. In this book I have used British rather than American terminology. I apologise for inadvertent offence caused by this.

Recommended Reading

Arnold, Catherine, *Bedlam: London and its Mad* (Pocket Books, 2009)

Aristotle, *The Politics* (Penguin Classics, 1981)

Avalos, Hector, Sarah J. Melcher and Jeremy Schipper (eds.), *This Abled Body: Rethinking Disabilities in Biblical Studies* (Society of Biblical Literature, 2007)

Barton, Carlin A., *The Sorrows of the Ancient Romans* (Princeton University Press, 1993)

Bayley, Michael, *Mental Handicap and Community Care* (Routledge and Kegan Paul, 1973)

Bayley, Michael, *What Price Friendship?: Encouraging the Relationships of People with Learning Difficulties* (Hexagon Publishing, 1997)

Bowlby, John, *Child Care and the Growth of Love* (Penguin, 1965)

Burkert, Walter, *Structure and History* (University of California Press, 1979)

Burleigh, Michael, *Death and Deliverance* (Pan, 2002)

Campbell, Jane, and Mike Oliver, *Disability Politics* (Routledge, 1996)

Cathcart, Brian, *The Case of Stephen Lawrence* (Viking, 1999)

Chakraborti, Neil, and Jon Garland, *Hate Crime: Impact, Causes and Responses* (Sage, 2009)

Christie, Nils, *Beyond Loneliness and Institutions* (Norwegian University Press, 1989)

Collins, Jean, *The Resettlement Game* (Values Into Action, 1993)

Darwin, Charles, *The Descent of Man* (London, 1871)

Davis, Lennard, *Enforcing Normalcy* (Verso, 1995)

Foucault, Michel, *Madness and Civilisation* (Routledge, 2001)

Gallagher, Hugh Gregory, *By Trust Betrayed: Patients, Physicians and the License to Kill in the Third Reich* (Henry Holt, 1990)

Gaskill, Malcolm, *Witchfinders: A Seventeenth-Century English Tragedy* (John Murray, 2005)

Goffman, Erving, *Stigma: Notes on the Management of Spoiled Identity* (Pelican, 1968)

Goffman, Erving, *Asylums* (Penguin, 1968)

Graham, Peter, and Fritz Oehlschlager, *Articulating the Elephant Man: Joseph Merrick and His Interpreters* (Johns Hopkins University Press, 1992)

Homer, *The Odyssey* (Penguin, 1967)

Howell, Michael, and Peter Ford, *The True Story of the Elephant Man* (Penguin, 1983)

Iganski, Paul, *Hate Crime and the City* (Policy Press, 2008)

Kevles, D.J., *In the Name of Eugenics* (Harvard University Press, 1985)

Kramer, Heinrich, and Jakob Sprenger, *Malleus Maleficarum* (Germany, 1487; Dover Publications, 1971)

Lapper, Alison, *My Life in my Hands* (Simon and Schuster, 2005)

Levack, Brian, *The Witch-Hunt in Early Modern Europe* (Longman, 1993)

Levin, Jack, and Jack McDevitt, *Hate Crimes: The Rising Tide of Bigotry* (Plenium, 1993)

Lifton, Robert Jay, *The Nazi Doctors: Medical Killing and the Psychology of Genocide* (Basic Books, 2000)

Midelfort, H.C. Eric, *A History of Madness in Sixteenth-Century Germany* (Stanford University Press, 1999)

Morris, Pauline, *Put Away: A Sociological Study of Institutions for the Mentally Retarded* (Routledge and Kegan Paul, 1969)

Ogden, Daniel, *The Crooked Kings of Ancient Greece* (Duckworth, 1997)

Oswin, Maureen, *The Empty Hours* (Penguin, 1971)

Perry, Barbara (ed.), *Hate and Bias Crime: A Reader* (Routledge, 2003)

Plato, *The Republic* (Penguin, 1974)

Pliny, *Natural History* (Penguin, 2004)

Pring, John, *Silent Victims* (Gibson Square, 2004)

Reinders, Hans, *Receiving the Gift of Friendship* (Eerdmans Publishing, 2008)

Schmidt, Ulf, *Karl Brandt: The Nazi Doctor* (Hambledon Continuum, 2007)

Schweik, Susan, *The Ugly Laws: Disability in Public* (New York University Press, 2009)

Scull, Andrew, *Museums of Madness* (Allen Lane, 1979)

Showalter, Elaine, *The Female Malady* (Pantheon Books, 1985)

Sinason, Valerie, *Handicap and the Human Condition* (Free Association Books, 1992)

Snyder, Sharon L., and David T. Mitchell, *Cultural Locations of Disability* (University of Chicago Press, 2006)

References

Introduction

1 http://news.bbc.co.uk/1/hi/england/gloucestershire/6284184.stm.
2 Katharine Quarmby, *Getting Away with Murder* (Scope, 2008), available at http://www.scope.org.uk/help-and-information/publications/getting-away-murder.

Chapter One: The Scapegoating of Kevin Davies

1 http://news.bbc.co.uk/1/hi/england/gloucestershire/6284184.stm.
2 http://www.british-history.ac.uk/report.aspx?compid=23274.
3 http://www.gloucestershire.gov.uk/inform/index.cfm?articleid=94990.
4 http://archive.disabilitynow.org.uk/search/z07_09_Se/KevinDavies.shtml.
5 Ibid.
6 Prosecutor's statement, obtained from Elizabeth James, 12 July 2010.
7 Coroner's report, obtained from Elizabeth James, 12 July 2010.
8 http://www.dailymail.co.uk/news/article-467223/Couple-imprisoned-epileptic-man-shed-months-starved-death.html.
9 http://archive.disabilitynow.org.uk/search/z07_09_Se/hatecrimes.shtml.
10 Prosecutor's statement, obtained from Elizabeth James, 12 July 2010.
11 Judge's summing-up, obtained from Elizabeth James, 12 July 2010.
12 Mitigation for Amanda Baggus, obtained from Elizabeth James, 12 July 2010.
13 http://www.disabilitynow.org.uk/201cwhy-shouldnt-people-be-angry-they-are-not-getting-justice.
14 Coroner's verdict, obtained from Elizabeth James, 12 July 2010.
15 http://www.disabilitynow.org.uk/latest-news2/old-news/davies-case-ruled-not-to-be-hate-crime.

Chapter Two: The Greek and Roman Legacy

1 http://news.bbc.co.uk/1/hi/england/london/4247000.stm.

2   Alison Lapper, *My Life in My Hands* (Simon and Schuster, 2005), 246.

3   Ibid.

4   D.M. Jones, quoted in Todd M. Compton, *Victim of the Muses: Poet as Scapegoat, Warrior and Hero in Greco-Roman and Indo-European Myth and History* (Center for Hellenic Studies, 2006), http://www.gifthub.org/the-pharmakos-ritual.html.

5   W.J.W. Koster, quoted in Compton, *Victim of the Muses*, http://www.gifthub.org/the-pharmakos-ritual.html.

6   Daniel Ogden, *The Crooked Kings of Ancient Greece* (Duckworth, 1997), 15.

7   Ibid., 16–17, from the *Scholia of Aeschylus, Seven Against Thebes*.

8   W.J.W. Koster, quoted in Compton, *Victim of the Muses*, http://www.gifthub.org/the-pharmakos-ritual.html.

9   Soranus, quoted in Martha L. Rose, *The Staff of Oedipus* (University of Michigan Press, 2003), 33.

10   Plutarch, *Lycurgus: The Father of Sparta*, http://classics.mit.edu/Plutarch/lycurgus.html.

11   Ibid.

12   Plato, *The Republic* (Penguin, 1974), 460c, 241.

13   Aristotle, *The Politics* (Penguin, 1962), 1335b, 443.

14   Rosemary Garland Thompson, quoted in Rose, *The Staff of Oedipus*, 34.

15   Ogden, *The Crooked Kings of Ancient Greece*, 13.

16   Plato, *The Republic*, 459e, 240.

17   http://news.bbc.co.uk/1/hi/world/europe/4080822.stm.

18   Plato, *The Republic*, 407d, 171.

19   Plato, quoted in Rose, *The Staff of Oedipus*, 47.

20   Nicole Kelly, 'Deformity and Disability in Ancient Greece', in *This Abled Body: Rethinking Disabilities in Biblical Studies*, ed. Hector Avalos, Sarah J. Melcher and Jeremy Schipper (Society of Biblical Literature, 2007), 36.

21   Frederick Hall, *The Pedigree of the Devil* (London, 1883), 178–9.

22   Erving Goffman, *Stigma: Notes on the Management of Spoiled Identity* (Pelican, 1968), 11.

23   Ibid., 15.

24   Philo, *The Special Laws* (William Heinemann, 1968), 114–15.

25   Walter Burkert, *Structure and History* (University of California Press, 1979), 72.

26   Carlin A. Barton, *The Sorrows of the Ancient Romans* (Princeton University Press, 1993), 146.

27   Ibid., 68.

28   Ibid., 86.

29   Pliny, quoted in Nicole Kelly, 'Deformity and Disability in Ancient Greece', in *This Abled Body*, 40.

30 Barton, *The Sorrows of the Ancient Romans*, 169.

31 Pliny, quoted in Frederick Elworthy, *The Evil Eye* (John Murray, 2004), 419.

32 Barton, *The Sorrows of the Ancient Romans*, 174.

33 Robert Garland, *The Eye of the Beholder: Deformity and Disability in the Graeco-Roman World* (Duckworth, 1995), 41.

34 Pliny, *Natural History* (Penguin, 2004), 83.

35 Ibid., 91.

36 Neal H. Walls, 'The Origins of the Disabled Body: Disability in Ancient Mesopotamia', in *This Abled Body: Rethinking Disabilities in Biblical Studies*, 19.

37 Ibid., 21.

38 Lennard J. Davis, *Enforcing Normalcy* (Verso, 1995).

39 Walls, 'The Origins of the Disabled Body: Disability in Ancient Mesopotamia', in *This Abled Body*, 30.

Chapter Three: Sin, Disability and Witch-Hunting

1 http://www.witchtrials.co.uk/matthew.html.

2 Malcolm Gaskill, *Witchfinders: A Seventeenth-Century English Tragedy* (John Murray, 2005), 49.

3 Brian Levack, *The Witch-Hunt in Early Modern Europe* (Longman, 1993), 142.

4 Ibid., 143.

5 Reginald Scot, *Discoverie of Witchcraft* (London, 1854), 320.

6 Levack, *The Witch-Hunt*, 150.

7 Ibid., 141.

8 Leviticus, 21: 17–20.

9 Samuel II, 5: 8.

10 Thomas Hentrich, 'Masculinity and Disability in the Bible', in *This Abled Body: Rethinking Disabilities in Biblical Studies*, ed. Hector Avalos, Sarah J. Melcher and Jeremy Schipper (Society of Biblical Literature, 2007), 150.

11 Thomas More, *Four Last Things, Part 1* (London, 1552), http://www.thomasmorestudies.org.

12 Andrew Scull, *Museums of Madness* (Allen Lane, 1979), 18–19.

13 Heinrich Kramer and Jakob Sprenger, *Malleus Maleficarum* (Dover Publications, 1971), 45.

14 http://www.sacred-texts.com/pag/mm/mm01_06a.htm.

15 Martin Luther, quoted in M. Miles, 'Martin Luther and Childhood Disability in 16th Century Germany', *Journal of Religion, Disability & Health*, 2001, http://www.independentliving.org/docs7/miles2005b.html.

16 Luther, quoted in Miles, 'Martin Luther and Childhood Disability'.

17 Levack, *The Witch-Hunt*, 141.

18 Gaskill, *Witchfinders*, 137.

19 Ibid, 146.

20 Louise Jackson, 'Witches, Wives and Mothers: Witchcraft, Persecution and Women's Confessions in Seventeenth-Century England', *Women's History Review*, Volume 4, Number 1, 1995, 73.

21 Ibid., 67.

22 Fred Feather, *Tales from the Essex Police Museum* (Essex Family Historian Society, 2007), 1.

23 http://www.witchtrials.co.uk/names.html.

24 Local newspaper report, 17 September 1863, either the *Halstead Gazette* or the *East Essex and Halstead Times*, in Essex Police Museum files (Sible Hedingham witchcraft case).

25 Ibid.

26 William Shakespeare, *Richard III*, Act V, Scene VI, 78–83.

27 H.C. Eric Midelfort, *A History of Madness in Sixteenth-Century Germany* (Stanford University Press, 1999), 228–76.

28 Ibid.

29 Colin Barnes, 'Effecting Change; Disability, Culture and Art?' (Leeds University Disability Archive, 2003), http://www.leeds.ac.uk/disability-studies/archiveuk/Barnes/Effecting%20Change.pdf.

30 Midelfort, *A History of Madness in Sixteenth-Century Germany*, 243.

31 Ibid., 276.

32 http://www.mirror.co.uk/news/top-stories/2006/03/15/two-locked-up-for-happy-slap-killing-115875–16814404/.

33 http://www.bbc.co.uk/news/world-africa-10671790; http://news.bbc.co.uk/1/hi/uk/5244306.stm.

34 Gaskill, *Witchfinders*, 286.

Chapter Four: The Industrial Revolution, Asylums and Freak Shows

1 Catherine Arnold, *Bedlam: London and its Mad* (Pocket Books, 2009), 103.

2 http://www.slam.nhs.uk/about-us/history.aspx.

3 http://www.slam.nhs.uk/about-us/history/bethlem-royal-hospital.aspx.

4 http://www.outsiderart.co.uk/wain.htm.

5 http://www.slam.nhs.uk/news/latest-new-exhibition-at-bethlem-art-gallery.aspx.

6 Pauline Morris, *Put Away: A Sociological Study of Institutions for the Mentally Retarded* (Routledge and Kegan Paul, 1969), 9.

7   Susan Schweik, *The Ugly Laws: Disability in Public* (New York University Press, 2009).

8   Andrew Scull, *Museums of Madness* (Allen Lane, 1979), 78.

9   Arnold, *Bedlam*, 167.

10   Scull, *Museums of Madness*, 74.

11   Ibid.

12   Ibid., 77.

13   Ibid., 87–8.

14   Ibid., 81.

15   http://studymore.org.uk/mhhtim.htm#Phrenology.

16   Morris, *Put Away*, 21.

17   Scull, *Museums of Madness*, 126.

18   Michael Howell and Peter Ford, *The True Story of the Elephant Man* (Penguin, 1983), 22.

19   http://www.ncbi.nlm.nih.gov/pmc/articles/PMC2036365/pdf/medcht00007–0437.pdf.

20   Ibid.

21   Howell and Ford, *The True Story of the Elephant Man*, 92.

22   Autobiography of Joseph Merrick, reprinted as an appendix in Howell and Ford, *The True Story of the Elephant Man*.

23   *Treves and the Elephant Man*, reprint of *The Elephant Man* (Royal London Hospital, 2003), 6.

24   Ibid.

25   Ibid., 10–11.

26   Peter Graham and Fritz Oehlschlager, *Articulating the Elephant Man: Joseph Merrick and His Interpreters* (Johns Hopkins University Press, 1992).

27   Elaine Showalter, *The Female Malady* (Pantheon Books, 1985), 104.

Chapter Five: No Better than Poison: the Eugenics Movement and the Holocaust

1   http://www.telegraph.co.uk/education/3319981/Named-the-baby-boy-who-was-Nazis-first-euthanasia-victim.html.

2   http://www.lpb-bw.de/publikationen/euthana/euthana4.htm.

3   http://www.thepsychologist.org.uk/archive/archive_home.cfm?volumeID=21&editionID=166&ArticleID=1433.

4   Sharon L. Snyder and David T. Mitchell, *Cultural Locations of Disability* (University of Chicago Press, 2006), 13–16.

5   http://www.ncgsjournal.com/issue62/robinson.htm.

6   Charles Darwin, *The Descent of Man* (London, 1871), 168.

7   http://www.dnalc.org/view/1850-The-Feeble-Minded-by-Mary-Dendy-Economic-Review-July-1903-1-.html.

8   Francis Galton, *The Problem of the Feeble-Minded*, an abstract of the Report of the Royal Commission on Mental Deficiency, 1908

9   *Morning Post*, 16 October 1909, quoted at http://studymore.org.uk/xmad1909.htm.

10 http://www.winstonchurchill.org/support/the-churchill-centre/publications/finest-hour-online/594-churchill-and-eugenics.

11 Asquith papers, MS 12, folios 224–8, quoted in www.winstonchurchill.org.

12 http://www.winstonchurchill.org/support/the-churchill-centre/publications/finest-hour-online/594-churchill-and-eugenics.

13 Dr A.F. Tredgold, 'The Feeble-Minded – A Social Danger', *Eugenics Review* (1909–10), 97–104.

14 Hansard, Parliamentary Debates, 16 November 1914.

15 http://www.mencap.org.uk/page.asp?id=1895.

16 Daniel J. Kevles, *In the Name of Eugenics* (Harvard University Press, 1985), 114.

17 Ibid., 145.

18 Ibid., 160.

19 G.K. Chesterton, *Eugenics and Other Evils* (Cassell, 1922), 5.

20 Susan Schweik, *The Ugly Laws: Disability in Public* (New York University Press, 2009), 1–2.

21 https://scholarworks.iupui.edu/bitstream/handle/1805/1057/The%20Indiana%20Plan-%20OCR.pdf?sequence=1.

22 Henry H. Goddard, *Feeble-Mindedness: Its Causes and Consequences* (1914), 504–9.

23 http://www.hsl.virginia.edu/historical/eugenics/3-buckvbell.cfm.

24 http://www.winstonchurchill.org/support/the-churchill-centre/publications/finest-hour-online/594-churchill-and-eugenics.

25 Kevles, *In the Name of Eugenics*, 46.

26 http://www.eugenicsarchive.org/eugenics/.

27 http://www.eugenicsarchive.org/html/eugenics/static/themes/8.html.

28 Kevles, *In the Name of Eugenics*, 62.

29 http://www.eugenicsarchive.org/eugenics/.

30 http://www.dnalc.org/view/11219-T-Roosevelt-letter-to-C-Davenport-about-degenerates-reproducing-.html.

31 Kevles, *In the Name of Eugenics*, 107.

32 Walter Fernald, 'The Burden of Feeblemindedness', *Journal of Psycho-Asthenics*, 1912, 10.

33 Michael Burleigh, *Death and Deliverance* (Pan, 2002), 43.

34 http://www.ushmm.org/research/library/bibliography/?lang=en&content=people_with_disabilities.

35 http://www.roaring-girl.com/productions/resistance-conversations/watch/ (transcript also available).

36 Robert Jay Lifton, *The Nazi Doctor: Medical Killing and the Psychology of Genocide* (Basic Books, 2000), 40.

37 http://www.wce.wwu.edu/nwche/reviews/disabled.shtml.

38 http://www.ippnw.org/Resources/MGS/V2N3Seidelman.html.

39 http://www.bmj.com/content/313/7070/1453.full?ijkey=41686bee0524cf4585d4937822eaa36f737c7453&keytype2=tf_ipsecsha.

40 Hugh Gregory Gallagher, *By Trust Betrayed: Patients, Physicians and the License to Kill in the Third Reich* (Henry Holt, 1990), 23.

41 Kevles, *In the Name of Eugenics*, 116.

42 Ibid.

43 Robert Proctor, *Racial Hygiene: Medicine under the Nazis* (Harvard University Press, 1988), 180.

44 http://forum.axishistory.com/viewtopic.php?p=406436 (a copy of the order to kill, in German, is scanned on this website).

45 Gallagher, *By Trust Betrayed*, 7.

46 Ibid., 73.

47 Ibid., 227–8.

48 Ibid., 143.

49 Ibid., 173.

50 http://www.t4holocaust.com/t4story/t4story.html.

51 Gallagher, *By Trust Betrayed*, 21.

52 http://www.bmj.com/content/313/7070/1463.extract.

53 Ulf Schmidt, *Karl Brandt: The Nazi Doctor* (Hambledon Continuum, 2007), 118.

54 http://www.ess.uwe.ac.uk/genocide/reviewsh35.htm.

Chapter Six: Scandalous Institutions

1 Ann Macfarlane, 'Watershed', reproduced with the permission of the poet.

2 http://www.dh.gov.uk/prod_consum_dh/groups/dh_digitalassets/@dh/@en/documents/digitalasset/dh_4071453.pdf.

3 John Bowlby, *Child Care and the Growth of Love* (Penguin, 1965).

4 http://www.liberty-human-rights.org.uk/about/history/liberty-timeline.php.

5 http://studymore.org.uk/xpowell.htm.

6 *Report of the Committee on Local Authority and Allied Personal Social Services* (HMSO, 1968), 116.

7   http://www.sochealth.co.uk/history/Ely.htm.
8   *Report of the Committee of Inquiry into South Ockendon Hospital* (HMSO, 1974).
9   *Report of the Committee of Inquiry into Normansfield Hospital* (HMSO, 1978).
10 Personal communication, Andrew Groves, solicitor, 28 July 2010, including sworn testimony from witnesses.
11 http://news.bbc.co.uk/1/hi/england/norfolk/7090998.stm.
12 http://news.bbc.co.uk/1/hi/england/norfolk/7045190.stm.
13 Pauline Morris, *Put Away: A Sociological Study of Institutions for the Mentally Retarded* (Routledge and Kegan Paul, 1969).
14 Ibid., 99.
15 Ibid., 98.
16 Ibid., 187.
17 Ibid., 285.
18 Ibid., 315.
19 Ibid., 22–3.
20 Maureen Oswin, *The Empty Hours* (Penguin, 1971), 10.
21 Ibid., 65.
22 http://www.guardian.co.uk/news/2001/aug/01/guardianobituaries1.
23 Erving Goffman, *Asylums* (Penguin, 1968), 18.
24 Ibid., 24.
25 Ibid., 73.
26 http://studymore.org.uk/mhhtim.htm#BetterServices1975.

Chapter Seven: Brave New World?

1   Jane Campbell and Mike Oliver, *Disability Politics* (Routledge, 1996), 48.
2   Ibid., 52.
3   Ibid., 60.
4   http://www.leeds.ac.uk/disability-studies/archiveuk/finkelstein/presentn.pdf.
5   http://www.leeds.ac.uk/disability-studies/archiveuk/Hunt/Hunt%201.pdf.
6   Campbell and Oliver, *Disability Politics*, 62–3.
7   Ibid., 54.
8   http://www.leeds.ac.uk/disability-studies/archiveuk/finkelstein/A%20Question%20of%20Choice.pdf.
9   http://www.leeds.ac.uk/disability-studies/archiveuk/UPIAS/UPIAS.pdf.
10 http://www.leeds.ac.uk/disability-studies/archiveuk/finkelstein/presentn.pdf.
11 http://www.leeds.ac.uk/disability-studies/archiveuk/finkelstein/A%20Question%20of%20Choice.pdf.
12 http://www.leeds.ac.uk/disability-studies/archiveuk/evans/Independent%20Living%20Development%20in%20USA%20and%20Europe%202.pdf.

13 http://berkeley.edu/news/media/releases/2010/07/27_roberts.shtml; http://www.udeducation.org/resources/61.html.

14 Michael Devenney, 'The Social Representations of Disability', http://www.leeds.ac.uk/disability-studies/archiveuk/titles.html, 2005.

15 Ibid.

16 http://www.flickr.com/photos/ruhuman/2548485687/in/set-72157606166053944/.

17 http://www.flickr.com/photos/ruhuman/2563773498/in/pool-inaccessible; http://www.flickr.com/photos/ruhuman/3422054673/; http://jpgmag.com/stories/15541.

18 http://www.ukdpc.net/index.asp?pl=true&pfolder=94&sid=70.

19 Campbell and Oliver, *Disability Politics*, 193–4.

20 Ibid., 194–5.

21 Devenney, 'The Social Representations of Disability', http://www.leeds.ac.uk/disability-studies/archiveuk.

22 http://www.leeds.ac.uk/disability-studies/archiveuk/Shakespeare/social%20model%20of%20disability.pdf.

23 http://hansard.millbanksystems.com/lords/1962/feb/14/the-hospital-plan.

24 Andrew Scull, *Museums of Madness* (Allen Lane, 1979), 263–4.

25 http://news.bbc.co.uk/1/hi/uk/57659.stm.

26 http://news.bbc.co.uk/1/hi/health/229445.stm.

27 http://hansard.millbanksystems.com/written_answers/1979/mar/08/jay-committee-report.

28 http://news.bbc.co.uk/1/hi/health/229517.stm.

29 Jean Collins, *The Resettlement Game* (Values Into Action, 1993), 79.

30 http://www.timesonline.co.uk/tol/life_and_style/article1003314.ece.

31 http://news.bbc.co.uk/1/i/uk/57659.stm.

32 Collins, *The Resettlement Game*, 17.

33 Ibid., 46.

34 Ibid., 89.

35 Michael Bayley, *Mental Handicap and Community Care* (Routledge and Kegan Paul, 1973), 284.

36 Margaret Flynn, *Independent Lives for People with Mental Handicap: A Place of Their Own* (Cassell, 1989), 65.

37 Ibid., 118.

38 http://www.archive.official-documents.co.uk/document/cm50/5086/5086.htm.

Chapter Eight: The Terroring of Raymond Atherton: Freedom's Betrayal

1   http://www.wigantoday.net/news/feral_teenagers_beat_man_to_death_1_170398.

2   http://www.guardian.co.uk/society/2007/aug/15/guardiansocietysupplement.socialcare.

3   Ibid.

4   http://www.timesonline.co.uk/tol/news/uk/crime/article1610309.ece.

5   'Joint Review of a Serious Incident', Warrington Borough Council report, obtained under the Freedom of Information Act, 8 December 2010.

6   Ibid.

7   Ibid.

8   Ibid.

9   http://news.bbc.co.uk/1/hi/england/merseyside/7085654.stm.

10   http://www.mind.org.uk/campaigns_and_issues/current_campaigns/another_assault; http://www.mencap.co.uk/document.asp?id=12069&audGroup=&subjectLevel2=&subjectId=9&sorter=1&origin=subjectId&pageType=112&pageno=&searchPhrase=.

11   http://www.disabilitynow.org.uk/living/features/unequal-before-the-law.

12   http://news.bbc.co.uk/1/hi/england/tees/4720642.stm.

13   http://www.telegraph.co.uk/news/uknews/1546319/Four-drowned-man-they-thought-was-pederast.html.

14   http://news.bbc.co.uk/1/hi/england/lancashire/6369319.stm.

15   http://news.bbc.co.uk/1/hi/wales/south_east/6624515.stm.

16   http://news.bbc.co.uk/1/hi/england/south_yorkshire/6159034.stm.

17   http://news.bbc.co.uk/1/hi/england/cornwall/6917659.stm.

18   http://news.bbc.co.uk/1/hi/england/gloucestershire/6284184.stm.

19   http://news.bbc.co.uk/1/hi/england/leicestershire/7138147.stm.

Chapter Nine: Steven Hoskin and the Case of the Invisible Crime

1   http://www.cornwall.gov.uk/default.aspx?page=5609.

2   Ibid.

3   Ibid.

4   Ibid.

5   Ibid.

6   Ibid.

7   http://www.voiceuk.org.uk/pdfs/SupplementalEvidenceHumanRights_Disability_Hate_Crime.pdf.

8 Paul Iganski, *Hate Crime and the City* (Policy Press, 2008), 5.

9 http://www.publications.parliament.uk/pa/cm200809/cmselect/cmhaff/427/42703.htm.

10 Iganski, *Hate Crime and the City*, 1.

11 http://www.legislation.gov.uk/ukpga/2003/44/contents.

12 Jack Levin and Jack McDevitt, *Hate Crimes: The Rising Tide of Bigotry* (Plenium, 1993)

13 Melissa Mertz, quoted in K.T. Berrill, 'Anti-Gay Violence and Victimisation in the US: An Overview', in *Hate Crimes: Confronting Violence against Lesbians and Gay Men* (Sage, 1992), 25.

14 Neil Chakraborti and Jon Garland, *Hate Crime: Impacts, Causes and Responses* (Sage, 2009), 90.

15 http://www.mind.org.uk/campaigns_and_issues/current_campaigns/another_assault.

16 http://www.mencap.co.uk/document.asp?pageType=112&origin=.

17 *Hate Crime against Disabled People in Scotland: A Survey Report* (Disability Rights Commission and Capability Scotland, 2004).

18 *Annual Survey Results* (Royal National Institute for Deaf People, 2007).

19 *'Give Us a Break': Exploring Harassment of People with Mental Health Problems* (National Schizophrenia Fellowship Scotland, 2001).

20 Katharine Quarmby, *Getting Away with Murder* (Scope, 2008), available at http://www.scope.org.uk/help-and-information/publications/getting-away-murder, 10.

21 Ibid., 13.

22 http://www.daa.org.uk/index.php?page=test-about-us.

23 http://www.disabilitynow.org.uk/latest-news2/news-focus/old-news-focus/january/zero-tolerance.

24 http://www.disabilitynow.org.uk/the-hate-crime-dossier.

25 http://www.disabilitynow.org.uk/201cwhy-shouldnt-people-be-angry-they-are-not-getting-justice.

Chapter Ten: Brent Martin and the Tipping Point that Never Was

1 http://news.bbc.co.uk/1/hi/england/wear/7202351.stm.

2 http://www.scope.org.uk/help-and-information/publications/getting-away-murder.

3 Stephanie Condron, 'Gang Dragged Victim by Belt to his Death', *The Times*, 27 August 2007.

4 Personal communication, Northumbria Police, August 2008.

5 http://news.bbc.co.uk/1/hi/england/wear/7270808.stm.

6 http://www.disabilitynow.org.uk/latest-news2/news-focus/we-cannot-let-this-pass.

7 Katharine Quarmby, *Getting Away with Murder* (Scope, 2008), available at http://www.scope.org.uk/help-and-information/publications/getting-away-murder, 30.

8 http://www.disabilitynow.org.uk/living/features/unequal-before-the-law/?.

9 Quarmby, *Getting Away with Murder*, 11–12.

10 Ibid., 15.

11 Ibid., 16.

12 Paul Iganski, *Hate Crime and the City* (Policy Press, 2008), 86–94.

13 http://www.disabilitynow.org.uk/latest-news2/news-focus/old-news-focus/we-launch-hate-report.

Chapter Eleven: The Humiliation of Christine Lakinski: Women and Children First

1 Katharine Quarmby, *Getting Away with Murder* (Scope, 2008), available at http://www.scope.org.uk/help-and-information/publications/getting-away-murder.

2 http://www.dailymail.co.uk/news/article-489914/Yob-urinated-dying-woman-jailed-years.html.

3 http://www.hartlepool.gov.uk/egov_downloads/11.01.10_-_Cabinet_Minutes_and_Decision_Record.pdf.

4 Personal communication, Cleveland Police, 23 September 2010.

5 http://www.thestar.co.uk/news/Abused-wife39s-horror-death.1621794.jp.

6 Ibid.

7 British Crime Survey (Home Office, 1995), http://rds.homeoffice.gov.uk/rds/pdfs/hors191.pdf, 33.

8 Gill Hague, Ravi K. Thiara, Pauline Magowan and Audrey Mullender, *Making the Links* (Women's Aid, 2008), 13–19.

9 http://www.equalityhumanrights.com/uploaded_files/research/disabled_people_s_experiences_of_targeted_violence_and_hostility.pdf.

10 Personal communication, Louise Wallis, 5 October 2010.

11 Quarmby, *Getting Away with Murder*, 14.

12 *Justice Denied* (Mental Welfare Commission, 2008), http://www.mwcscot.org.uk/nmsruntime/saveasdialog.asp?1ID=1290&sID=732, 1.

13 http://news.bbc.co.uk/1/hi/england/london/7839280.stm.

14 http://www.dailymail.co.uk/news/article-1197143/Increased-sentences-rapists-poured-caustic-acid-16-year-old-victim.html.

15 http://www.disabilitynow.org.uk/living/features/behind-closed-doors.

16 Ibid.

17 E. Stanko, V. Kielinger, S. Paterson, L. Richards, D. Crisp and L. Marsland, 'Grounded Crime Prevention: Responding to and Understanding Hate Crime', in *Crime Prevention, New Approaches*, ed. J. Obergfell-Fuchs and H. Kury (Sage, 2003), 123–52, http://www.brown.uk.com/domesticviolence/stanko.pdf.

18 http://www.cps.gov.uk/legal/s_to_u/stalking_and_harassment/.

19 http://news.bbc.co.uk/1/hi/england/devon/8345159.stm.

20 http://www.bbc.co.uk/news/uk-england-devon-10750279.

21 http://www.cps.gov.uk/news/press_statements/cps_statement_on_james_watts/.

22 http://www.guardian.co.uk/society/2010/mar/15/stern-review-rape-less-focus-convictions.

23 Joan Petersilias, 'Crime Victims with Developmental Disabilities: A Review Essay', *Criminal Justice and Behaviour*, 2001, 28, 6, 655–94.

24 *Living in Fear* (Mencap, 2000).

25 *B is for Bullying* (National Autistic Society, 2006).

26 Quarmby, *Getting Away with Murder*, 41.

27 http://news.bbc.co.uk/1/hi/england/leicestershire/8268706.stm.

28 http://news.bbc.co.uk/1/hi/scotland/north_east/7497997.stm.

29 Quarmby, *Getting Away with Murder*, 43.

30 http://www.chroniclelive.co.uk/north-east-news/evening-chronicle-news/tm_headline=animals&method=full&objectid=19553202&siteid=50081-name_page.html

Chapter Twelve: The Hounding of Fiona Pilkington: the Hidden Victims of Hate Crime

1 http://www.scope.org.uk/help-and-information/publications/getting-away-murder, endorsements.

2 http://news.bbc.co.uk/1/hi/england/leicestershire/8261155.stm.

3 http://www.mirror.co.uk/news/top-stories/2009/09/28/inquest-verdict-on-fiona-pilkington-and-daughter-francesca-115875-21707985/.

4 http://www.lsr-online.org/reports?page=12.

5 http://news.bbc.co.uk/1/hi/uk/8273247.stm.

6 http://www.communitycare.co.uk/Articles/2009/09/30/112729/fiona-pilkington-scr-questions-safeguarding-adults-policy.htm.

7 http://www.ipcc.gov.uk/news/pr_160310_pilkingtonupdate2.htm.

8 http://localgovernmentlawyer.co.uk/index.php?option=com_conten

t&view=article&id=4353%3Apilkington-family-sue-police-and-two-councils&catid=55%3Acommunity-safety-articles&q=&Itemid=23.

9   http://www.timesonline.co.uk/tol/news/politics/article6851681.ece.

10 http://www.politics.co.uk/news/policing-and-crime/johnson-no-excuses-for-pilkington-deaths-$1330517.htm.

11 http://www.mirror.co.uk/news/top-stories/2010/01/28/pilkington-abuse-thug-walks-free-115875-22000515/.

12 http://www.telegraph.co.uk/news/uknews/crime/7086265/Fiona-Pilkington-gang-suspect-labelled-her-a-freak-court-told.html.

13 http://www.independent.co.uk/news/uk/crime/david-askew-a-human-tragedy-and-national-scandal-1920089.html.

14 http://www.disabledgo.com/blog/2010/09/police-force-blasted-for-astonishing-hate-crime-failings/.

15 Ibid.

16 http://www.ipcc.gov.uk/news/pr_190310_gmpaskew.htm.

17 http://www.hmic.gov.uk/SiteCollectionDocuments/Anti-social_behaviour_2010/ASB_IPS_20100923.pdf.

18 http://www.disabledgo.com/blog/2010/09/one-in-three-anti-social-behaviour-victims-are-disabled-says-report/.

Chapter Thirteen: Multi-Agency Chaos: Michael Gilbert and the Failure of Safeguarding

1   http://localgovernmentlawyer.co.uk/index.php?option=com_content&view=article&id=4046%3Asurvey-reveals-councils-increasing-charges-tightening-eligibility-criteria&catid=52%3Aadult-social-services-articles&q=&Itemid=20://.

2   http://www.dh.gov.uk/en/Publicationsandstatistics/Publications/PublicationsPolicyAndGuidance/DH_4008486.

3   news.sky.com/skynews/Home/UK-News/Headless-Body-Discovered-In-Blue-Lagoon-Arlesey-Bedfordshire/Article/200905215279470.

4   http://www.guardian.co.uk/uk/2010/apr/26/family-jailed-blue-lagoon-murder-michael-gilbert.

5   Personal communication, Bedfordshire Police, 21 April 2010.

6   http://www.timesonline.co.uk/tol/comment/columnists/guest_contributors/article7113995.ece.

7   Jill Manthorpe and Stephen Martineau, *Serious Case Reviews in Adult Safeguarding* (Social Care Workforce Research Unit, King's College London, 2009), available at http://www.kcl.ac.uk/content/1/c6/06/75/83/ManthorpeandMartineau2009SCR.pdf.

8 http://www.communitycare.co.uk/Articles/2009/10/20/112913/adult-safeguarding-referrals-up-and-jobs-for-disabled-down.htm.

9 http://news.bbc.co.uk/1/hi/england/leicestershire/7138147.stm.

10 Information received under Freedom of Information Act, from Leicester City Council, 16 July 2010.

11 http://www.devonlmc.org/uploads/File/2010/LSCB/multi-agency_safeguarding_hub.pdf.

12 http://www.cqc.org.uk.

13 http//www.disabledgo.com/blog/2010/08/solar-centre-abuse-scandal-family%E2%80%99s-anger-at-health-trust/.

14 Ibid.

15 http//www.communitycare.co.uk/Articles/2010/11/23/115871/Poor-services-have-had-performance-records-wiped-admits.htm.

16 http://www.cqc.org.uk/newsandevents/newsstories.cfm?FaArea1=customwidgets.content_view_1&cit_id=36683.

17 Personal communication, CQC, 25 October 2010.

18 http://www.cqc.org.uk/_db/_documents/cornwall_investigation_report.pdf; http://www.cqc.org.uk/_db/_documents/Sutton_and_Merton_inv_sum_Tag.pdf.

19 http://www.cqc.org.uk/_db/_documents/CQC_learning_disability_strat_plan_2010-15.pdf, 25.

20 http://www.lawcom.gov.uk/docs/cp192_outline.pdf.

Chapter Fourteen: Mate Crime: the Importance of Friendship

1 http://www.arcuk.org.uk/1000646/default/safety+net.html.

2 Hans Reinders, *Receiving the Gift of Friendship* (Eerdmans Publishing, 2008), 5.

3 Ibid., 6.

4 Nils Christie, *Beyond Loneliness and Institutions: Communes for Extraordinary People* (Norwegian Press, 1989), 101–2.

5 http://www.scie-socialcareonline.org.uk/profile.asp?guid=11785d44-559f-4de7-ad70-240255f305e0; http://ici.umn.edu/index.php?projects/view/52.

6 http://www.scope.org.uk/news/comres-poll.

7 Michael Bayley, *What Price Friendship?: Encouraging the Relationships of People with Learning Difficulties* (Hexagon Publishing, 1997), 21.

8 http://www.thenorthernecho.co.uk/news/local/darlington/8400464.Three_jailed_for_torture_attack_on_man/.

Chapter Fifteen: Motivations

1 Katharine Quarmby, *Getting Away with Murder* (Scope, 2008), available at http://www.scope.org.uk/help-and-information/publications/getting-away-murder.

2 http://news.bbc.co.uk/1/hi/wales/south_east/6624515.stm.

3 http://news.bbc.co.uk/1/hi/england/gloucestershire/6284184.stm.

4 Quarmby, *Getting Away with Murder*, 35; http://www.timesonline.co.uk/tol/news/uk/crime/article1610309.ece.

5 http://www.disabilitynow.org.uk/the-hate-crime-dossier.

6 http://www.guardian.co.uk/uk/2010/mar/01/couple-die-mobility-scooter-rugby.

7 Paul Longmore and Elizabeth Bouvia, 'Assisted Suicide and Social Prejudice Issues', *Issues in Law and Medicine*, 1987, 3, 141.

8 Barbara Perry (ed.), *Hate and Bias Crime: A Reader* (Routledge, 2003), 168.

9 Ibid., 105–6.

10 Ibid., 128.

11 Carl Hovland and Robert Sears, quoted in Perry (ed.), *Hate and Bias Crime*, 469–70.

12 Ibid., 470.

13 Jack Levin and Jack McDevitt, *Hate Crimes: The Rising Tide of Bigotry* (Plenium, 1993).

14 http://www.ncjrs.gov/App/Publications/abstract.aspx?ID=204396.

15 www.homeoffice.gov.uk/crime-victims/reducing-crime/hate-crime.

16 Neil Chakraborti and Jon Garland, *Hate Crime: Impact, Causes and Responses* (Sage, 2009).

17 H. Willems, quoted in Perry (ed.), *Hate and Bias Crime*, 39.

18 Gail Mason, 'Hate Crime and the Image of the Stranger', *British Journal of Criminology*, 2005, 838.

19 Quarmby, *Getting Away with Murder*, 39.

20 http://www.disabilitynow.org.uk/201cwhy-shouldnt-people-be-angry-they-are-not-getting-justice.

21 http://www.crfr.ac.uk/spa2009/Roulstone%20A,%20Thomas%20P,%20Balderston%20S,%20Harris%20J%20-%20Hate%20is%20a%20strong%20word%20-%20a%20critical%20policy%20analysis%20of%20disability%20hate%20crime%20in%20the%20British%20%20criminal%20justice%20system.pdf.

22 http://www.crimeandjustice.org.uk/opus191/cjm66-stanko.pdf.

23 Barbara Faye Waxman, 'Hatred: The Unacknowledged Dimensions in Violence

Against Disabled People', *Sexuality and Disability*, 1991, 185–7.

24 http://www.timesonline.co.uk/tol/comment/columnists/guest_contributors/article7113 995.ece.

Chapter Sixteen: Locations

1 Sue Thompson, Tom Shakespeare and Michael Wright, 'No Laughing Matter: Medical and Social Factors in Restricted Growth', *Scandinavian Journal of Disability Research*, 2010, 12, 1, 19–31.

2 http://www.equalityhumanrights.com/uploaded_files/research/disabled_people_s_experiences_of_targeted_violence_and_hostility.pdf.

3 http://webarchive.nationalarchives.gov.uk/+/http://www.dft.gov.uk/pgr/statistics/datatablespublications/trnstatsatt/antisocialcrime.

4 http://webarchive.nationalarchives.gov.uk/+/http://www.homeoffice.gov.uk/crime-victims/reducing-crime/hate-crime/index.html.

5 http://www.equalityhumanrights.com/uploaded_files/research/disabled_people_s_experiences_of_targeted_violence_and_hostility.pdf.

6 Rae Sibbit, *The Perpetrators of Racial Harassment and Racial Violence* (Home Office, 1997), 139.

7 Katharine Quarmby, *Getting Away with Murder* (Scope, 2008), available at http://www.scope.org.uk/help-and-information/publications/getting-away-murder, 21.

8 Ibid.

9 http://www.equalityhumanrights.com/uploaded_files/research/disabled_people_s_experiences_of_targeted_violence_and_hostility.pdf.

10 Ibid.

11 http://www.chiefprivacyofficers.com/uploads/2/6/6/5/2665080/thesis.pdf.

12 http://blog.indexoncensorship.org/2010/02/25/google-italy-disability-privacy/.

13 http://www.theage.com.au/news/national/outcry-over-teenage-girls-assault-recorded-on-dvd/2006/10/24/1161455722271.html.

14 http://www.cbc.ca/world/story/2010/02/24/italy-google-autism.html.

15 http://www.cps.gov.uk/news/press_releases/138_10/index.html.

16 Personal communication, Home Office, from Network for Surviving Stalking, September 2010.

17 http://www.beds.ac.uk/news/2010/sep/100920-cyber-stalking.

18 http://www.huffingtonpost.com/katharine-quarmby/the-retard-controversy-ov_b_467766.html.

19 http://www.mencap.org.uk/news.asp?id=14930.

20 http://www.dailymail.co.uk/tvshowbiz/article-1337095/Katie-Price-wants-

apology-Frankie-Boyles-sexual-slur-disabled-son-Harvey.html.

21   http://www.dailymail.co.uk/tvshowbiz/article-1171536/They-called-Susie-Simple-singing-superstar-Susan-Boyle-laughing-now.html.

22   http://www.dailymail.co.uk/tvshowbiz/article-1189954/Britains-Got-Talent-backlash-Priory-clinic-boss-attacks-producers-Susan-Boyle-suffers-breakdown.html.

23   http://www.guardian.co.uk/tv-and-radio/2010/may/30/britains-got-talent-suicide-fear.

24   http://www.guardian.co.uk/music/2010/may/30/susan-boyle-the-dream.

25   http://www.whitehouse.gov/the-press-office/2010/12/21/presidential-proclamation-stalking-awareness-month.

26   http://www.convergencecornwall.com/downloads/publications/12.pdf.

27   http://www.gloucestershire.gov.uk/inform/index.cfm?articleid=94990.

28   http://www.cartoplus.co.uk/sunderland/text/02_plan_people.htm.

29   http://www.hartlepoolmail.co.uk/news/THE-11TH-POOREST-PLACE-IN.613462.jp.

30   http://www.leicester.gov.uk/sys_upl/documents/departments/dpt_2787.pdf.

31   http://news.bbc.co.uk/1/hi/england/tees/4720642.stm.

32   http://www.chroniclelive.co.uk/north-east-news/evening-chronicle-news/tm_headline=animals&method=full&objectid=19553202&siteid=50081-name_page.html.

33   http://news.bbc.co.uk/1/hi/england/wear/7177716.stm.

34   http://news.bbc.co.uk/1/hi/england/tees/7002627.stm.

35   http://www.independent.co.uk/news/uk/crime/woman-jailed-for-32-years-for-torture-murder-1876187.html.

36   http://www.disabilitynow.org.uk/the-hate-crime-dossier.

37   http://www.visionsense.co.uk/files/Download/Disablist%20Hate%20Crime%20in%20the%20North%20East%20Vision%20Sense%20FINAL%20Report%202009.pdf.

38   http://www.imd.communities.gov.uk/.

39   http://www.popcenter.org/library/crimeprevention/volume_04/03-Felson.pdf.

Chapter Seventeen: Leading the World?

1   http://www.speaker.gov/newsroom/legislation?id=0341.

2   http://www.whitehouse.gov/the-press-office/remarks-president-reception-commemorating-enactment-matthew-shepard-and-james-byrd-.

3   http://www.matthewshepard.org/our-story.

4   http://www.startribune.com/local/42977107.html?page=2&c=y.

5   http://www.startribune.com/local/48078197.html?page=1&c=y.

6   http://www.adl.org/99hatecrime/offender_motivation.pdf; http://www.
    nytimes.com/1999/02/17/nyregion/8-are-charged-in-tormenting-of-
    learning-disabled-man.html?pagewanted=2.

7   http://www.washingtonpost.com/wp-dyn/content/article/2010/11/03/
    AR2010110306636.html.

8   http://www.chron.com/disp/story.mpl/front/5823669.html.

9   http://www.cbsnews.com/8301–504083_162-5409420-504083.html; http://
    www.wvpubcast.org/newsarticle.aspx?id=11740.

10 Ryken Grattet and Valerie Jeness, 'Examining the Boundaries of Hate Crime
    Law: Disability and the "Dilemma of Difference"', in Barbara Perry (ed.), *Hate
    and Bias Crime: A Reader* (Routledge, 2003), 285–6.

11 http://www.fbi.gov/about-us/cjis/ucr/hate-crime/2008.

12 http://www.fbi.gov/news/pressrel/press-releases/2009hatecrimestats_112210.

13 http://archive.chicagobreakingnews.com/2010/01/1-arrest-in-86-chicago-
    nursing-home-rape-cases-since-july-07.html.

14 http://www.dallasnews.com/sharedcontent/dws/news/texassouthwest/
    stories/DN-disabled_08tex.ART.State.Edition1.4799330.html.

15 http://www.justice.gov/opa/pr/2010/November/10-crt-1291.html.

16 http://www.osce.org/odihr/documents/40203.

17 http://www.osce.org/odihr/documents/73636.

18 http://news.bbc.co.uk/1/hi/world/europe/4045359.stm.

19 http://njca.anu.edu.au/Professional%20Development/programs%20by%20
    year/2010/ Sentencing%202010/Papers/Mason.pdf.

20 http://www.winnipegsun.com/news/world/2010/03/10/13178451-winsun.
    html.

21 http://www.news.com.au/national/peter-kipniak-jailed-for-
    abducting-and-raping-an-intellectually-disabled-man/story-e6frfkvr-
    1225853712636#ixzz16CA96KWn.

22 http://www.acpo.police.uk/asp/policies/Data/084a_Recorded_Hate_
    Crime_-_January_to_December_2009.pdf.

23 http://www.stophateuk.org/talk/.

24 http://www.stophateuk.org/.

25 http://www.cps.gov.uk/publications/equality/.

26 http://www.cps.gov.uk/publications/docs/CPS_hate_crime_report_2010.pdf.

27 http://www.mind.org.uk/news/233_high_court_finds_crown_prosecution_
    service_to_be_discriminating_against_victims_with_mental_health_problems.

28 http://www.equalityhumanrights.com/legal-and-policy/formal-inquiries/
    inquiry-into-disability-related-harassment/.

29 *Snapshot of Hate Crime in Lancashire* (Crown Prosecution Service, 2009).

30 http://www.disabledgo.com/blog/2010/08/ukdpc-uncovers-widespread-reports-of-hate-crime-deaths/.

31 Anne Novis, *Bigger Picture Report* (UKDPC, 2009).

32 http://rds.homeoffice.gov.uk/rds/pdfs10/hosb1210chap5.pdf.

Chapter 18: Not Them But Us: Society's Challenge

1 http://www.turning-point.co.uk/News/Pages/Publicstilldiscriminate.aspx.

2 http://www.enham.org.uk/pages/research_page.html?section=00010015.

3 Valerie Sinason, *Mental Handicap and the Human Condition* (Free Association Books, 1992), 38 and 209.

4 http://www.dailymail.co.uk/news/article-1317400/Virginia-Ironside-sparks-BBC-outrage-Id-suffocate-child-end-suffering.html.

5 Sinason, *Mental Handicap and the Human Condition*, 138.

6 http://www.education.gov.uk/consultations/downloadableDocs/EIA%20Final.doc.

7 http://news.bbc.co.uk/1/hi/wales/7606111.stm.

8 Ibid.

9 Nadeem Badshah, 'Horror at the Hands of Healers', *Eastern Eye*, 23 July 2010.

10 http://www.disabilitynow.org.uk/living/features/licensed-to-abuse-a-question-of-dishonour; http://www.anncrafttrust.org/Forced_Marriage_of_People_with_Learning_Disabilities.html.

11 Ibid.

12 http://www.respond.org.uk/campaigns/Forced_Marriageof_People_with_Learning_Disabilities.html.

13 http://www.dailymail.co.uk/debate/article-1314130/The-epidemic-hate-crimes-vulnerable-reveals-callousness-heart-society.html; http://www.dailymail.co.uk/debate/article-1317786/Caring-disabled-daughter-enriched-lives.html.

14 Sinsaon, *Mental Handicap and the Human Condition*, 257.

15 http://www.scie.org.uk/publications/knowledgereviews/kr11.asp.

16 http://www.bbc.co.uk/news/education-11757907.

17 http://www.leeds.ac.uk/disability-studies/archiveuk/Booth/parents%20with%20lea%20diff.pdf.

18 http://www.telegraph.co.uk/news/newstopics/politics/conservative/8114432/Iain-Duncan-Smith-My-welfare-reforms-are-Beveridge-for-today-with-a-hint-of-Tebbit.html.

19 Personal communication, John Pring and Anne Novis, November 2010.

20 http://www.disabledgo.com/blog/2010/07/treasury-fails-to-remove-disablist-comments-from-cuts-website/.

21 http://www.prospectmagazine.co.uk/2010/10/wrong-thinking-on-disability-fraud/.

22 http://www.cps.gov.uk/publications/prosecution/assisted_suicide.html.

23 http://www.guardian.co.uk/society/2010/nov/28/assisted-dying-falconer-commission.

24 http://www.bbc.co.uk/news/10358650.

25 Sinason, *Handicap and the Human Condition*, 38.

Chapter 19: Ways Forward

1 Hugh Gregory Gallagher, *By Trust Betrayed: Patients, Physicians and the License to Kill in the Third Reich* (Henry Holt, 1990).

2 http://www.guardian.co.uk/society/2009/jun/12/mental-illness-health-attitudes.

3 http://www.radar.org.uk/leadership/empproject.aspx.

4 http://www.disabilitynow.org.uk/latest-news2/campaigns/justice-system-failing-on-hate-crime.

5 http://www.inclusive-solutions.com/circlesoffriends.asp.

Index